Liturgy is meaning + structure.

Liturgy and the Moral Self

THEO - Lit/Asc

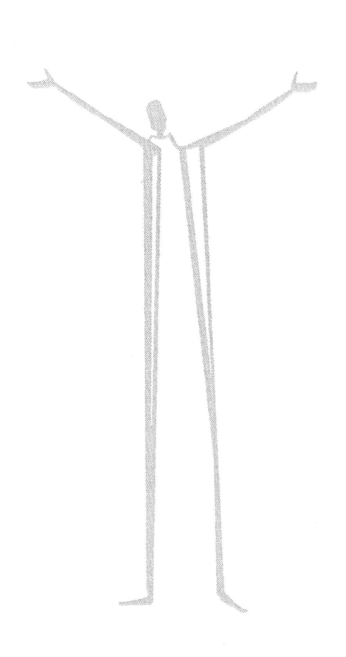

E. Byron Anderson, Bruce T. Morrill, S.J.,

Editors

LITURGY
AND THE MORAL SELF

Humanity at Full Stretch Before God

Essays in Honor of Don E. Saliers

A PUEBLO BOOK

The Liturgical Press Collegeville, Minnesota

A Pueblo Book published by The Liturgical Press

Design by Frank Kacmarcik, Obl.S.B.

Library of Congress Cataloging-in-Publication Data

Liturgy and the moral self : humanity at full stretch : essays in honor of
    Don E. Saliers.
        p.   cm.
    "A Pueblo book."
    Includes bibliographical references.
    ISBN 0-8146-6168-8 (alk. paper)
    1. Liturgics.   2. Public worship.   3. Christian ethics.   4. Man
(Christian theology)   5. Saliers, Don E., 1937–   . I. Saliers, Don E.,
    1937–   . II. Anderson, E. Byron.   III. Morrill, Bruce T.
BV178.L58   1998
264—dc21   97-52051
                                                                            CIP

Contents

Contributors

E. BYRON ANDERSON, Assistant Professor of Worship and Director of Community Worship, Christian Theological Seminary, Indianapolis, Indiana

ROBERTA C. BONDI, Professor of Historical Theology, Candler School of Theology, Emory University, Atlanta, Georgia

REBECCA S. CHOPP, Charles Howard Candler Chair of Theology, Emory University, Atlanta, Georgia

PETER E. FINK, S.J., Professor of Sacramental Theology, Weston Jesuit School of Theology, Cambridge, Massachusetts

STANLEY M. HAUERWAS, Gilbert T. Rowe Professor of Theological Ethics, The Divinity School, Duke University, Durham, North Carolina

HENRY H. KNIGHT, III, Assistant Professor of Evangelism, Saint Paul School of Theology, Kansas City, Missouri

GORDON W. LATHROP, Charles A. Schieren Professor of Liturgy, Lutheran Theological Seminary, Philadelphia, Pennsylvania

STEVEN J. LAND, Academic Dean and Professor of Pentecostal Theology, Church of God School of Theology, Cleveland, Tennessee

BRUCE T. MORRILL, S.J., Assistant Professor of Theology, Boston College, Chestnut Hill, Massachusetts

GAIL RAMSHAW, Professor of Religion, LaSalle University, Philadelphia, Pennsylvania

DON E. SALIERS, Franklin Nutting Parker Professor of Theology and Worship, Candler School of Theology, Emory University, Atlanta, Georgia

MARY EWING STAMPS, Episcopal House of Prayer, Collegeville, Minnesota

JAMES F. WHITE, Professor of Liturgical Studies, The Graduate School, Drew University, Madison, New Jersey

PAUL WESTERMEYER, Professor of Church Music, Luther Seminary, St. Paul, Minnesota

BRIAN WREN, Hymnwriter and Theologian, Biddeford, Maine

Foreword

It is with great respect and delight that I write this Foreword to a book that gives witness to the scholarly career of Don Saliers. Respect because I, like others who learn from him, have high regard for his profound intertwining of philosophy, theology, and liturgy. Delight because to know him is to experience that about which he writes: a life formed through Christian patterns, lived in glory to God and sanctifying creaturely things. And, in this Christian *ordo,* a Festschrift could not simply offer salutations to Don Saliers' work, so we have here a collection of essays reflecting on his key essay, "Liturgy and Ethics: Some New Beginnings," which appeared in the *Journal of Religious Ethics* (Vol. 7, no. 2, Fall 1979) and is included here beginning on page 15.

I have been asked to invite others into this reading by making some brief observation of how the essay "Liturgy and Ethics" and the accompanying essays relate to practical theology and liberation theology. To do so, let me presuppose that the readers understand and accept some basic assumptions in Saliers' theology. For instance, Saliers assumes that theology begins, not in an apologetic or kerygmatic moment, but in the teaching of the Christian pattern, the identifying and ordering of the Christian way, coded and performed in worship. Thus the readers must understand that in these essays theology does not prove God through speculative abstraction, but rather theology gestures to God through the communal symbolic, ritual, and cultic acts of how Christians know God and world.

Saliers' assumptions about Christian *homo religiosus* are quite startlingly antimodern and yet not quite postmodern. For Saliers and most of the accompanying authors in this book, Christians are formed into the community by ritual patterns that seek neither to solve nor to celebrate moral ambiguities and logical contradictions in the created order. The Christian community worships God and serves the world in the rich and diverse textures of life.

So over against the modern "man," elevated as universally rational and ideally alone, and alongside our postmodern condition, marked by aimless wandering and collaged by pastiche, Saliers sketches the outline of a distinctly Christian anthropology. In this anthropology the individual is shaped in and through the patterns and practices of belonging to a community that is itself shaped and formed by belonging to God. The ordering of life's feelings, actions, and thoughts, for Saliers, moves from the body through language to deeds, not, as in most modern and postmodern anthropologies, vice versa. As Gordon Lathrop notes in his essay in this volume, the geography of Christian liturgy is quite distinct from the other maps by which most of us live our lives.

This unabashed richness and realistic ambiguity with which the community lives and performs make these essays practical theology, though of course with a decidedly Christian shape! Ecclesial practices become the primary arenas of the Christian life; the point of such practices is to order the fullness of life rather than to adhere to some notion of univocal coherence. Christian practices, with the accompanying diverse array of stories, myths, and symbols, embrace the many dimensions, times, desires, and diseases of life itself.

In the liturgy, tradition gathers through the present toward the future, just as God brings all creation toward Godself. This gathering and bringing in liturgy and life is what theology "knows" of God. This knowledge, while it is certainly cognitive, is never merely rational or even linguistic. The range of what we know about liturgy's embrace and God's giftedness requires our ability to name God in all that we do.

As the Christian community forms and performs its liturgy, the affections of the believers are formed and shaped. Prayer and ritual action form the particular affections of adoration, solidarity, and holiness. These affections, shaped and formed by life as prayer, embrace ethics as a holiness of life—both the life of the believer and the community as well as the life of the sanctified creation. As Stanley Hauerwas observes, "To learn to worship truthfully that God [whose justice is to be found in Jesus' cross and resurrection] requires that our bodies be formed by truthful habits of speech and gesture. To be so habituated is to acquire a character befitting lives capable of worshiping God" (below, p. 101).

Such Christian affections become the place of morality and, by extension, the moral imagination. Saliers contends that one never has merely formal principles of ethics, but rather one is embedded in the ethical life of the community, represented in myths and stories, shaped and formed around practices and virtues. Shaped to stand before God, the body bows in prayer in the intimacy of partaking in liturgy. In this intimate partaking, the moral imagination of reverence and solidarity is nurtured.

This moral imagination, from the body in the mind, to use Mark Johnson's phrase, is the requirement of Christian ethics. Because of this basic continual patterning and performing, Christians see and act in the world in specifically Christian ways: "Normatively considered, good liturgy is the fundamental imaginal framework of encounter with God in Christ which forms intentions in and through the affections which take God in Christ as their goal and ground" (Saliers, "Liturgy and Ethics," below, p. 24).

Within this imaginal framework, the transformation of life occurs, even if only eschatologically. This transformation, remembered, performed, longed for in the liturgy, is the wellspring of desires for the liberation of all that suffers. For, as Saliers suggests in his work, the Christian pattern teaches one, shapes one, to have an attitude of awesome wonder and deep recognition of suffering and death. When the community prays (in life as well as in worship), continually lifting to God those who suffer, the world in its actuality is held, openly and honestly, before God (see below, p. 21).

Saliers explains why any and all theology has to be liberation theology: Christians pray and thus live for the release of suffering of all creation, anticipating God's glory in that new day promised still to come. Saliers doesn't begin his liturgical liberation theology with a formal theory of justice but in the prior founding of sanctifying grace of all creaturely things before God. Thus, he requires us to understand why justice is important for creation and why the quest for justice is an intrinsic part of Christian holiness. Likewise, liturgically speaking, God's grace is for those who have too much, their spiritual senses dulled and their souls rubbed raw by consumerism. For these Christians, liturgy implies a freedom from this bondage of nothingness, offering a grace satisfying and at the same time requiring a life formed with God's ordering.

Saliers' work, as the authors included in this volume so aptly demonstrate, has many gifts for all of us. For clergy, these essays will help explain what clergy do in the basic, most nourishing aspects of their ministerial work of leading the church in worship. For theologians, these essays will suggest a remaking of theology, more along the lines of refashioning than reconstructing, in the sense that theology will not build new spaces as much as it will refashion the enduring spaces, full of character and memory, to invite vital forms of holy Christian dwelling. For theological educators, baffled by what to do with seminarians who arrive in need of catechesis before ministerial formation can occur, Saliers' theology may well be one of the few resources on the scene that suggest ways to combine forming Christian experience and performing Christian worship and service. For all of us Christians, Saliers' work calls us to a specificity of Christian ways of living that is written on our bodies before it is expressed in our words, communally as well as individually.

REBECCA CHOPP
Candler School of Theology
Emory University
Atlanta, Georgia

Part 1

The Prophetic Challenge

Introduction

For some thirty years, Don Saliers has served the Church and academy as scholar, teacher, pastor, musician, and poet. In this time he has shaped a generation of pastors, musicians, scholars, and teachers. Saliers has spent most of this time with the faculty of Candler School of Theology at Emory University as professor of theology and worship, serving formerly as dean of the seminary chapel and now as director of the graduate program in sacred music. He has led the way as part of a distinctively United Methodist but ecumenically formed and minded liturgical team in crafting trial liturgies, liturgical supplements, and the resources for a denominational book of worship that, over twenty-five years, have reshaped United Methodist worship.

As a liturgical theologian, musician, and editor, Saliers has participated in a variety of ecumenical ventures, including the United Methodist/Roman Catholic bilateral dialogue on the Eucharist and the Milwaukee symposia on music in worship, and serves on the editorial boards of *Worship* and *Weavings*. He has shaped Christian prayer even as his life continues to reflect the depth and shape of that prayer. Both within and beyond the confines of the Emory campus, many know him as a "strong, loving, and wise" worship leader, lecturer, and writer, always gracious and inviting, encouraging Christian people to life "at full stretch" before God.

We believe that this combination of life and work is cause to honor Don Saliers on the occasion of his sixtieth birthday. Even so, at one point in preparing the initial proposal for this book, we asked ourselves and were asked by publishers how, even why, we would celebrate in such a volume the work of a person who not only is a number of years from retiring but also is in the midst of a productive period of writing. Our reply is that the most appropriate response to one whose work summons us to life "at full stretch" is to engage and stretch that work ourselves. Therefore, we have set out to honor Saliers by taking specific themes in his writing as the starting point for our own reflections. In particular, we take up a series of questions around the relationship of liturgy, ethics, and the Christian person as Saliers himself names these.

As we turn to these specific questions, however, it will be helpful to review briefly three themes in Saliers' work that shape the essays presented here. The first theme is the relationship between prayer *(lex orandi)* and belief *(lex credendi)* and, from this, the relationship between liturgical practice and theological reflection. The second is Saliers' understanding of the relationship between prayer and the "deep affections" of the Christian person. The third is his understanding of the relationship between prayer, affection, and liturgical aesthetics.[1]

PRAYER AND BELIEF

The relationship between prayer and belief, *lex orandi* and *lex credendi*, has been amply addressed in recent scholarship on liturgical theology.[2] The most frequently stated form of what we might call "Prosper's axiom," *lex supplicandi statuat lex credendi*, is usually translated as "The law of prayer constitutes the law of belief." Some, following Aidan Kavanagh and Alexander Schmemann, argue that this statement effectively subordinates the law of belief to the law of worship, even as the two laws remain in dialectical relationship with each other. Others, such as Edward Kilmartin, are less willing to subordinate belief to worship and argue for a more fully mutually critical relationship.

More recently, Kevin Irwin has introduced a third term into the relationship, the *lex vivendi*, or "law of living." Irwin thereby presses us to see the connection between the practices of prayer, belief, and ethical action; that is, Christian liturgical practice is not only oriented to-

---

[1] Our goal here, therefore, is not to review all of Saliers' work, a complete bibliography of which we provide at the end of the book, but to summarize the part of his work that sets the stage for our discussion.

[2] In particular, see Paul de Clerck, "'Lex orandi lex credendi.' Sens original et avatars historiques d'un adage equivoque," *Questions Liturgiques* 59 (1978): 193–212; Kevin Irwin, *Context and Text: Method in Liturgical Theology* (Collegeville, Minn.: The Liturgical Press, 1994) 55–56; Aidan Kavanagh, *On Liturgical Theology* (New York: Pueblo Publishing Co., 1984) 91–92; Edward Kilmartin, *Christian Liturgy*, vol. 1, *Theology and Practice* (Kansas City: Sheed & Ward, 1988) 96–97; and Alexander Schmemann, *Introduction to Liturgical Theology* (Crestwood, N.Y.: St. Vladimir's Seminary Press, 1966).

ward Christian belief but also toward the life of Christian persons and communities in and with the world.

In all these there is a clear argument either for the priority of Christian practice (liturgy and prayer) over Christian theory (theological reflection) or for a critical relationship between the two. Irwin's argument suggests a slightly different move, however. By the addition of the third term, *lex vivendi*, it is possible to consider both liturgy and theology as forms of Christian practice that, together, we must hold in critical tension with ethical praxis.

Where do we situate Saliers in this conversation? First, like Kavanagh and Schmemann, Saliers argues in a number of ways for the priority of the law of prayer to the law of belief, even as they remain in critical tension with each other. In regard to the priority of the law of prayer, liturgical prayer does two things. It is, first, a normative practice of the Christian community that establishes the experiential and theological framework for Christian belief. As Saliers wrote in *The Soul in Paraphrase*, "Worship . . . is itself a rule-keeping activity for the language of religious belief. It keeps the paradigmatic descriptions of God, the self, and the world in place."[3]

Second, liturgical prayer provides the first place, a place prior to the academy, in which the Christian community speaks theologically. Liturgical prayer is the "logically required context for the utterance of theological truths" and "the most fitting context for asserting things about God."[4] In a way that parallels the work of recent praxis theologies, Saliers argues that, as with any social practice, the practice of liturgical prayer is the object of theological reflection. That is, it is "the prayed and enacted signs" which carry "the significance that was elaborated in various cultural and historical contexts" and which must continue to be elaborated in our current context.[5]

Just as in praxis theologies, however, practice does not have the only voice. Theological reflection, even as it is sourced and normed by liturgical prayer, is itself a critical voice in their interrelationship. In this regard Saliers wrote: "When misunderstandings about God arise,

[3] Don Saliers, *The Soul in Paraphrase: Prayer and the Religious Affections* (New York: Seabury Press, 1980; reprint, Cleveland: OSL, 1991) 82. Several essays that follow, especially those of Anderson and Ramshaw, suggest how this is so.

[4] Ibid.

[5] Don Saliers, *Worship as Theology: Foretaste of Glory Divine* (Nashville: Abingdon Press, 1996) 55. See the Morrill essay below, p. 67ff.

theology emerges as a distinct kind of thought. Theology provides a grammar for the affective content and shape of the praying. . . . Theology is a way of understanding the One addressed in prayer."[6] This statement was perhaps more programmatic for Saliers' work than he may have realized when he wrote it. By engaging in what we might call practical liturgical theological reflection,[7] Saliers attempts to articulate the normative character of liturgical prayer even as, increasingly, he is critical of the deficiencies of that prayer as it is being practiced. In his most recent work, he points in particular to the deficiencies in liturgical prayer for naming or speaking of the Triune God when that prayer, especially in recent Protestant practice, turns away from or rejects biblical language and sacramental practice.

As Saliers also argues, such rejection of Christian tradition results not only in deficient or misunderstood prayer but also in an impoverished theology. By holding prayer and theology in critical tension with each other, Saliers reminds us, on the one hand, that "liturgy is not simply doctrine well dressed and ornamented," theology made, as it were, attractive for common consumption by the uninitiated; but he also reminds us, on the other hand, that "without the primary orientation of liturgy and life to the glory of God," theology and doctrines are little more than abstract intellectual programs.[8] More succinctly, Saliers summarizes the interrelationship of prayer and theology, practice and theory, with these words: "Doctrine without experience is empty; religious experience without doctrine is blind."[9]

This connection between doctrine and experience, prayer and theology, leads Saliers, like Irwin, to introduce a third term into the relationship: the "internal, conceptual link between liturgy and ethics,"[10] which Saliers calls the *lex agendi*, or law of ethical action. Here Saliers' concern for the "primary theology" enacted in and co-constituted by liturgy and life, "the worship of God in cultic enactment and service

---

[6] *Soul in Paraphrase*, 77.

[7] As have both Kevin Irwin, *op. cit.*, and Gordon Lathrop in *Holy Things: A Liturgical Theology* (Minneapolis: Fortress Press, 1993). Also see Lathrop's essay below, p. 41ff.

[8] *Worship as Theology*, 210, 203.

[9] *Soul in Paraphrase*, 20.

[10] "Liturgy and Ethics: Some New Beginnings," *Journal of Religious Ethics*, vol. 7, no. 2 (Fall 1979) 174; see below, p. 16.

of God in life,"[11] seems to relativize the role of "secondary" theological reflection. That is, even in the midst of his liturgical theological reflections, Saliers returns again and again to the links between Christian liturgical practices and Christian praxis. Programmatically, this link is summarized in what he calls the ordering principle of Christian prayer: "Prayer begins with praise and thanksgiving and issues in love."[12] Prayer is, for Saliers, a way of intending the world, of undertaking a way of existing in the world, and the means by which we articulate our expectations for the future of the world.

Although Saliers makes the link between liturgy and ethics clear in the essay reproduced here, it is interwoven throughout his writings, especially in *Worship as Theology,* where he returns to and reworks the themes of this essay. His theological reflections provide a litany on liturgy and ethics: "Eucharistic praise [is an] intention-action pattern for human existence." Shall we respond *Amen?* "Liturgy [is] a rehearsal for the way we are to become related to one another and to the world." And again, *Amen.* "Prayer as praise must be linked with prayer as love of neighbor." *Amen.* There is "no true service of others without praying with Christ for them."[13] *Amen.* These comments all come in Saliers' discussions of the character of liturgical prayer, not in specific discussions of liturgy and ethics. When he does turn explicitly to this link, he writes:

"Patterns of prayer, reading, proclamation, and sacramental action are precisely the practices of communal rehearsal of the affections and virtues befitting 'life in Christ': the baptized life of faith in the world. This is no mere 'imitation of Jesus.' Rather, communal worship is a participation in the mystery of God's life poured into the human condition. The symbolic forms and actions of liturgy are the school for conceiving and receiving such a pattern of life."[14]

With these comments Saliers seems to displace theological reflection, even in the midst of such reflection, from its often dominant place as the critical dialectical voice with liturgical practice as named in the relationship *lex orandi, lex credendi.* If we consider it in light of

---

[11] *Worship as Theology,* 16.
[12] *Soul in Paraphrase,* 71.
[13] *Worship as Theology,* 98, 102, 134, 135.
[14] Ibid., 176.

the third term, *lex agendi*, theological reflection seems either to merge with prayer as another Christian practice or to disappear under the critical weight of praxis. Nevertheless, as a practical liturgical theologian, and as we also find in praxis theologies, Saliers uses theological reflection as a mediating voice between liturgical practice and ethical praxis. When the three terms—*orandi*, *credendi*, and *agendi*—are considered together, we begin to get a sense of what the apostle Paul intended by his injunction to "pray always" and what Origen intended by his argument that we consider "the whole of the saint's life as prayer."

PRAYER AND THE CHRISTIAN AFFECTIONS

If the intrinsic link between liturgy and ethics functions as an ongoing litany or perhaps as one of the distinctive melodies developed throughout Saliers' work, then his concern for liturgy as the "rehearsal of the affections and virtues befitting 'life in Christ'" provides something of the deep harmonic structure which he continues to develop and upon which he is constantly improvising.[15] From his first book, *The Soul in Paraphrase*, through his most recent, *Worship Come to Its Senses*, Saliers develops an argument for the relationship between prayer and the formation of the Christian affections. What, then, does he mean by the Christian affections?

Saliers' primary definition and descriptions of the Christian affections occur in *The Soul in Paraphrase*. There he is careful to distinguish what he means by "affection" from what is more commonly understood as emotion or feeling. By "affection" Saliers' concern is with "deep emotions" in contrast to "passing enthusiasms," sentiment, or "the interior consolations of experience." Deep affection is "a basic attunement which lies at the heart of a person's way of being and acting." Christian affection is "a comprehensive phenomenon of life by which we understand the world in and through a sense of the world. Affections thus always combine evaluative knowledge of the world

---

[15] Ibid. Here we are reminded that Saliers' work is, as yet, unfinished. As such, "Liturgy and Ethics" and *The Soul in Paraphrase* function as the introduction and first theme of the sonata; *Worship and Spirituality* (Philadelphia: Westminster, 1984; 2nd ed., Cleveland: OSL Publications, 1996) a secondary theme; *Worship as Theology* the development; and *Worship Come to Its Senses* (Nashville: Abingdon Press, 1996) as the coda! Will the next movement be an adagio or a scherzo? What is the shape of this lifelong symphony?

and self-awareness." The affections, in contrast to feeling and sentiment, provide the "motives and wellsprings of desire and action."[16] Such seems to be Paul's argument in 1 Corinthians 12–13. The deep affections, faith, hope, and love, are those things that abide throughout the Christian life, through times of sorrow and joy, of personal failure as well as success, of illness and death as well as health.

The deep affections of the Christian life form over time. Their formation requires more than the evocation of "lively feeling" or immediate physical sensation, as some who call for "more exciting" worship seem to suggest.[17] Rather, their formation requires participation in those practices that form deep memory, that draw us into the history of suffering and hope, exodus and liberation, death and resurrection. They require an honesty of prayer and life that is unsustainable by feeling and sentiment. They summon us to what Saliers calls a "passional knowing—a process of being formed in specific affections and dispositions in the way we live that manifests what is known about God."[18] They summon us, as we have already suggested in the discussion of the link between liturgy and ethics, to our "sharing a form of life in which the affections, desires, and dispositions to act are oriented toward God's promises."[19]

As faithful and true Christian prayer moves us to the "glorification of God and the sanctification of humanity," so, too, it provides what Saliers calls "the fundamental imaginal framework of encounter with God in Christ which, in the power of the Holy Spirit, forms intentions in and through the affections oriented to God revealed in Christ as their goal and ground."[20] To be thus formed in Christian prayer is to be formed in the deep affections of the Christian life, in the form of life that goes with the practice of prayer. Formation in the Christian affections is the formation of the Christian person in one's primary humanity "at full stretch before God."

In a day concerned more with promoting "good" feelings, enthusiasm, self-certainty, and self-fulfillment, Saliers' concern for the formation of the deep affections of the Christian life is perhaps most radical

---

[16] *Soul in Paraphrase*, 4–9.
[17] *Worship as Theology*, 178; *Worship Come to Its Senses*, 86.
[18] *Worship as Theology*, 86.
[19] Ibid., 178.
[20] Ibid., 176.

in his attention to the formation of those affections that address the apparent lack of certainty in the Christian life. In summoning the Christian community from what he calls "presumptive prayer," Saliers summons us to liturgical practices of invocation, beseeching, lamentation, and confession by which, in addition to thanksgiving and praise, we name the fullness of human life, our experiences of pain and sorrow as well as our experiences of joy, our experiences of God's absence as well as God's presence. Our liturgical formation in the deep patterns of gratitude, holy fear, joy, love of God, and love of neighbor sustains what feeling, sentiment, and sensibility cannot, because, unlike the former, they are embedded deeply in the human heart and soul. The formation of Christian persons in the patterns of Christian affection enables them to sing and pray, in Dietrich Bonhoeffer's words,

"And when this cup you give is filled to brimming
with bitter sorrow, hard to understand,
we take it thankfully and without trembling,
out of so good and so beloved a hand."[21]

PRACTICING A LITURGICAL AESTHETIC

How is it that Christian persons come to receive the cup of bitter sorrow "thankfully and without trembling"? Saliers argues that it is the "art" of liturgical prayer that draws us into the affective life, into a deep pattern of feeling, and into an aesthetic, a patterned form of perception. Here Saliers juxtaposes the senses of mystery, awe, and wonder, the awareness of human suffering, anger, sorrow, and humility with attempts to worship with "the showy, the pompous, the self-serving, the mawkish, the cleverly casual, or the thoughtlessly comfortable forms of art."[22]

In a day in which Christian worship is increasingly inundated with the promises of new technologies such as synthesizers and other electronically amplified instruments, projectors and large-screen video images, "how to" books on "contemporary" worship, in a day of increased attention to the place of the arts in worship as means to provide "experience," Saliers argues that it is the "art" of worship it-

[21] "By Gracious Powers," trans. Fred Pratt Green, in *The United Methodist Hymnal* (Nashville: The United Methodist Publishing House, 1989) 517.
[22] *Worship as Theology*, 195.

self that patterns the deep and durable affections of the Christian life. It is the practicing of a liturgical aesthetic that forms the Christian affections.

We might describe this liturgical aesthetic, at its simplest, as those liturgical forms and practices that draw us into and cultivate the depths of the Christian life. But Saliers is more specific, offering criteria with which to evaluate the faithfulness or truth of our liturgical practices. As he warns us about the dangers of excitement, lively feeling, and artistic pleasure as goals of liturgical planning, so, too, he cautions us about substituting seriousness and intentionality in our practice for depth, truth, and power. On the one hand, Saliers warns that "continuing to pray and sing biblically impoverished texts that may also lack aesthetic power, no matter how seriously done, cannot guarantee a deepening of spiritual growth and discernment of what it is to be the church today."[23] On the other hand, he writes:

"Some aspects of our worship, even whole liturgies enacted, please in virtue of their aesthetic properties, but they cannot withstand prolonged spiritual analysis. Some artistic 'enhancements' in worship may be elegant, but are easily forgotten. But liturgical celebrations that have 'deep souls' always yield new discoveries."[24]

Elsewhere Saliers warns against confusing "delight in the things of God" with "entertainment or the frivolity of mere self-expression."[25] These warnings and cautions may seem overly negative, yet the observations behind them reveal problems with Christian worship in North America that neither liturgists nor Church growth experts will fix with another "how to" manual.

While he does not offer such a manual, Saliers does suggest a set of questions about liturgical practice that, when worked through, may reveal the "deep soul" of the liturgy and "yield new discoveries" about our life with God in Christ.[26] In place of efficiency and enthusiasm, Saliers points us to emotional and symbolic authenticity and gospel faithfulness. He asks us to consider:

---

[23] *Worship and Spirituality*, 31.

[24] *Worship as Theology*, 205.

[25] *Worship Come to Its Senses*, 47.

[26] The following questions draw from Saliers' article "Aesthetics, Liturgical" in *The New Dictionary of Sacramental Worship*, ed. Peter Fink, S.J. (Collegeville, Minn.: The Liturgical Press, 1990) 30–39.

Do the materials and forms employed in the liturgy "reflect the beauty and dignity of the rites they intend to serve?"

Does the language used permit an "overplus of poetic meaning" and the multiplicity of meaning inherent in symbol?

Are ritual actions performed in a manner appropriate to wonder and adoration rather than perfunctory, business-like efficiency?

Are the style and quality of the music appropriate to the nature of the rites and of the assembly?

Does the music permit or offer the potential for surprise, tension, and durability such as to encourage the "imaginative power and metaphoric range" of the texts to which it is wedded?

Is there consistent care for "each element and to their interrelation in the whole pattern of the liturgy?"

Finally, is the artfulness of this liturgy "congruent with the self-giving of God in our humanity at full stretch?"[27] It is in this final question that we find Saliers drawing us once again to the vital links between liturgical practice, the formation of the Christian affections, and the beauty and excellence of the moral life.

SYMPOSIUM: LITURGY AND THE MORAL SELF

In this brief review we have suggested that, through his work as a practical liturgical theologian, Don Saliers consistently articulates a liturgical theology that unites prayer, belief, and ethical action. Liturgical practice, to the extent that it succeeds in cultivating the formation of the deep affections of the Christian life, orients the Christian person to a life of praise and gratitude to God that overflows in love and care of neighbor. Such a liturgical aesthetic and ethic yields a life befitting our life in Christ; a life practiced in "the beauty of holiness."

Almost twenty years ago Saliers published an essay in which he challenged both the Church's and the theological academy's understandings of the relationship between liturgy and ethics. On the one hand, he argued, the way in which believers pray and worship is "often radically in conflict with how [they] live." On the other hand, scholars have reinforced "this gap between the 'rhetoric' and the 'reality' of liturgical worship" by enlisting "the easy assumptions of sociology and psychology of religion in our time."[28] As a corrective, he

---

[27] *Worship as Theology*, 198.
[28] "Liturgy and Ethics," p. 16 below.

posited a normative claim and exploration of the conceptual and intrinsic—not merely external and causal—relationship between liturgy, spirituality, and ethics. Through their many and varied practices of prayer and worship, believers are, according to Saliers, formed over time in the deep affections that mark the life of Christian faith.

To honor Don Saliers on the occasion of his sixtieth birthday, we seek in *Liturgy and the Moral Life* to respond to his prophetic challenge and prescriptive invitation to theological work that is "framed in terms of the double focus of liturgy—the glorification of God and the sanctification of [humanity]." The perennial Christian question, a problem since the days of Paul's correspondence to the Corinthians, must be rendered explicit today: "To what extent ought the church as liturgical community make moral and ethical transformation of persons and society the purpose of worship?"[29]

We begin our symposium with Saliers' essay "Liturgy and Ethics: Some New Beginnings." The essays that follow take up the challenges he offers, grouped to reflect the themes and particular emphases of his work discussed above. As a symposium, the authors engage a variety of theological disciplines (historical, systematic, practical, liturgical, ethical, linguistic, musical) in the effort to understand and envision how liturgy, spirituality, and aesthetics entail practices that form Christian subjects in a character worthy of the gospel, that bring humanity to "full stretch" in its life before God. As our intent is not only to honor Saliers but also to engage his work as work in progress, we have invited him to offer the last word, bringing the symposium to a conclusion with his response.

[29] Ibid., p. 28 below.

13

Don E. Saliers

Liturgy and Ethics: Some New Beginnings[1]

Can someone confess faith in God without worshiping God? If someone should answer, "Of course," this signals a fundamental miscon-
ception. *Either* it means to "confess faith in God" has not been
grasped; *or* that person has something other than Judaism or Christianity in mind. To declare loyalty to the God of Abraham, Moses, the
prophets and Jesus of Nazareth is to find one's existence oriented in
the attitudes, beliefs, emotions and intentions which target that God
and no other god. To confess faith here means that the confessor is
oriented in gratitude, trust and obedience to the biblical God. That is
to say, for anyone confessing faith in the sense relevant to our concerns, the God witnessed to in the Scriptures and by the central
Church tradition is their proper worship.

Beginning with our first question is meant to draw attention to an
internal connection between "confessing faith" and worship. To acknowledge and to declare faith in God is to worship God. This ac-
cents confession as a living idiom of human existence rather than as
an abstract theoretical project. Being disposed toward the God who is
confessed in Christian Scripture and Tradition is both formed and expressed in worship and prayer. Worship and prayer are the rule-
keeping activities which keep verbal professions of faith true to their
object. *Lex orandi, lex credendi* is therefore not simply a slogan, but is
itself a methodological remark for our work.

Questions concerning Christian ethics and the shape of the moral
life cannot be adequately understood apart from thinking about how
Christians worship. Communal praise, thanksgiving, remembrance,

[1] Reprinted by permission of Religious Ethics, Inc., from the *Journal of Religious Ethics*, vol. 7, no. 2 (Fall 1979). Copyright 1979 by Religious Ethics, Inc.; all
rights reserved.

confession and intercession are part of the matrix which forms intention and action. This matrix of personal agency constitutes a focal
point in any investigation of the liturgical life of a religious community. Concepts such as remembering, praising, and giving thanks to
God rightly belong to the study of liturgy, and have come increasingly to occupy the forefront of research and constructive work in
liturgical theology. But there has to date been a paucity of dialogue
between liturgical studies and ethics, even though it seems obvious
that there are significant links between liturgical life, the confession
of faith, and the concrete works which flow from these.

How we pray and worship is linked to how we live—to our desires,
emotions, attitudes, beliefs and actions. This is the normative claim of
all communities intending to be faithful to Scripture and to the inner
norms of the Church's declaration of faith. Yet how we pray and worship is, empirically considered, often radically in conflict with how we
live. Such is the description of what is the case sociologically. Upon
this gap between the "rhetoric" and the "reality" of liturgical worship
we have recently had no end of commentary. In fact, most views of
the connection between liturgy and ethics picture the relation as external or causal. This approach is reinforced by the easy assumptions of
sociology and psychology of religion in our time.

Our question is, therefore, how to effect the dialogue between
liturgical studies and ethics. This essay is one attempt to open the
conversations at a level beyond the recital of the slogan *lex orandi, lex
est credendi*. The fundamental conviction undergirding these pages is
that, properly considered, there is an internal, conceptual link between liturgy and ethics. At the foundations of Christian faith and
throughout Jewish teachings, liturgy and ethics are bound together
internally. That is, the link is not causal and extrinsic, but conceptual
and intrinsic. Our problem is how to articulate this without doing injustice to the complexity of other relationships between liturgy and
ethics which can be described.

A second assumption undergirding these pages is that norms and
practices in ethics are never *simply* ethical. The concretization of the
moral life requires a vision of a world, and the continuing exercise of
recalling, sustaining and reentering that picture of the cosmos in
which norms and practices have meaning and point. In short, the
possibility of religious ethics (or, for that matter, of any significant societal understanding and practice of the good) rests upon available

mythoi—stories and narratives of human existence in which a picture of the moral good and associated ideas are expressed. In particular, Christian moral intention and action are embedded in a form of life which is portrayed and shaped by the whole biblical story. Such a narrative understanding of the world found in Hebrew and Christian Scripture provides a way of placing human life *in conspectu Dei,* before the face of God. Such narratives are not ethical systems or lists of rules and principles as such; rather they portray qualities of being-before-God which are focused upon features of God such as holiness, righteousness, and lovingkindness.

It may be objected that a description of the moral life can indeed be given in complete independence from liturgical considerations. This may be empirically possible. But if this is done, certain essentials fall away; indeed, certain conceptual confusions concerning religious ethics result. Thus my central thesis is: *The relations between liturgy and ethics are most adequately formulated by specifying how certain affections and virtues are formed and expressed in the modalities of communal prayer and ritual action. These modalities of prayer enter into the formation of the self in community.* Beliefs about God and world and self which characterize a religious life are dramatized and appropriated in the mode of the affections and dispositions focused in liturgical occasions. (I do not intend to argue that any one specific historic tradition of liturgical worship such as Greek Orthodox, Reformed, or Roman Catholic is itself normative, though any specific historic liturgy or tradition of communal prayer may furnish certain paradigms. There are, after all, good and bad, more adequate and less adequate liturgical patterns and structures.)

I *Xu worship is Conporate*

Worship is something Christians do together, not just because of religious duty, but because it is their way of remembering and expressing their life unto God. But it is also a characterizing activity. It takes time and place and people. When worship occurs, people are characterized, given their life and their fundamental location and orientation in the world. Worship characterizes human beings who recall and give expression to a story about the world. The language of this story teaches us to describe all creatures in the world as God's. Worship forms and conveys the awareness of God and the orders of creation and history.

To put the point in a slightly different way, worship both forms and expresses persons in the beliefs, the emotions and the attitudes appropriate to the religious life. It shapes the Christian affections and provides a way of expressing the perceived realities of existence as received by those who are at the disposal of such beliefs, emotions and attitudes. In any adequate explication of the meaning and point of Christian worship, both the forming and expressing side must be made clear.

Worship, then, is something Christians do together, not just from religious duty (though this may be a sociological fact), but because it is the primary communal mode of remembering and expressing the Christian faith and the Christian story. In the very activity of re-presenting and rehearsing features of existence described in the Scriptures, worshipers articulate their fundamental relations to one another and to the world. Worship is thus necessarily normative. At the same time, not all who participate in its language and action are shaped by it. This is a remark about the concept of "understanding" the world in and through the Christian story. Not all who say the words and participate in the stylized activities fully understand what it is to say and do these things and to *mean* them. Faith is related to "understanding," but in complex ways.

In corporate worship, Christians engage in activities which articu-late and shape how they are to be disposed toward the world. Those who say they love God but who are *not* disposed to love and serve the neighbor are misunderstanding the words and actions of wor-ship. In 1 John we read that anyone who claims to love God and hates the neighbor is a liar. That is a conceptual remark and not an empirical observation about what Christians may or may not do most of the time. It links saying, doing and understanding in wor-ship with a way of life. "Not everyone who says to me, Lord, Lord, will enter the kingdom." To speak of and to address God in the voca-tive of prayer means to undertake a certain way of existing, and to be a certain way towards other persons. This linkage between learning to address God in worship and learning to be disposed toward the world and other human beings "in his name" is easily neglected.

To this point, we have spoken of prayer and worship interchange-ably. Obviously, not everything in worship is, strictly speaking, a prayer. There are lessons, hymns, sermons, gestures of giving and re-ceiving, acts of reconciliation and exhortations. But surely the heart

18

of corporate worship is prayer. We can learn what to say about the nature of Christian worship by thinking about the range and scope of what it means to pray. Prayer covers the entire range of human experience, from extremity to extremity, and much everydayness between. The Lord who teaches the Church to pray himself ranged from "hallowed be thy name" to "My God, why?" The psalms provide the great common hymnal and prayerbook for the praise of God, as well as describe experience of those struggling to live with God in faith.

Regarded from a human point of view, prayer is the activity in which human beings explore their life "unto God." It is much more than words. In uttering the words of prayer, we are doing something, performing an act. To thank God, to praise God, to confess, to intercede—all these are ways of gesturing the self in and through words. What is done with the words is part of the meaning of what is said. Unless we grasp the point of saying such things to God and about God, we will not have fully understood the language of Scripture and theology, or at least its fundamental *telos.* Let us recall briefly, then, something of the primary range of prayer so that we may better describe the meaning and point of worship.

The primary mode of prayer in all Jewish and Christian liturgy begins in praise and thanksgiving. The formulary of the Jewish *berakah* underlies the gesture of common prayer: "Blessed art Thou, O Lord our God. . . ." This form of words speaks God's name in gratitude and praise for who God is, and for the specific occasions in the world given to us. Inherent in this mode of praying is a fundamental receptivity to the world as God's domain—a world bestowed. Liturgically we may wish to distinguish the logic of praising from the logic of giving thanks; but for our purposes they can be assimilated under the more generic *berakah,* or blessing prayer. Christian eucharistic prayers display their origin and shape in this primordial acknowledgment of God.

The prayer of praise and thanksgiving is intrinsic to understanding the nature of God within the religious life; it is essential to human self-understanding as well. In learning to pray this way, human beings are disposed in gratitude toward the world and their place in the orders of existence. Such praying mitigates against the natural fear of regarding everything as having strings attached. So far as prayer is first and last speaking God's name in thanks and praise, it is required for truthfulness in Christian life and theology. Worship is,

19

in this sense, a continual practice in naming God, thereby keeping an essential aspect of the concept of deity in both thought and affection: God is the giver of life, the source of good.

But prayer is also recalling and retelling. Prayer in corporate worship recalls who God is and what God has done. It is grounded in the corporate memories of the religious community. Huub Oosterhuis has put this point well:

"When the bible prays, the whole of creation is listed and the whole of God's history with man is brought up again. When we pray, with the bible, we appeal to creation and to the covenant. We call God to mind and remind him who he is and what he has done. What God used to mean . . . in the past includes a promise for the future, the promise that he will mean something for us as well, that he will be someone for us."[2]

 So prayer is praise and thanksgiving: the acknowledgment of God for who God is. But secondly, prayer recalls and re-presents the story of God's mighty deeds in relationship to the world and to humanity.

In the classical eucharistic prayers of the first six centuries, both East and West, the shape and substance of prayer is *anamnetic*. That is, Christians give thanks to God in the action of the eucharist or Lord's Supper precisely by reciting the story of creation and redemption in the vocative of addressing God.[3] Such prayers of great thanksgiving are recitals of the *mirabilia Dei*, rendering the past as present: "Do this, for my anamnesis."

 Thirdly, prayer is acknowledgment and confession of who we are in God's sight. For to address God and *mean* what we say is to recognize our status. Praying thus explores and continually reveals the infinite qualitative difference between God and human beings. A

---

[2] Huub Oosterhuis, *Your Word Is Near,* trans. N. D. Smith (New York and London: Newman Press, 1968) 8.

[3] A detailed study of these eucharistic prayers yields a rich set of data for our inquiry. The recital of creation and redemption serves to portray the world in which human response to God has point and meaning. Different liturgical traditions or families of eucharistic prayers show differing relations between praise of God for creation and specific thanksgiving for the works of redemption. The West, generally speaking, concentrates upon the redemptive work of Christ, while the Eastern liturgies accent the glory of God and the extent of God's power and splendor in the created order.

central paradigm for this feature of communal worship is found in the language of Isaiah in the temple. In response to the vision of God's transcendent holiness he exclaims, "Woe is me, for I am a man of unclean lips, and I dwell in the midst of a people of unclean lips." This same modality of prayer is found in various confessional sequences and is reflected in the Collect for Purity: "cleanse the thoughts of our hearts by the inspiration of thy Holy Spirit, that we may perfectly love Thee. . . ."

Confessing sin and untruth to God occasions insight into the indelibly human features of the moral life. If praising and thanking are essential to our humanity, so is confession. The language of confessing unto God gives shape to our own self-description: "We have followed too much the devices and desires of our own hearts, we have offended against thy holy laws. . . ." "Lord, have mercy upon us." What interests us here is the manner in which descriptions and ascriptions of God are intrinsic features of the language of repentance, desire, praise and longing. The emotions of the believer—sorrow over sin, gratitude, joy in the forgiveness of God—are made clear in and through language which attributes holiness and mercy to God. Praying brings an entry into the language such that dispositions to feel, intend and to act are formed.

Finally, though not exhaustively, liturgical prayer is found in the mode of intercession. Praying for others requires looking clearly and honestly at the world as it is, and entails awareness of the suffering of others. In interceding for the world, the liturgical community identifies with others and, at the very least, is formed toward pity and compassion. In this sense, communal prayer, rightly exercised, covers the entire range of circumstances and events, good and evil. As a corporate act of intercession, praying holds the world in its actuality, before God. It is a worldly activity. The strenuousness of true intercessory prayer results in a truthful perception of the world's moral ambiguity. We will return in more detail to the relationship of intercessions and the moral imagination in section III.

Christian worship, through a complex symbolic pattern of words and gestures in its ritual actions, both forms and expresses dispositions belonging to the life of faith in God. These dispositions show a double aspect discerned in the four modes of prayer just observed. The affections take God as their ground and object, and they are ingredient in the moral regard toward the neighbor and toward the world as the arena of God's activity. Thus, love of God and neighbor are correlate in the very forms of language and action addressed to God—especially so in the eucharistic context. Such dispositions are requisite features of understanding who God is and what God commands from those who worship him. In tracing out the grammar of the language and action of specific liturgies—e.g., rites of initiation, daily offices, rites for marriage and burial, the eucharist, et al.—we begin to encompass the inner logic of the Christian life.

Specific rites also express the community's life before God and thus bring to consciousness a wide range of life experience in the world of lived moral conflict. There are tensions between the meanings articulated in such rites and the life-meanings which persons bring to worship. On the one hand there are normative patterns of affection and virtue commended and formed in the liturgical prayer of the community. As God is holy so the worshipers are called to be holy. On the other hand the worshipers' intentions and actions fall short, and their affections never become pure motives for welldoing in everyday life. There is always a gap between the ideal values inherent in the prayers and rites and their existential realization. But just at this crucial point a dialectic is built into adequate forms of communal prayer. Recognition of the gap is itself part of what is formed and expressed in the affections belonging to repentance.[4]

II   Xn worship outcome is moral life

The Christian life can be characterized as a set of affections and virtues. There are limits and possible misunderstandings in such a characterization, but for purposes of drawing attention to the internal relations between liturgy and ethics it is essential. From the outset we must conceive virtues and affections in their specific determination in response to the person and work of Jesus Christ. The Christian moral life is the embodiment of those affections and virtues which are intentional orientation of existence in Jesus Christ.

---

[4] This is why reformed rites in our time must continue to struggle with penance and confession of sins, even though we have rightly restored in several traditions (Roman Catholic, Episcopalian, Methodist and Lutheran) the non-penitential and joyous sense of thanksgiving in the texts and actions of the eucharistic rites.

We cannot understand the moral life here simply as conformity to a set of rules, even though teachings and rules for appropriate attitudes and actions are involved. Nor is it sufficient to speak of the imitation of the pattern of behavior given in the gospel portraits of Jesus. Neither the achievement of moral ideals per se nor the adoption of a view of life adequately accounts for the shape of the Christian moral life. An actual reorientation of sensibility and intentional acts is involved, as well as a new self-understanding and a "world-picture." How we understand ourselves in the world and how we ought to live in relation to society, the neighbor and the self—all these are ingredient in our conception of the Christian moral life.

Affections and virtues grounded in the saving mystery of Christ constitute a way of being moral. Thus gratitude to God, joy in the saving works of Christ, hope, penitence and love of God and neighbor are all grounded in the narrative of who Jesus was and is. The exercise of such affections requires a continual re-entry of the person into the narrative and the teachings which depict the identity of Jesus Christ. As I have proposed, the modalities of prayer and liturgical action are the rule-keeping activities of the affections. Liturgy provides both a rehearsal of the narratives and a continual re-embedding of persons in the language of faith.

In a recent study Stanley Hauerwas has argued persuasively that the continuity and identity of self embodied in our character have profound moral significance. The individual Christian character, he contends "is formed by his association with the community that embodies the language, rituals, and moral practices from which this particular form of life grows."[5] The heart of the matter in the form of the Christian life is coming to understand who God is and what his intentions for human beings are as revealed in Jesus Christ. This coming to understand is precisely what good liturgy and faithful communal prayer provide. Hauerwas borrows a phrase from John Dewey—"deliberate rehearsal"—to express the necessary process of bringing every aspect of character into harmony with God's intention for us in Christ.[6] This phrase, I contend, is an apt description of the imaginative power of good liturgy for the formation of character. The

---

[5] Stanley Hauerwas, *Character and the Christian Life: A Study in Theological Ethics* (San Antonio: Trinity University Press, 1975) 210.

[6] Ibid., 213–214.

various modalities of prayer discussed above are linked with the deliberate rehearsal of the great narratives of creation and redemption in Christian liturgy. Patterns of prayer, reading, proclamation and sacramental action are precisely such occasions of communal rehearsal of the affections and virtues befitting "life in Christ." This is no mere mimesis, no simple "imitation of Christ." Rather such worship is best understood as a participation in the symbols of faith which is effected and signified by the words and actions of Christ.

Responding to some remarks on the fundamental symbols of faith made by H. Richard Niebuhr, Hauerwas speaks of the "enlivening of the imagination by images that do justice to the central symbol of our faith."[7] The primary formation and expression of the enlivened Christian imagination is worship. Normatively considered, good liturgy is the fundamental imaginal framework of encounter with God in Christ which forms intentions in and through the affections that take God in Christ as their goal and ground.

Yet it is also true that Christian liturgical prayer must respond to a world in which moral ambiguity abounds. Archbishop Anthony Bloom has reminded us that "prayer is not simply an effort which we can make the moment we intend to pray; prayer must be rooted in our life and if our life contradicts our prayers, or if our prayers have nothing to do with our life, they will never be alive nor real."[8] Not only does prayer shape intentions in accordance with the central symbols of faith, it must be accountable to the way we make actual decisions.

The connection between liturgy and the ethics of character we have been sketching leads to the inner connection between praying and being. How honestly such a form of life confronts the suffering and gladness of the world is something which liturgy itself cannot guarantee. Spiritual self-deception is always possible because praying is always done in the human sphere of forces. Prayer and praise in heaven, we may assume, no longer fall prey to deceit. In hell, self-deception has become a way of life. Prayer that seeks withdrawal from the realm of human forces—social, economic and otherwise—and seeks only to enjoy the symbols of faith fails to exercise fully the religious affections as motives in well-doing. To be moved by the

7 Ibid., 233.

8 Anthony Bloom, *Living Prayer* (Springfield, Ill.: Templegate Publishers, 1966) 123.

24

love of God in Christ requires engagement with the principalities and powers of the world.

A powerful expression of this point is given in the high priestly prayer of Jesus which appears in John's Gospel. In addressing the Father, Jesus says, "I do not pray that thou shouldst take them out of the world, but that thou shouldst keep them from the evil one" (John 17:15). The prayer of Christian liturgy faces the world's ambiguity and evil. But it is precisely in the world that God is to be glorified by doing the works of Christ. Worship ascribes glory to God alone; but unless the glorification is shown in works of justice, mercy and love faithful to God's commands, Christ's liturgy is not fully enacted. At times the tension between cultic and ethical activity must be rediscovered. At other times, their coinherence and mutual reciprocity must be shown forth. The glory and holiness of God is shown both in the otherness of God as the object of prayer and worship, and in the servanthood of those who are formed in the central symbol of the faith.

In our time, there is a tendency to define prayer primarily by its effects and by our own consequent actions in the world. The prayerful life is shown by its fruits, though it can never be reduced to its results. When praying becomes a special instrument for getting things done, such a conception is not far from magic. A one-sided concern for the effectiveness of prayer leads, in Urban Holmes' phrase, to a spirituality of "prayer as production."[9]

Despite such misunderstandings, prayer and worship do respond to a broken and often inexplicable world. Christian prayer is beholding the world in light of the narrative, told, enacted and pondered in Scripture, proclamation and liturgical rites. It is linked both to the raw needs of conflict and to the world beheld as the arena of God's activity. The question may not be "to what?" does prayer respond but "to whom?"

The issue is whether we pray what we mean and mean what we pray without being drawn into the way in which God views the world. The meaning of praying is not a simple matter of saying the words. To pray is to become a living text before God. In this sense, meaning what we pray requires more than the onset of lively emotions. Meaning what we pray involves sharing a form of life in which

[9] Urban Holmes, "A Taxonomy of Contemporary Spirituality" in *Christians at Prayer*, ed. John Gallen (Notre Dame: University of Notre Dame Press, 1977).

the affections and dispositions are oriented toward God. Discovering the meaning of what we pray in communal worship includes the discovery of our loves, fears, hopes, and the situations over which we will weep and rejoice together.

Consider a simple analogy: what do we say and *mean* by "I love you"? Sometimes we say the words without much feeling. A good friend may then remind us, "Once more with feeling, please." We may be able to say it with a little more affection. But the test of the language of love cannot be measured by a one-time episode in its use. While the various "feelings" connected with, say, romantic love may wax and wane, they are not put to the test; but the love is put to the test. Is it not that over a long period of loving and giving, misunderstanding and being understood, being preoccupied and yet forgiven and loved again, that we say "How much this love has come to mean"? Here the utterance is far more than words said with feeling. The language of love becomes access to truth (or falsehood). A lifetime's learning to grow in love may be required to catch the deeper echo of what it means to experience the range of human loves. How much more is the love ingredient in the Christian story not measured by episodic intensities, but by steadfast love. Of God, the Psalmist continually sings, "For his love endures forever." From this, intense affectivity may flow; and, upon occasion, from a proleptic experience the dispositions for more enduring love may be laid down in a life. That is, from an overwhelming experience of being mercifully loved and accepted, a person may find new capacities for steadfast love suddenly in place. Yet the holy affection of love, as Jonathan Edwards would point out, consists in the ongoing exercise of that love over time.

In the letter to the Thessalonians (1 Thess 5:16), St. Paul exhorts them to a Christian way of life. He first lists the things which prevent life in Christ. They are familiar: we are to avoid evil in all its forms, to put away revenge, malice and the dark emotions and vices. We are to put on mutual respect and love. In the midst of the exhortation, he calls upon the people to "rejoice always, pray constantly, give thanks in all circumstances." He commands the emotions of joy, gratitude and love. These are not the kinds of affections which can be simply worked up as a matter of feeling. For he calls forth a deeper joy which can abide all circumstances, good or ill. The constant prayer, of course, is not an incessant pouring forth of words about God and the affections; rather it is a life lived prayerfully and with attention to those features of the gospel for which one can be constantly grateful, and in which one can continually rejoice despite the rise and fall of all worldly enthusiasms.

Prayer begins in gratitude, and its constancy in season and out of season is linked to the constancy of its object—God's love in Christ. As the Psalmist sings, "For his love endureth forever." This holds, I think, for all Christian prayer. To pray is to give oneself to the Christian story in such a way that there is an internal link between the emotions and virtues exercised in that life and the meaning of the texts, prayer and symbols enacted in the rites. Prayer will be on occasion, and perhaps for long periods of time, dry and "meaningless" in the popular sense of that term. Where affectivity is lacking, we may lose sight of the story, and its power and reach may be in eclipse for such periods in one's life. Such a lack of meaning cannot itself be overcome by cultivating "feelings" apart from recovering the depth of the story in allowing our moral lives to be qualified and shaped by it. The "meaninglessness" here must always be met with a waiting, an attending to the Word of God.

To pray to God in the various modalities entailed in communal worship requires living in light of the Christian gospel such that we may rejoice whatever the circumstances and persist in hope. To pray constantly is to be disposed in this world before the face of God. Prayer is thus not an *aid*, psychological or otherwise, to the living of a spiritually healthy or ethically sensitive life. It is not a motivating set of techniques. Rather, prayer is part of having a life formed in joy, gratitude, awe and compassion. These capacities which one learns to call "gifts" when they are rightly understood are directed to God and all God's creation. We respond to the world and to others because we behold them before the face of God. Yet God is never "contained" in prayer. After all this has been said, the connection between liturgy and ethics is qualified by the fact that liturgy is an eschatological gesture and utterance—it is proleptic and does not presume to "possess" or to "dispense" God.

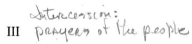

III

We have explored how the prayer of Christian liturgy is formative and expressive of the ethics of Christian character. Liturgy as cultus must bear within itself a prophetic self-awareness because *how* and *what* we pray is also a response to the world as the arena of moral ambiguity and agency. It is time to render an implicit question explicitly: To what extent ought the Church as liturgical community make moral and ethical transformation of persons and society the purpose of worship? Is the ultimate thing to be said about the liturgy of Jesus Christ that it is service and love toward humankind? The answer, of course, can only be framed in terms of the double focus of liturgy— the glorification of God and the sanctification of human beings. The glory of God is shown both in right praise and in the servanthood of those who worship in the name of Jesus Christ.

Let us consider a specific mode of prayer-action which raises these questions most clearly, namely, the intercessions or "prayers of the faithful." The restoration and renewal of the prayers of the people in recent liturgical reforms helps focus a central reality: Christ is in the midst of his people praying with and for them. Here is an explicit mode of prayer in which the attention is upon the needs of the world. This mode of prayer, as we established in the previous section of the essay, comes in response to the divine identification with the lowly, the suffering and the forsaken. The prayers of intercession are themselves a declaration that God in Christ identifies with the suffering needs of a fallen humanity. Here is a specific place of formation of identity as those who pray with Christ the intercessor.

Without prayers for others, our worship cannot discern the fullness of how God is to be glorified by doing his works in the world. The presence and self-giving of God in the liturgy of Word and sacraments cannot be disassociated from the neighbor in need. St. Paul makes this clear, for example, in his criticism of the church at Corinth, whose eucharists were a profanization of the body and blood precisely because they did not attend to another. To forget the others in the presence of Christ's self-giving is to participate unworthily. To recognize Christ's power and presence in Word and eucharist is to confess his presence in the hurt and suffering of the neighbor as well. The former, rightly acknowledged and praised, discloses the latter. In this sense, intercessory prayer is linked to the continuing action of Christ both in liturgy and in the world. This link gives us an insight into the relation between true liturgical spirituality and Christian moral vision.

Prayers for others in the context of Christian worship show forth a fundamental Christological orientation: As Christ had compassion, so must we; as he encountered the brokenness of others, so must we; as he loved even in the face of death, so must we. In these specific ways we are being formed, not simply in the rhetoric of the prayer texts (whether liturgical or "free"), but in a way of regarding the world. The meaning and direction of our affections is always twofold: toward those in need whom God in Christ loves and with Jesus who prays in our midst—the mediator and high priest. Intercessions are the practice and exercise of being turned to discern and act in the direction in which God's love looks and moves.

Four aspects of intercessory prayer constitute its "grammar" and require rediscovery in every age. First, we encounter dimensions of ourselves as praying with and for others. Prayer, for the early Church, was never an isolated action. The notion of "closet" prayer—the interior prayer of the purified heart—focuses upon the integrity of praying, not its personal privacy. Praying was always in community, even when it was prayer alone. The distinction between individualistic devotional prayer and the Church's common prayer was foreign to the early Church.

Prayer for others requires a truthfulness about who we are in relation to others as well as a vulnerability born of empathy. There are religious communities of prayer where counterfeit vulnerability of self-indulgence abounds. Spiritual pulse-taking can and should never substitute for being disposed in love toward others. Thus, encounter with these dimensions of the self are part of understanding and praying.

Secondly, only in and through solidarity with those in need can we mean what we pray in intercession. In exercising the human capacity for identification with others, this mode of praying can grow in maturity and insight into God's grace. The meaning of prayers for others, therefore, is not so much the style of praying as it is the manner of being disposed in compassion.

Thirdly, we gain a moral intentionality in addressing the world to God. We ask God to remember those for whom we pray. We cannot simply "enjoy" the forms of prayer and the affections of empathy. Those who pray must learn, outside the rooms of prayer, the reality of commending others to the grace and mercy of God. The development of this capacity can only be learned over time and circumstances as we engage the needs of others. The most difficult thing is that those who pray are called to trust God beyond their own highest capacity for pity and compassionate service. To intercede is to be attentive to God's hidden ways with the world.

Finally, to intercede without allowing the ministries of the community to be visibly represented in the body renders prayers inadequate to their intent and object. "The community of the people of God," Karl Barth reminds us, "speaks to the world by the fact of its very existence as a community of prayer."[10] It serves the world and speaks "by the simple fact that it prays for the world." Thus is manifest the *reason* for praying—Christ goes before us and promises to be encountered in the hurt and the needy. Where encountering the reality of human need is not part of the experiential background in intercessory prayer, no amount of lovely text—said or sung—will suffice.

Intercessory forms of prayer force us to recognize that religious faith must be lived in the world of power, conflicting passions and moral ambiguity. In our age and cultural circumstances prayer as praise must be connected with prayer as love of neighbor. This, we may observe, is the perennial tension between prayer and action in the Christian life. But our argument implies two further points relevant to this tension. First, the stress on love of neighbor does not entail the diminishment of love and adoration of God. Love of God and love of neighbor are not two sides of a balancing scale of affections. The commandment cannot be taken this way. The summation of law and prophets does not put love of God and neighbor in inverse ratio one to the other.

Secondly, we should not assume that the tension between prayer and action is the same as the contrast between contemplation and action. This identifies prayer completely with "contemplative prayer." It is far more illuminating to speak of the contemplative and envisioning dimensions of all genuine Christian prayer in the liturgy.

Here we see that tensions are built into the Christian moral life shaped by common prayer. This is because the concept of praying is internally connected with the call to holiness at the heart of the Christian gospel. This constitutes the focal point of Christian existence: Christ's own life is one of active prayer and prayerful action. It

---

[10] Karl Barth, *Evangelical Theology: An Introduction* (New York: Holt, Rinehart and Winston, 1963) 38.

is thus fitting to speak of his whole life as a prayer—a continual self-offering in love and obedience to the Father. In exploring what Christ's life (liturgy) signifies, we ponder anew the necessity of understanding prayer and action not in opposition but in tension required by living particular moments in the stream of life which is oriented toward the full stature of God in Christ.

Prayer is itself one activity among others within the Christian life. So there is a temporal contrast: now the community prays and worships, now it engages in works of love and mercy. But this assumes a connection between faith and works which is conceptual and not merely causal or consequential. In light of our thesis concerning liturgy and the formation of Christian affections, faith without works is not so much "dead" as it is self-preoccupied and self-stultifying. Holy affections which do not become the wellspring and motive for action turn in upon themselves; in short, they are not holy affections.

It is crucial to mark a contrast between being and doing within the Christian life. But we also need a contrast between the prayerful life and a life without prayer. These are not conflicting but complementary contrasts. The pervasiveness of prayer can be construed as a mark of Christian moral maturity only insofar as it expresses a wholehearted orientation of life in the person and work of Christ. We are led therefore to extend the concept of prayer (and worship) from its application as specific acts of piety to its application over the whole of one's life. As the early patristical theologians are fond of saying, the whole of the life of a saint is one continuous prayer. We began with praying in the ordinary sense of specific acts of worship and find ourselves necessarily drawn to a sense of prayer which encompasses all of one's feeling, knowing and doing. "The glory of God is the living man." Thus Irenaeus of Lyons asserted once for all against future heresies the fundamental truth we have been exploring in our reflections on the intercessory modes of prayer.

Christian prayer in each of its modes—praise, thanksgiving, confession, intercession, and others—manifests the double focus of glorification and sanctification. Thus we cannot oppose the joy of contemplating heavenly things (the enjoyment of the divine moral excellency of God) and the grim courage of active mission in the world. Both contain a joy which flows forth from having one's affections fixed upon the creating and redeeming self-giving of God.

Prayer is congruent with the human character of divine revelation. The divine self-communication does not destroy the world in coming to it. Likewise the Word and grace of God does not destroy or reduce our humanity in being received. This is why the giving of oneself to God in true worship is intimately linked with prayer as self-giving in works of mercy. The whole of human life is offered and the whole of God's self-giving is to be the orienting vision of the moral life.

The fruits of the Spirit are always embodied in intentions and action, and can never be adequately kept as private consolations. The deep affections of thanksgiving, joy, gratitude and love constitute the Christian community's continuing prayer over time and are part of the continuing dialogue with God. To worship God and to love God entail worldly embodiment. The gifts of the Spirit are bestowed as capacities to know and to recognize God everywhere, even God's hidden glory in the groaning of creation for its liberation from sin and death.

But the secret hidden from the eyes of the world which animates the moral life and our being in the world lies more deeply still. Prayer responds to the world of suffering and dense ambiguity. Its animating principle is hidden from the plain view untutored in suffering and compassion. Neither is it contained by the highest religious ecstasy. The Word and Spirit of God comes in forms compatible with our being human moral agents. But always in the process of transformation, sanctification and glorification by the God to whom all things are returning.

IV

It is, we must admit at the end, misleading to speak of the relation between liturgy and ethics as though there were only one essential link to be explicated. There are a multitude of connections between liturgy as enactment of the defining story of faith and the lived narratives of the moral life. There are many relationships descriptively available. We may investigate worship as motivator of moral behavior, or liturgy as political act. Liturgy can be viewed as the promulgator of an ideology, or at least of specific moral and ethical policies. These and other kinds of accounts of the relation between liturgy and ethics are possible. Our concern, however, has been with the conceptual relationship.

The reciprocity of liturgy and the moral life is traced through affections and virtues formed and ritually enacted in various modalities of prayer. We have thus entered into questions pertaining to theories of virtue and the ethics of character rather than into matters of obligation or consequences. This line of reasoning is clearly related to the doctrine of sanctification, though by no means is it limited to one specific doctrinal formulation. The glorification-sanctification dialectic cannot be understood apart from the determination of the self which is graced.

Human persons are formed in myriad ways. But in the Christian life, the mystery of redemption in the death and resurrection of Christ is the basis and source of the formation of the person. The orientation and process of maturation are therefore never a matter of adopting right behavior or conforming to a priori systems of ruled actions. The qualities of formed character and the exercise of the virtues require the ongoing deliberate rehearsal of the identifying stories and actions of God. What remains to be done is the detailed analysis and specification of how the context of liturgy—rightly prayed and celebrated—is the school of the affections, and, more particularly, what constitutes faithful and unfaithful liturgy in the formation of the Christian life.

There are questions yet more difficult and far-reaching which we have not raised here. Some of these constitute the immediate agenda for the ongoing dialogue between liturgical theology and ethics. For example, in the face of the inhuman and the demonic powers, can the liturgical order of language and action still animate moral imagination and ethical judgment? What traditions and what ecumenically emerging patterns of worship are most conducive to moral maturity and social wisdom? These questions are yet ahead of us.

When liturgy is regarded primarily as a means to moral exhortation or ethical motivation, it loses its essential character as praise, thanksgiving and anamnetic enactment of the mystery of faith. Instrumentalist definitions of worship, whether Protestant or Roman Catholic, founder upon this rock. As it has been observed, when the Church marries the spirit of the age, she will be left a widow in the next generation.

Surely the worship of God in forms which call forth obedience to the gospel and open ears and hearts to the prophetic Word of God forces the issue upon us. Worship is not merely *cultus*—it cannot be and remain faithful to its ground and goal. In the New Testament it is clear that all of Christian existence is a rendering of service unto God. The sacrifice of praise and thanksgiving is already ingredient in the formation of moral dispositions. In fact, the biblical concept of sacrifice is more than a merely cultic concept—it has immense ethical ramifications. There is a unity of *leitourgia* and *diakonia*—of worship and the doing of good works—implied by the narrative recital of God's covenant and history with the world. The focal point remains God's gracious turning toward humankind. The human response of worship articulates a glorification of God in and through all that is human.

All this being said, it is stubbornly the case that the liturgical life of the Christian community cannot be reduced to ethical implications of the cultus either. Liturgy is the non-utilitarian enactment of the drama of the divine-human encounter. At the heart of this is our response to the divine initiative and to the divine goodness into which the prayerful life is drawn. As James Gustafson has remarked, ". . . when one's being is rightly tending toward or intending God, when one's love is rightly directed, there will also be a right intention and direction of specific projects. Thus, what one is by virtue of God's creation, . . . can become realized to some extent in the moral life as one has the right objects of love."[11] How the life of worship and prayer helps to give direction toward the good and toward those right ends has been, in part, the burden of these remarks.

Within the historical ebb and flow of ecclesial life, we cannot nor should we do away with the contingent relationships between liturgy and the realization of the good by Christians. The gap between the worship of religious communities and their works of justice, mercy and love is so great at times as to generate the prophetic rebuke of all liturgy. "Take away from me the melody of your songs . . . but let justice roll down like waters . . . !" The prophetic relativizing of the cultus is always contained within the very narrative and the Word by which the Church prays, proclaims and enacts.

Part of our mutual task as liturgical theologians and as Christian ethicists is to keep the language and rites of Christian worship clear and resilient with respect to the moral life. This is why both Jewish

[11] James Gustafson, *Can Ethics Be Christian?* (Chicago: University of Chicago Press, 1975) 75.

and Christian ethicists need to attend more closely to the connection between ritual life and the normative/descriptive ambiguities within the discipline of ethics. "The glory of God is the living man." But Christian liturgical life also needs to be judged even while it provides the matrix which shapes the affections and virtues requisite for the moral life.

Part 2

Liturgical Theology:
Tradition, Practice, and Belief

Introduction

In this section we explore the relationships between the traditions and patterns of prayer and belief. Two questions are common to the following essays. First, what is the relationship between description and prescription in the work of liturgical theology? Second, what does it mean for liturgical practice to be "authentic" or "faithful" in the present context of Christian diversity? The challenge inherent in both questions concerns what is normative in liturgical practice for the ethical formation of believers. The traditions and patterns of prayer and belief, as means of orienting persons in and to the world, carry ethical consequences for Church and person.

Using the metaphors of geography and mapmaking, Gordon Lathrop argues that the primary link between Christian worship and ethics lies in the liturgy's power, in both its *ordo* and practice, to orient persons and assembly in relation to the world and to Christ. Lathrop asserts that Christ must be the principal referent through which all other ethically oriented elements of the liturgy are applied to the assembly and its members, reorienting even their religious maps through the juxtapositions intrinsic to worship grounded in Trinitarian faith.

James White challenges Lathrop's focus on liturgical *ordo* and, additionally, the ecumenical quest for consensus in Christian worship. White criticizes these attempts, as well as the work of liturgical theologians, for focusing too narrowly on sacramental worship, single traditions, and limited periods in history. He argues that observations of the complexities and varieties within and among traditions of worship do not lend themselves to the normative statements of liturgists but, rather, invite more description of the ways in which American Christians actually worship.

Bruce Morrill develops an argument, similar to Lathrop's, that what is normative is not the particular style of Christian liturgical practices, such as result in claims for a renewed "traditionalism."

Rather, what is normative is the tradition of the dynamic, transformative encounter with Christ in the power of the Spirit as remembered and actualized in liturgical practice. The authenticity or faithfulness of a community's liturgical practice, then, is to be measured against its concrete way of life as the body of Christ.

Henry Knight, Steven Land, and Stanley Hauerwas take up the question of liturgical authenticity and faithfulness from the perspective of Methodist understandings of personal and social holiness. Knight and Land provide an overview of the theologies of sanctification and worship developed in the Wesleyan and Holiness Movements, developing insights into the practices that constitute "holiness of heart and life." For them, the crucial activity of witnessing to the gospel depends upon being morally constituted as a witness through ongoing participation in a worshiping community. Knight and Land describe the forms that worship takes in these traditions, as well as the characteristic affections to which these worship practices give rise.

Stanley Hauerwas posits that the separation of evangelism and ethics from worship is a fundamental misunderstanding of the Church's mission. The crucial issue for the Church today is neither growth in membership nor debates over contemporary or traditional styles of worship nor whether worship can be changed. The question, rather, concerns the "faithful character" of the Church's worship. It is truthful worship of God that enables the Church to give truthful witness about the world to the world.

Gordon Lathrop

"O Taste and See":
The Geography of Liturgical Ethics

The Christian liturgy orients its participants in the world.[1] Such orientation provides the primary and essential connection between worship and ethics, a connection that can be understood as far more compelling than mere lists of rules, far more interior to the liturgical interactions than prescription or causality. Indeed, many Christians who have engaged in liturgical renewal in the twentieth century have done so with explicit interest in the communal orientation to justice and to social action that the newly strong symbols may give. And some have believed that the renewed, ecumenically rooted liturgy can indeed respond to Suzanne Langer's appeal for public symbols that hold and orient us in material and social realities.[2]

Such orientation has been a classic Christian hope for what is to happen in the assembly for worship. Indeed, at root the word "orientation" can be used to denote that ancient Christian practice of locating the assembly and its building or space so as to place it in the world, toward the east. Such a practice was clearly intended to give the assembly a cosmic setting, interpreting the four directions, the lines toward the "ends of the earth," as *created*, and interpreting the east, the place of the sunrise, as standing for God's *time*. To face east in prayer was to

---

[1] This paragraph is thoroughly dependent on the work of Don E. Saliers in "Liturgy and Ethics: Some New Beginnings," *The Journal of Religious Ethics*, vol. 7, no. 2 (Fall 1979) 173-189 and reprinted above, pp. 15–35. See especially p. 17 above: "When worship occurs, people are characterized, given their life and their fundamental location and orientation in the world." What follows here is intended as an homage of thanks for this article and for all of Don Saliers' work.

[2] Suzanne Langer, *Philosophy in a New Key: A Study in the Symbolism of Reason, Rite, and Art* (Cambridge: Harvard Univ. Press, 1978) 288–289. Langer, of course, despaired of such symbols being provided by the churches.

41

be in the world which God had made, on the earth, under the sun and the moon, before God, expecting the open and manifest coming of the day of God in the coming of the risen Jesus Christ. To be in the assembly, toward the east, was thus to bear witness in the world, while waiting and, yet, while receiving that Coming One already. Worship, by its repeated insertion of the gathering into these directions, thus "oriented" the community in both time and space and, thereby, in a world of meaning and meaningful action.[3]

But this orientation has also been expressed much more personally in the history of Christian liturgy. In the mid-fourth century instructions to newly baptized adults that have been preserved for us as the *Mystagogical Catecheses* of Cyril of Jerusalem, that old bishop proposed that receiving communion itself was to be an "orientation" of the senses toward a world held in the extravagant mercy of God.

"After these things, you hear the cantor, in a sacred tone, inviting you to the communion of the holy mysteries and saying, 'O taste and see that the Lord is good.' . . . Come near, therefore, . . . making the left hand a throne for the right, as if it were about to receive the King, and having hollowed the palm, receive the body of Christ, answering with the Amen. After you have then, with certainty, sanctified your eyes by the touch of the holy body, eat. . . . Then, after your communion in the body of Christ, come near also to the cup of the blood. Not extending your hands but bowing and saying the Amen, in the manner of worship and reverence, be sanctified also by partaking in the blood of Christ. While the moisture is still on your lips, touch it with your hands and sanctify your eyes and your forehead and the rest of your means of perception."[4]

The One who is Lord of all, by enacting the opposite of "kingship," by giving himself away in love, is now also "Lord" here, in the hands and heart of the communicant. The Christian macrocosmic orientation is also now reflected in the microcosm of this believer, who is repeatedly gifted and "characterized" by sheer grace.

[3] "The concretization of the moral life requires a vision of a world, and the continuing exercise of recalling, sustaining and reentering that picture of the cosmos in which norms and practices have meaning and point."—Saliers, "Liturgy and Ethics," p. 16 above.

[4] Cyril of Jerusalem, *Mystagogical Catecheses*, 5:21-22.

But this microcosm does not thereby turn inward. The Christian individual is henceforth to experience the world, through all of his or her means of connection to the world, through the actual *senses*, as under the same gift, as covered with the blood of Christ. Indeed, two of these senses have already been addressed: "O taste and see that the Lord is good," sings the cantor in inviting the people to communion, quoting Psalm 34 (and 1 Peter 2:3) and wonderfully proposing that this *meal* might be healing to our *sight*, a sensual reorientation in the world. That such eating helps us to see—or, indeed, in other contexts, that reading and hearing can be a kind of eating—these, of course, are surprising metaphors for *faith*. But the metaphors carry within themselves a strong and intended further connotation: such faith is lively orientation in the world. If all things are henceforth seen, sensed, as covered with the blood of Christ, if henceforth faith sees, amidst all things, that the creating and redeeming God is good, the ethic of Christians follows. This faith must be active in love.[5]

Amidst the repeated exchanges of holy things and holy people, the very exchanges of Christian assembly, each subject is invited to a new relationship to the world, a new orientation in the world.

One way further to consider such orientation of persons and assembly as the primary link between worship and ethics is to apply a metaphor. We may discuss the *geography* of the liturgy. Worship is, of course, no topography lesson, no essay on the interdependence of land mass, living creatures and weather, no exercise in map-reading, route-finding, "orienteering." But such a metaphor can surprise us into seeing the many indications of location, direction, time, and physical interdependence with which classic liturgy is full. The metaphor may invite us into once again evaluating the importance of these indications for our basic orientation in the world that God has made.

There are indeed limitations to the metaphor: we need to see that liturgy is not writing and study, not any kind of "graphy"; the liturgy may be more like binoculars, map, and compass together in the hands of a group that is actually walking in the field. Or it may be

---

[5] Thus, the gesture of communion practice, as proposed and interpreted by Cyril, is an example of "how certain affections and virtues are formed and expressed in the modalities of communal prayer and ritual action."—Saliers, "Liturgy and Ethics," p. 17 above.

the group's seeing a distant peak, finding a nearby spring, and, with that help, reading the map and walking carefully and accurately in the world. But many human communal rituals do have a "geography," song lines that run out from the songs of the ritual across the land, dreams that see the land itself as it was or as it will be. It is useful to ask if we can say anything about that geography in the case of Christian ritual.

It will be important to remember that a good modern geographer knows that maps are interpretations and that mapmaking is an exercise in power. If we ask about the "maps" that Christian worship may propose, we also need to ask about the power that is being exercised here and about the criticism of that power. Nonetheless, like all human beings, we need such communal interpretations of our surrounding space in order to live. Furthermore, a good modern geographer knows that time, and not just space, is involved in any understanding of location and in any map, and that location involves the interdependence of all the creatures nearby. Similarly, our "geography" will not be complete without a sense of liturgical orientation that connects to the past, to the future, to all the surrounding communities of creatures, even to the cosmic and geologic location of the earth itself. And geographers know that one place can be mapped in many different ways and not all maps tell the truth.[6] Our liturgical "geography" will need to ask about its own correspondence to the truth and its own relationship to the other maps, perhaps some of them false or misleading, by which we live.

For we all do live among and by many different geographies. We sit, of an evening, before the television set and its images of a sporting event, a political convention, the Academy Awards. Suddenly we are in a geography: the playing field or the distant hall is the center; our living room is at the periphery. We get a good view of the center, we think, but we know that we have no effect upon that center, except as part of someone else's calculations of mass-marketing, mass-polling tallies. We are marginal. So is our living room. The trees and animals and setting sun outside our window are out of scope entirely.

Or, by means of bridge or ferry we drive up to the watery border between, say, Maine and New Brunswick, and, with the assent of the

---

[6] Mark Monmonier, *How to Lie with Maps* (Chicago: University of Chicago, 1991; 2nd ed., 1996).

44

authorities, we cross as it were into another world, another flag flying to mark its space. It is indeed another economic world, or it is at least slightly so, with demarcated lines of commerce, currency, taxation, political authority. But it is not another world at all to cormorants, gulls, guillemots, osprey, seals, whales, even many of the human residents of these island, bayside, and riverside communities. Some of them find the border as nearly insignificant as those wandering herders, the Maasai, find the invisible line between Kenya and Tanzania. By which geography shall we live? Which tells the truth? The answers, while sometimes obvious, are never easy.

There are many other geography-making tools within our experience. Novels, films, concert halls, the brief but repeated narratives of television advertisements, astrology columns, astronomy reports— they all map our sense of the world, our lines of connection and meaning, of good and bad, of home and away-from-home. Cultural celebrations, multicultural hopes, and the "race" categories available on official forms map our sense of our neighbors and of the lines between us. Highway systems, train lines, and vast suburban malls create our sense of the city, move us through it, map it for us, neglecting decaying neighborhoods and older, less consumption-determined public spaces. These geographies also imply patterns of action. These orientations in the world also bring an ethics along. The sheer force of their presence and repetition in our lives may form us to think that such an ethics is inevitable, "natural," taken for granted.

Among these maps stands the Christian liturgy. The danger has been that we have neglected to see the ways in which the assembly for worship orients us in the world. No, the danger is deeper: that the orientations we have allowed our religious rituals to give us have been almost exclusively interior orientations to the Self, a map of the human heart without a macrocosm, without exterior references except to a World Away From Here, "heaven," we may call it. Such orientations, of course, have nothing much to do with mapping the community of life outside our window, and they largely leave unchallenged and untransformed the maps created by television, advertising narratives, highway systems, racial categories, and national boundaries.

It is not our business here directly to criticize any of these other mapping systems. Let it be said simply: they all have their important uses and their dangerous untruths. But it is our concern to ask whether Heaven and the Self are the only directions that authentic Christian liturgy knows. The assertion being made here is that the renewed Christian liturgy, the liturgy which is the result of recent ecumenical study and ferment and which has influenced the books and the practice of many different churches in North America, is full of lines that run out to the world, full of a communal orientation that is also a personal ethical formation.

What are those lines? What orientations occur in the liturgy? It would be a useful and important exercise to catalogue and analyze the ways in which "orientation" occurs in the classic and renewed liturgy of Christians.[7] Such a catalogue would need to include, at least, the narrative heart of the meeting, the intercessory prayers for all the world, the collection for the poor and for action in the world, the utterly basic shared meal with enough for everyone, the sense of baptismal "citizenship" in the city of God, the musical genre of the meeting, the architecture and arrangement of the meeting room, and the connections between this assembly and other such assemblies.

If an assembly for worship is making clear and strong use of the simplest form of the ecumenical ordo for liturgy—word, table, baptism remembered, all amid a participating community—it has in its midst the tools of a geography. In fact, it is dwelling in an enacted map. The narratives of the Scriptures can provide a sense of the world as being before God.[8] They can provide each local place with a past and with a future, held in God's own hands. The intercessory prayers may behold the actual world in the light of that narrative, holding it in hope and beseeching before God.[9] The collection can be understood as not "for" God nor for us here, but as intended for the

---

[7] "What remains to be done is the detailed analysis and specification of how the context of liturgy—rightly prayed and celebrated—is the school of the affections, and, more particularly, what constitutes faithful and unfaithful liturgy in the formation of the Christian life."—Saliers, "Liturgy and Ethics," p. 33 above.

[8] "Christian moral intention and action are embedded in a form of life which is portrayed and shaped by the whole biblical story. Such a narrative understanding of the world found in Hebrew and Christian Scripture provides a way of placing human life in conspectu Dei, before the face of God. Such narratives are not ethical systems or lists of rules and principles as such; rather they portray qualities of being-before-God which are focused upon features of God such as holiness, righteousness, and lovingkindness."—Saliers, "Liturgy and Ethics," p. 17 above.

[9] Saliers, "Liturgy and Ethics," pp. 27–30 above.

46

hungry and for action in the world, in response to the truth about God and the world. It can thus be part of a "songline." The meal itself can locate the assembly within the economies necessary for eating. It can use local food. Then, by its simple gesture of feeding everyone with limited food, especially when related to the ancient Christian practice of giving most of the food and money away, the meal may make one feature of our geography unforgettable: people need to eat and many people are ill-fed. And when baptism is remembered or enacted, a belonging which is open to all, which defies flags and boundaries and racial categories and even religious purities, may come to help us redraw our maps.

More: the use of the ancient yet growing repertoire of Christian hymnody and of diverse ways to do the whole liturgical action musically can mean that the song of this assembly will link it to other moments in cultural history and cultural geography. Thus there may be created at least a slightly greater complexity against any tendency among the participants to map the world too simply from a monocultural perspective.

More: if this assembly makes use of an even slightly renewed space, the building itself could coordinate with the map proposed by the *ordo*. This can be so whether or not the building makes actual use of the old Christian practice of "orientation"—though that may be desirable if the assembly can be helped to understand the locating, mapping purpose of this ancient eastward positioning. This local place will, however, also be oriented in other ways. At its best, it will be important, holy, not marginal to the supposed "reality" and magnitude of distant, televised events. Its holiness can come to expression by its ability to house a community, each one in personal dignity, around the central matters of the *ordo*, and to do so with a sense of openness toward God's future, a sense of accessibility to strangers, and a sense of responsibility to the surrounding natural world. This building will need to be about being here in open community, not about going away, not about being an essentially unlocated Self or a Self as the only location. Such mapping of the world can be seen in the humblest of Christian buildings when they are used well for the interactions of word, baptism, prayer and meal.

More: in its use of the *ordo*—indeed, perhaps even in its concrete use of hymnals and worship books—this assembly will be in communion with many other assemblies around the world. That communion—thus, that *geography*—will be indicated also by the nature of its leadership (leaders recognized, at least, by the topographically extensive communion or denomination of which the assembly is part) and the wording of its prayers (for example, ". . . for the well-being of the churches of God and for the unity of all, let us pray to the Lord . . ."). Indeed, urgent longing for a greater communion, for Christian unity in witness and action, may be one of the characteristics of this community's prayer and thus of its proposed ethical map.

Such are some of the principal lines that may run from the Christian liturgical assembly into the whole world, creating a sense of space and time, an *ethos* in which meaningful action may occur.[10]

It is of course true that we can obscure the geography proposed to us by this assembly. We can reduce the use of Scripture in our gatherings to single verses functioning as ideological supports, not as rich narratives placing us and all the world before God. We can blunt the force of the intercessions, the collection, or the meal as referring to the concrete needs of the world. We can reduce the frequency of the Supper. We can understand baptism as establishing, not ending, ritual purity and the line between ourselves and others. We can refuse to see the connections provided us by our song, our gathering space, our community linkages. We can avoid doing justice in the actual conduct of the meeting, by our choice of leaders for the sake of their power according to other mapping systems, or by our refusal of hospitality.

But if we simply receive, unobscured, the regular and repeated gift of these basic elements of ecumenical Christian assembly, we will be receiving an orientation in the world. What is more, even when they are obscured, these root elements of the mapmaking liturgy may break out their occlusion to indicate location and direction to some of the participants in the assembly. The Scripture, read even in fragments, may speak a liberating word about the truth of God and the world. The Supper, even protected and minimized, may connect a communicant to the hunger of the world and to our common need before God. The very use of the genre *prayer*, regardless of its content, may indicate the orientation of the world.

[10] On the *ethos* of the liturgy, see especially Don E. Saliers, *Worship as Theology: Foretaste of Glory Divine* (Nashville: Abingdon Press, 1994).

Still, a healthy liturgical practice will be one that tries to allow these central, orienting matters to stand forth in clarity. It will be one that tries to let the practice of the meeting itself at least approximate something of the justice and mercy that liturgy clearly hopes for in all the world. It is not that the goal of the meeting is ethical formation. The central matters of renewed liturgy are central for more fundamental reasons, because they are central to Christian identity. But when these central matters—the *ordo* and its setting—are allowed to stand forth in clarity, the result is inevitably an ethos, a topography, a map. The renewal of the liturgy in clarity, simplicity, and focus around the central things is thus a matter of some urgency, not least because such a renewal will also orient the community in God's world.

This centered liturgy does not bring along an established, narrowly articulated ethical or political agenda. How the liturgy has an ethical meaning—and how it is to be acted out in the course of our lives—admits of quite different formulations. But the orientation in the world already gives points of reference and directions of significance that will be shared by the resultant courses of ethics: that this is God's world, not ours; that we are fellow creatures, along with many others; that the care for the earth and the use of what we need in the world are given to us all in common; that our creatureliness and our insertion in the community of creatures indicate limits on our existence; that none of the boundaries we draw between ourselves are ultimate; that all the boundaries must be judged before God.

Still, such directions are not necessarily followed. Even fervent participants in a liturgy do not always act on its indications. Worse, we all are consummately skilled in self-deception about whether we are so acting. And worse yet, the lines into the world that we may sense as established by one or the other of the centers of the liturgy may turn out to be false geography, in need of radical judgment.

The story of the Taiping Rebellion in mid-nineteenth century China could serve as sobering instruction to those who care about the connection of liturgy and ethics.[11] Hong Xiuquan and the other "kings" of Taiping knew much of the biblical story, largely read from Protestant tracts. They were quite capable, in the manner of the best

---

[11] See, most recently, Jonathan D. Spence, *God's Chinese Son: The Taiping Heavenly Kingdom of Hong Xiuquan* (New York: W. W. Norton, 1996).

modern Easter Vigil, of applying the Exodus story to themselves.
They had a "sabbath" liturgy too: they read the Bible and proclama-
tions of the "kings"; they recited the Ten Commandments; they
prayed and offered incense and flowers and food to God. They also
baptized, thereby establishing, fiercely, the pure and disciplined
ranks of the faithful with a kind of "catechumenate." They were not
so good at putting the words about and from Jesus next to that baptism. And they had no Lord's Supper. In fact, the "Heavenly King"
and his court ate quite apart from the people, as the men were supposed to eat quite apart from the women. But they did indeed discover in the biblical story and in their own dreams a kind of map. It
led from rural southern China, by way of violence, destruction, and
ultimately the deaths of millions of people, to their establishment as a
brief imperial court in the ancient city of Nanjing. (The court itself
witnessed thousands of executions, commanded by the Heavenly
Father, including the death of the East King, who was the mouth of
the Father, the brother-in-law of Heaven, and the very presence of the
Holy Spirit, and the further retaliatory deaths of the North King and
the South King!) This empire proposed itself as coextensive with the
realm of the Heavenly Father, the "elder brother" Jesus, and the
heavenly younger brother, Hong Xiuquan himself. Such a "Christian"
geography needs to be pondered seriously.

But such biblically justified mapmaking does not belong only to
other times and other peoples. A biblical account of the "chosen
people," for example, might be read in our assembly, with all the best
liturgical sense that the texts read here should indeed be read of us.
The account may not be further corrected by any other reference to
passages about the mission and responsibility of the "chosen," about
the judgment and overthrow of the "chosen," about outsiders and
strangers, about God among the strangers. Then the liturgical use of
the "chosen" can participate—and has so participated—in establishing a geography marked by the uncriticized exercise of our own
power, marked by boundaries in need of judgment. But, just as with
the Taiping leaders, to our own consciousness there is no God available to do the judging, for God is none other than the one who has
chosen *us*!

Or, the force of the water-washing that is baptism may be taken
quite seriously. Indeed, in good liturgical form, a great deal of water
may be used, and we may be brought to see that a massive purifica-

tion is taking place here, just as in Taiping. But then we are the purified. And does that not clearly draw a line, a map, a topography, in
which the unpurified are somewhere else?

Or, the holiness of our space for worship may indeed be intensified.
Holiness, God, is here, in the center of our room. But then does the resultant map of the world not have very large spaces for the profane?

Draw a line that includes us and excludes many others, and Jesus
Christ is always on the other side of the line.[12] At least that is so if we
are speaking of the biblical, historic Christ who eats with sinners and
outsiders, who is made a curse and sin itself for us, who justifies the
ungodly.

This reference to Jesus Christ must be seen as the principal contribution of healthy Christian liturgy to Christian ethical mapmaking.
Talk about the "chosen people" in Christian liturgical use can never
be directly applied to "us." The Christian assembly must use such
language with great respect for its history of use among the Jews, for
the Jewish moral seriousness about the burdens the language brings,
and for modern Jewish interest in seeing the language transformed in
its reference. But among Christians, such talk, even biblical talk, must
be run through Christ, through his stance with the little ones and the
outsiders, through his cross, indeed through the crucified one, the
one made to be among criminals and the unclean, himself being the
one "chosen" by God, on whom the Spirit rests, from whom the
Spirit pours.

Furthermore, the experience of the centered holiness of the liturgical building must always be discovering the disorienting, eccentric
reference at the heart of the meeting. The one around whom we
gather when we actually use the building, the one who is present for
us in the hearing of the Scriptures and the celebration of the sacraments, is himself always also away from here, identified with those
who are outside our circle, outside all circles. In him, the Spirit blows
where it will. In him, every place, even and especially the most god-
forsaken, is before God.

And baptism must never be seen as simply "purification." Indeed,
the words that accompany the washing, the words that make it a
"sacrament," will make of the washing a participation in the cross of

[12] This remarkable dictum comes from the systematic theologian Duane Priebe
of Wartburg Theological Seminary, Dubuque, Iowa.

Christ and thereby an end to ideals of ritual purity. Baptism by water and the word, rather, is an immersion in identification with all the needy ones of the world. Such identification makes of the Church that is created by baptism a paradoxical society, a centered society of the open door, the Spirit-formed "body" of the one in whom God is reconciling all things, a community carrying its own contradiction.

Healthy Christian liturgy, for this Christological and Trinitarian reason, is full of juxtapositions. Texts are put next to texts, in tension, and that whole is put next to an oral proclamation of Jesus Christ. The meal follows the word service. Thanksgiving is conjoined with lament, song with silence, people with leaders. The water-washing always follows or precedes a lengthy immersion in the word that is about Jesus. "Direction" is thus found in the liturgy by means of a kind of triangulation: this mountain peak actually seen near this spring, read in relationship to map and compass, yields an accurate reading of direction. Only by the use of at least two things may we avoid being immediately misled. These liturgical pairs lead to a "third" thing: to prayers before God for the world, to mission and service in the world. That third thing can be seen as a lively expression of the geography established by the juxtapositions of the liturgy.

One can say that Christian liturgy, at its best, receives our senses of direction, our maps, our geographies, and radically reorients them.[13] Such reorientation is the most important form of liturgical mapmaking. We may come expecting centered holiness, and we are given a direction away from here. We may come looking for God-in-the-distance, and we are given God-in-our-midst. We may come for us and we are given them. We may come for them and we are given ourselves, our selves truly, in community, before God, not cut off from them. We come to a cultic event and we are given, in the context of the cult, the radical critique of the cult.[14] We bring religious expectations to "chosen people" in the Scriptures, "holiness" in our

[13] "Neither the achievement of moral ideals per se nor the adoption of a view of life adequately accounts for the shape of the Christian moral life. An actual reorientation of sensibility and intentional acts is involved, as well as a new self-understanding and a 'world-picture.'"—Saliers, "Liturgy and Ethics," p. 23 above.

[14] "The prophetic relativizing of the cultus is always contained within the very narrative and the Word by which the Church prays, proclaims and enacts." Saliers, "Liturgy and Ethics," p. 34 above.

architecture, "purity" in our baptisms, and find these geographic designations profoundly revalued.

These reorientations correspond exactly to the central and identifying faith of the Church in Jesus Christ, to his parables, to his cross and resurrection, to his contradiction and reorientation of words like "lord," "messiah," "salvation," and "holiness." These geographic reorientations correspond exactly to the Church's Trinitarian faith. They arise in an assembly that is enlivened here by that Spirit which blows over the face of all deeps. They occur in an assembly around the presence here of that crucified and risen one who holds all the stars and all the needy in his hands. They thus position the assembly before the face of the God who is more than our own projections. These reorientations belong to the geography of Trinitarian faith.

So Cyril teaches Jerusalem's neophytes—and with them, teaches us as well—that communion itself has given us a map. This map includes its own critique of all mapmaking power by referring to the one who is Lord by being no lord at all. This is thus a reoriented map. This is a map that locates us in time as well as space, inviting us to wait confidently amidst all things for the healing of all things and to run out, in all our actions, toward the coming of that healing. This is a map given in juxtapositions: Christ's healing of our eyes with food, Christ's food next to his words about the food, this little food next to all the hungry world. O taste and see.

James F. White

How Do We Know It Is Us?

Several years ago, people in the historical preservation movement adopted a slogan: "How Do We Know It Is Us?" The point was that unless we preserve a sufficient stock of the built environment, we stand to lose our identity as a people. When long-familiar buildings disappear, a community forgets who it is. I don't know how many buildings this slogan helped to save, but it does suggest a dilemma that people concerned about liturgy also have discussed increasingly in recent years.

There have been many concerns in the last two decades to articulate just what we mean by authentic Christian worship, prompted, no doubt, by an avalanche of changes that have left some doubts as to whether what was left was still identifiably us. Presumably, one of the alternatives was worship that was not authentic, maybe not in spirit and truth. The presence of Jewish and Muslim worship in most American cities makes us realize that we have to be specific; there are other kinds of worship than Christian. And worship has to be distinguished from other Christian activities such as catechesis, undeniably Christian but not worship. I shall examine where these discussions have led us so far and offer my critique.

THE EFFORT TO DEFINE A CONSENSUS

The most concerted effort to define authentic Christian worship has come in terms of those seeking to find a consensus. And the most thorough effort has come through those working with the Faith and Order Commission in the World Council of Churches. But it has not been alone; many bilateral and multilateral conversations have gone on between many Churches. Worship, particularly sacramental worship, has been a main concern of many of these conversations.

The chief monument of this effort has been the document *Baptism, Eucharist and Ministry* (BEM).[1] This was submitted to the Churches for response in 1982, and six volumes of responses have been published. BEM deals with such topics as the institution, meaning, practice, and celebration of baptism as well as baptism and faith; the institution, meaning, and celebration of the Eucharist; and matters both liturgical and theological in ordination. Throughout, the effort has been to reach the maximum degree of consensus possible, while admitting the stubborn areas that resist this, such as baptism of believers only or the ordination of women.

In this approach, convergence leading to consensus is considered highly desirable. Divergences and disagreements are seen as impediments to the final "goal of visible Church unity." Disagreements, such as that over "the sign of the gift of the Spirit" in baptism, are acknowledged, but the thrust is to maximize the areas of agreement. There is no suggestion that the Churches might be better served by more disagreements or variances in practice. The movement is centripetal, not centrifugal. Some of the responses to BEM have welcomed such convergence; others have failed to recognize in the text their own faith and practice. It seems to be a natural assumption of ecumenism that homogeneity is better than heterogeneity.

Individual theologians have taken up the same concerns. One of the most brilliant recent attempts has been the beautifully written volume *Holy Things: A Liturgical Theology*[2] by Professor Gordon W. Lathrop of Lutheran Theological Seminary in Philadelphia. A major concern of Lathrop's is to define the *ordo* of Christian worship, a term employed by Alexander Schmemann, the Russian Orthodox theologian who taught at St. Vladimir's Orthodox Theological Seminary in this country.[3] In elucidating "the Pattern of the *ordo*, that ritual ordering and 'shape of the liturgy'"[4] Lathrop begins with the week and Sunday and the juxtaposition of word and sacrament, then moves on to the "classical structure of Christian prayer itself," the connection of teaching and baptism, and the *ordo* of the liturgical year with its center in Easter.

[1] Geneva: World Council of Churches, 1982.

[2] Minneapolis: Fortress Press, 1993.

[3] *Introduction to Liturgical Theology* (Portland, Maine: The American Orthodox Press, 1966) 28–39.

[4] Lathrop, *Holy Things*, 33.

Lathrop shows how meaning occurs through structures, that is, the way things relate to one another. He is particularly concerned to portray those things that have endured in Christianity ever since the New Testament or at least since Justin Martyr in the second century. Lathrop tries to unearth the meaning behind the forms of ritual patterns that have endured throughout the centuries. For each generation, the *ordo* is a challenge to "renewed religious intensity and renewed religious critique." Lathrop may have achieved the finest available description of classical Christian worship.

Many others have written liturgical theologies in recent years: Geoffrey Wainwright, Aidan Kavanagh, Don E. Saliers, David W. Fagerberg, Kevin W. Irwin, and David N. Power, to name but a few. These represent magnificent theological accomplishments. *Unfortunately, most liturgical theology tends to be historically naive, just as much liturgical history may be theologically unsophisticated.* Most liturgical theologies are based on a single period of a single tradition. And frequently it is an idealized version of that tradition. In most cases, it is something similar to what theologians envision to be the realities of post–Vatican II Roman Catholic worship or its near counterparts. Few represent the Eucharist as an occasional service for most American Christians. Rarely do liturgical theologies take account of the enormous complexities and varieties within a single tradition, let alone between them.

The fact that there are at least twelve major traditions of Eastern and Western Christian worship in North America alone makes generic statements almost impossible. And when one considers the multitude of ethnic and cultural styles within those traditions, generalities become still more difficult. One can do a liturgical theology for a carefully defined tradition at a given time and place. For example, the United Pentecostal Church, International can give evidence for the unity in the Godhead on the basis of their practice of baptism in the name of Jesus only. But one cannot make normative statements on that basis for any other Church. At best, one can be descriptive: this is prayed and believed by these people at this time and place. But one cannot leap to a normative declaration: this is what all Christians believe.

Unfortunately, the attempts at finding convergences or consensus have the effect of ignoring the worship of most North American Christians. Do we want to say that what happens in most churches in the United States on a Sunday morning is "baby worship," since it does not match some ecumenical or historical standard? Do we want to say that a preaching service each week and Thirteenth Sabbath Lord's Supper (as among Seventh Day Adventists) is not authentic Christian worship? Do we disqualify those for whom the major events in the liturgical year are Children's Sunday, Homecoming, Revival, and Rally Day (none of which, as yet, has been commercialized)?

We face a basic problem in ignoring the worship of most North American Christians. Large segments of North American Christianity have no interest in ecumenism and are doing quite well without us. But though they ignore us, can we afford to ignore their worship? If we take seriously the premise that the way people pray expresses what they believe, then we have to be very deliberate in accepting the vast diversity of actual prayer practice, especially in North America. In trying to marginalize the worship life of so many millions, we have violated one of the basic motifs of *lex orandi*. But if we respect the varieties of prayer, it will change significantly the way liturgical theology is done.

Part of the problem results from following too uncritically the dogmatism of Alexander Schmemann. Any scheme that totally ignores the worship life of about sixty percent of American Christianity is highly questionable. To imply that the *ordo* of Christian worship is missed by all those for whom the Eucharist is an occasional service, for whom the pragmatic Christian year makes more sense than the traditional Christian year, is indeed risky business.

Actually the basis of liturgical theology ought to be empirical observation of what the Church actually does. But if one excludes from consideration, even condescending consideration, what the majority of American Christians call worship, such selective use of evidence makes the empirical basis of liturgical theology very dubious. To call infant baptism a "benign abnormality," despite the fact that probably ninety percent of Christians ever baptized were baptized as infants, seems to impose other concerns than what the Church does in reality. It makes what the Church should do operative instead, that is, it introduces normativity. Impartial observation would seem more objective. The consequence has been to make liturgical theology, all too often, a minority report.

It occurs to me that the place to begin is not with actual worship traditions but with something more basic, albeit more elusive. I speak of spiritualities that underlie American worship, just as bedrock underlies fertile soils. The history of religion in American might well be described as the history of competing spiritualities. These crisscross beneath various worship traditions such as Methodist, Anglican, Reformed, etc. Thus, competing spiritualities are not to be confused with denominational allegiances, although frequently they have much in common.

I shall try to describe a few North American spiritualities, without trying in any way to produce an exhaustive list. I realize that some may overlap. As with traditions, it is easier to define the center than the edges. But if I can give some indication of the underlying strata of American religious life, it might prove helpful.

Most familiar to my readers would be a sacramental spirituality, or in reality, a *Eucharistic spirituality*. There are certainly large numbers of Americans whose chief experience of the divine is at Mass or Holy Communion. I wish I could say that there is a baptismal spirituality, but no one seems to have seized that part of Luther, who began each day recalling his baptism and lived in that comfort. In recent years a Eucharistic spirituality has focused on receiving communion in the Mass. For previous generations of Roman Catholics, communion was detachable, and various devotions, such as little visits to the Blessed Sacrament, could rely on spiritual communion alone.

One can find a Eucharistic spirituality among most Orthodox, many Anglicans, some Lutherans, and a few Methodists and Presbyterians. It may not be as secure among Roman Catholics as one might assume. A recent poll by the *New York Times* showed[5] that seventy per cent of Roman Catholics under forty-five years of age were Zwinglians in Eucharistic theology, and Zwingli was satisfied with four communions a year. On the other hand, there are indications that some Methodists, for example, are returning to their Wesleyan roots in demanding a weekly Eucharist.

A second kind of spirituality has more adherents in this country. I call it a *Word–centered spirituality*. It is found in vast reaches of American Protestantism, where one goes to church primarily to hear if

[5] *New York Times*, June 1, 1994, 1A and 12A.

there is any Word from the Lord. Most obviously this is centered in preaching, but God's Word may be heard in readings, psalmody, hymnody, and prayer. A Word–centered spirituality is becoming increasingly important in Roman Catholic circles as three Scripture readings and improved preaching have become common. It may in time mark a major shift away from purely arbitrary authority in doctrinal matters. Preaching functions as faith expression in black parishes, Catholic or Protestant, where it becomes genuine dialogue as preacher and people wrestle meaning out of God's Word for today.

Our third type of spirituality I call *Spirit-centered.* This takes many forms, from Quaker silent waiting on God to the ecstatic speech of Pentecostals. In any case, all seem to have transcended the inhibitions of Enlightenment mentality in order to experience a God who acts here and now in their midst. Such worship is filled with unexpected possibilities, for one never knows whom the Spirit will use or what gifts will be manifest. Liturgical democracy is a weekly reality with these people. Little distinguishes Catholic Pentecostals from Protestant Pentecostals. One Spirit moves in their midst in many forms of divine–human encounter.

Not all would agree, but I believe there is a strong *community–centered spirituality* in much North American worship. At its worst, this is the club ecclesiology most apparent in ethnic Catholic parishes. Hungarian and Irish parish churches in our city perch on adjoining blocks. At its best, a community–centered spirituality is a recognition that one experiences Christ in one's neighbors. After all, the promise is that it only takes two or three for Christ to be present. It is discouraging to read of Catholics who claim a greater sense of community in the coffee hour than in the Mass. But there is a deep instinct here that one encounters Christ in other people. The Quakers stress the necessity of "seeing of the faces one of another," as in Robert Barclay's metaphor that more candles gathered together produce more light.[6]

I think that it is possible to speak of a *musical spirituality.* This is not an aesthetic matter but a reality which is found in many Protestant congregations and the lack of which is bemoaned in *Why Catholics Can't Sing.*[7] The easy answer is that Catholics, unlike Protestants, do not have a long tradition of congregational singing. Indeed, many

---

[6] *An Apology for the True Christian Divinity,* "Prop. 11th Concerning Worship."
[7] Thomas Day (New York: Crossroad, 1991).

Protestants find that the most normal and natural way to express religious feeling is in song. Whether one rejoices or mourns, it is best done in hymns. And in life's crises, words of hymns often come to mind before those of Scripture.

One of the newest developments, the so-called worship and praise type of service, only confirms the power of a musical spirituality. In such services literally half of the worship time is devoted to music. The music is addressed to God but the words speak heavily to humans, sometimes with a mantra–like intensity. And much of this musical spirituality can be drawn upon during the week outside of common worship.

These are samples of the underlying strata of spiritualities in American religion. I call them competing spiritualities because they often seem to vie for people's allegiance. At the same time, Eucharistic, communal, and musical spiritualities often overlap in various individuals. Eucharistic and Spirit-centered spiritualities frequently coincide here, although usually at different hours. So they are by no means mutually exclusive, although often with strong centers of gravity. Thus most Methodists would be more likely to have a Word–centered spirituality than a Eucharistic one, even though John Wesley combined the two.

DEFINING AUTHENTIC CHRISTIAN WORSHIP

If there are so many underlying spiritualities beneath the ground in American worship, what unites them? What are the criteria for determining what is authentic Christian worship?

At the highest level, we are frustrated because one cannot query God, the object of our worship, to find what forms are most pleasing. As far as we know, there is considerable latitude, although child sacrifice seems to meet with certain resistance! Indeed, the Bible seems much firmer in condemning various forms of idolatry than in prescribing forms of worship. The English Puritans did their level best to make Scripture into a book of rubrics, but they only proved the impossibility of the task. So we must presume that any worship offered in Spirit and in truth is pleasing to God.

Another approach is to look at the human side. As Pius X said, worship both glorifies God and sanctifies humans.[8] The human

---

[8] "Tra le sollecitudini," *The New Liturgy,* ed. R. Kevin Seasoltz (New York: Herder and Herder, 1966) 4.

dimension is almost as hard to estimate as the divine. All forms of Christian worship seem to be effective in producing saints, maybe equally so. I am tempted to put the Quakers in first place because they have seen so clearly the connection between worship and justice. George Fox died two centuries before Virgil Michel was born. His followers were the first to oppose slavery and to achieve the equality of women, all on the basis of their worship. Yet Quaker worship is the most ascetic of all, doing without visible sacraments, hymns, or sermons. But they certainly have no monopoly on sanctity, and it is common to all worship traditions and all spiritualities.

For me, the hardest test case is the service of the Jehovah's Witnesses. Can I call worship what seems to me to be almost entirely a process of catechesis? It may be authentic, and probably is Christian, but is it worship? Most of the service consists of reading and responding to passages dealing with doctrine. I find it much easier to recognize Muslim services as worship, although definitely not Christian.

Are we any closer, then, to defining authentic Christian worship? I think we must avoid definitions that say the canon is fixed. This is the problem with trying to make an *ordo* our basis of definition. That method means that the canon is closed, although even Karl Barth could claim that, in theory at least, the canon of Scripture is still open. As Richard McBrien is fond of saying, we may only be in an early period of Church history. Who knows how many sacraments there are? No one did for the first three-fifths of Church history to date. Not until a textbook writer tried to be precise about God's activity was anyone counting.

The same may be true for worship in general. Not only are we in danger of unchurching the majority of American Christians if we give too precise a definition, but we also risk missing what we can learn about worship from fringe groups. It took the Shakers to remind us that Christian worship can be ecstatic dance, although there are only eight Shakers left. The Brethren Churches have reminded us for two centuries that the Lord's Supper always occurs in the context of servitude manifested in footwashing. Some of us have forgotten much of our own tradition. Methodists might do well again to shout over the presence of the King in the camp.

So what criteria can we use to pinpoint authentic Christian worship? I would say the first criterion is survival. Maybe the answer is to wait and see if this thing be of God. If a form of worship survives more than the original generation, it must have some validity as a means of humans relating to God. We may dislike the Church-growth approach to worship, but if it is still flourishing a dozen years from now, we must concede it a certain validity.

Like a self-pruning tree, many branches that are no longer productive disappear in worship. We no longer practice the lifelong penance of the early Church; extreme unction is no longer almost exclusively a rite for the dying. Some practices may disappear for reasons purely irrelevant to the Christian content, as in some burial customs. And some things forgotten may be well worth retrieving, such as the adult catechumenate. But survival, especially over generations or centuries, must be respected. Four hundred seventy years of Anabaptist worship or a century of Pentecostalism deserves a place in the liturgical sun.

The consequence is that we need to spend much more time in describing rather than prescribing. Liturgical theology has leaned to normative rather than descriptive statement. What do lay people really mean when they say having the Eucharist every Sunday would make it less meaningful? Liturgists have been trained to argue against that frequent assertion. But maybe lay people are telling us that life cannot sustain a weekly high, but that monthly or quarterly rhythms are true to life. After all, birthdays would mean much less if they occurred monthly instead of yearly. And when Catholics give the "wrong" answer about Eucharistic theology, are they really telling us they live in the Enlightenment and to expect them to do otherwise is presumptuous?

This brings us back to the efforts at consensus or the exclusive focus on the *ordo.* If we take history seriously, we cannot be so definite. The first rule of history is that history is messy. Indeed, while we can assert that sacraments are important to Christian worship, they are not essential. Otherwise we have learned nothing from the Quakers. Quakers, of course, should not say that silent waiting on the Spirit is essential to authentic Christian worship, although few of them would be so assertive. I happen to cherish the Eucharist, but I can understand other forms of communion with God.

Nor would we assert that the liturgical year is essential to Christian worship. The Puritans abolished the traditional liturgical year except the weekly observance of Sunday. But I know of no group that has had a stronger sense of the immediacy of God's saving acts in the midst of their own time. Why keep Christmas when you could celebrate God's most recent gifts by thanksgiving? Even the written Word of God sometimes seems tame when its Author is present at a Quaker meeting. Most of those who lead in prayer would be astonished to learn that there is a classical bipartite form. Many things that make sense to liturgical scholars do not seem all that important to real people.

Beyond survival, what seems to be essential in Christian worship? Are there some things that do seem to be universal and constant, that is, everywhere and at all times? I would say there are a few, but they are very broad and general rather than precise and specific.

The first essential of authentic Christian worship is *coming together in Christ's name*. Christian worship is a public act done by assembling, congregating, meeting. There is an intentionality in the *ecclesia*, those who are called out from the world. It is so obvious that we usually forget it, but the most important thing that happens in Christian worship is that believers come together. Over the centuries, hundreds of thousands of Christians have been willing to die for the act of coming together in Christ's name. Their crime was not in what they did in worship but in making worship possible by assembling.

I recently was studying eighteenth–century meetinghouses in New England. Two places are treated with great elaborateness: the pulpit and the doors. The iconography of the elegant pulpit is probably conscious; the ornate doorways are a bit more subtle. But what I think they are saying is that every individual who enters to worship is performing an important liturgical function: forming the body of Christ. And therefore the most elaborate pediments, pilasters, and panels that the community could afford adorn these entrances; sometimes three doorways are treated with equal dignity. We have rediscovered some of these insights in church architecture today, with an intentional focus on gathering space.

A second requisite for authentic Christian worship would be *expectation of encounter with the divine*. This may occur in many ways. Prayer may be the most obvious, but it is by no means the only form. I have been, with a bit of surprise, in services in which prayer had completely disappeared. It plays a very minor role, if any, in seeker services. That does not mean that prayer is irrelevant to evangelization, but it is hardly a chief focus in some instances.

By way of contrast, I would say that most Protestants attend worship with an expectation of being edified, whereas Catholics come with the hope of being sanctified. These terms are not opposites by any means, even in their Greek and Latin ancestors. What unites them is the expectation of encounter with God. Edification relates more to a Word–centered spirituality, sanctification to a Eucharistic spirituality. Both words and actions have one purpose: to bring us into the presence of God. Thus there is a common expectation but by different means.

Thirdly, I would say that authentic Christian worship can take *an enormous variety of forms,* some of which we have experienced in the past and many more that we may discover in the future. Many types of worship have evolved in the past; the past five centuries have been the most productive in history. Roman Catholicism, the Byzantine Rite, the other Eastern rites, and the nine Protestant traditions are all options in various parts of the United States. As Christianity becomes more and more global, other options will certainly become available as more people are Christianized.

The problem is not that we have too many traditions but rather too few. As we become more aware of the rich variety of human cultures, we become more aware of the need to find ways of expressing Christian worship that are congenial to a wide variety of cultures. Many if not most of these will rely on the *ordo* as articulated by Western Christians in our time. But this is no guarantee that they are any more or less authentically Christian than, say, some of the independent Churches of Africa. Indeed, someday we may be judged by what those Churches have contributed.

Fortunately, in our time of global communication, we can all share more readily in the gifts of Pentecostals in Chile or monks in Russia. In theory the canon is still open. So we must be open, too, to accept God's gifts in whatever form and from whatever source to create authentic Christian worship.

Bruce T. Morrill, S.J.

The Struggle for Tradition

There is at present a typical and widespread struggle over the word and concept of "tradition" as Christians think about the role and significance of liturgical celebration in their lives. My own experience in recent years of conducting workshops and lecture series on the reform of the Church's liturgy in Roman Catholic parishes in the Archdiocese of Atlanta has led me to reflect upon this typical situation. My effort to explore how the liturgy should draw people into a dynamic, transformative encounter with Christ in the power of the Spirit often met with conflicting reactions. Almost predictably I found myself challenged by one or several persons who were disenchanted (at best) with the reformed rites and who missed what they often described as the solemnity and mystery of—and here the terminology is important—the old, *traditional* Latin Mass. On the other hand, there were individuals who would express their disappointment with the continued formalism of their parish liturgy and wish that more interpersonal gestures, such as holding hands at the Lord's Prayer, and more contemporary music could be adopted.

To the former group, I was a reformer quoting modern Church documents (Vatican II's Constitution on the Sacred Liturgy or the General Instruction of the Roman Missal) to the neglect of tradition (no matter how much I cited the Constitution's self-described mandate of "faithful obedience to tradition"[1]). From the latter the cautions and, at times, criticisms I raised about some popular ways of trying to make liturgy "relevant" elicited such reactions as, "Why, you're not a *traditionalist*, are you?"

---

[1] The Constitution on the Sacred Liturgy, no. 4. In *Vatican Council II: The Conciliar and Post Conciliar Documents*, vol. 1, rev. ed., ed. Austin Flannery (Grand Rapids, Mich.: Eerdmans, 1992) 2.

Without doubt, the people taking these varied, often polarized positions on the liturgical reform are making an effort to own the tradition, to claim it for themselves. The danger, however, is that people can become so preoccupied with questions about the form of worship itself that there seems to be little chance for the liturgy to form them in the virtues and affections of Christian life, as Don Saliers argues the liturgy is meant to do. More specifically, the problem seems to lie in the degree of comfort being sought in relation to traditions in the liturgy that threaten to distort the living tradition given in Christ through the ongoing work of the Holy Spirit.[2]

In other words, the problem here is that people consider tradition to be located in the forms of liturgy itself. To a certain extent, of course, this is correct, since it is only through the performance of the ritual that the tradition can be passed on. The evidence, nevertheless, that Christian tradition is alive is found in the impact that the practice of worshiping God on the Lord's Day has upon its participants' lives during all the rest of their days. The authenticity of Christian liturgy, as an integral part of the Christian tradition, cannot be evaluated simply in terms of the rites themselves but, rather, can only be adequately assessed in relation to the ethical practice of Christians, that is, in their concrete way of life.[3]

What I hope to do in this brief essay is to go beneath and behind these struggles over traditional versus untraditional forms of worship in order to explore more fully the concept of Christian tradition in relation to the liturgy. I shall begin with consideration of the New Testament. Providentially, what seems to be the earliest Christian mention of tradition in a liturgical context dramatically makes my

---

[2] Biblical theologian Sandra Schneiders identifies the gift of the Holy Spirit that Jesus passed on to his disciples as the "foundational" sense of the word "tradition." For her discussion of three distinct but related meanings of the word "tradition," see Sandra M. Schneiders, *The Revelatory Text: Interpreting the New Testament as Sacred Scripture* (San Francisco: Harper Collins, 1991) 71–81. Systematic theologian Edward Schillebeeckx explores the relationship between Christian tradition and contemporary cultures in his *Church: The Human Story of God*, trans. John Bowden (New York: Crossroad, 1991) 33–45.

[3] Here I follow Don Saliers' use of the word "ethics" to refer to "the concrete way of life rather than the theoretical interpretations of ethical theory." See Don E. Saliers, *Worship as Theology: Foretaste of Glory Divine* (Nashville: Abingdon Press, 1994) 172.

point. In his First Letter to the Corinthians, Paul is dealing with conflict in the community and with inauthentic Christian behavior evident in the Eucharistic celebration.

What we find in 1 Corinthians 11 is not only one of the earliest definitions of tradition in the Church but also one of the first teachings about the Eucharist.[4] Paul is able to *hand on* (v. 23) to the Corinthians the origin of the Church's Eucharistic meal in Jesus' words and gestures at the supper on the eve of his death, that is to say, the tradition of the Eucharist. His passing on of the tradition, however, is occasioned precisely by the reports he has received concerning the community's Eucharistic celebration. Paul perceives the conventional social behavior of the wealthier Christians as defeating the very action of communion in the body and blood of Christ that they should be enacting. Paul calls on the wealthier members to recognize what they are doing when they feast together while the poorer members are unable to join in a lengthy meal in conjunction with the ritual sharing of the bread and cup (due not only to their meager finances but also an apparent lack of leisure time).[5]

Together, an indicative and an imperative quality comprise the tradition of the faith. The surety and faithfulness of what God has done for the Church, the Body of Christ with its many members, is received and passed on in the enactment of the sacramental meal. The faithfulness of believers to the divine gift of their salvation in Christ is realized in their living out of the imperative that this gift reveals. Mere attention, however, to the traditional form, to the words and gestures, of the Eucharistic ritual is not all that the command of remembrance entails. Unless these Christians grasp the meaning and live out the implication of the gift of salvation manifested in the Eucharist, it is not, as Paul bluntly puts it, the Lord's Supper that they are celebrating. They do not know what they are doing.

Selfish feasting to the neglect of the poorer members of the community betrays a character inimical to that of Christ, whom the community claims to commemorate in the performance of the Lord's

---

[4] In the following discussion of 1 Corinthians 11, I am dependent on the works of two Scripture scholars: Xavier Leon-Dufour, *Sharing the Eucharistic Bread: The Witness of the New Testament*, trans. Matthew J. O'Connell (New York: Paulist, 1987), especially pp. 203-229; and Jerome Murphy-O'Connor, "Eucharist and Community in First Corinthians," *Worship*, vol. 51, no. 1 (January 1977) 56–69.

[5] See Leon-Dufour, *Sharing the Eucharistic Bread*, 217.

Supper. Scripture scholar Jerome Murphy-O'Connor argues that Paul's concern to correct the failure of those Christians in Corinth necessitated his adding his commentary to the account of the Last Supper: "For as often as you eat this bread and drink this cup, you proclaim the death of the Lord until he comes" (11:26).

Concerning the word "proclaim" *(kataggelete)*, Murphy-O'Connor argues that analysis of the verb in various New Testament passages (1 Thess 1:8; Phil 2:14-16; 1 Cor 4:16-17, 11:1) disqualifies "any attempt to limit 'proclamation' to the purely verbal level."[6] The proclamation is of a definitive, completed event in history, but the act of proclaiming participates in the content and character of the message itself. The death of Jesus, in Paul's thought, is the consummate act of what was most characteristic of his life, a self-giving for others. The message or lesson of Jesus' life unto death is to be so fully assimilated by believers that the "dying" *(nekrosis)* of Jesus characterizes their own lives (see 2 Cor 4:8-11).

Only with the "realism of Paul's approach" to the message and life of the gospel in mind, Murphy-O'Connor argues, can one understand what he means when he says that partaking of the Eucharistic food is a proclamation of the Lord's death. "The attitude of those who eat and drink is essential to the proclamation, because if their imitation of Christ (11:1) is defective, then, as Paul expressly insists, 'it is not the Lord's Supper that you eat' (11:20)."[7] Paul thereby connects the meaning of the Eucharist with the kind of love and faithfulness to God and humanity that Jesus revealed in going to his death. The carrying on of the Eucharistic tradition bears the implication of carrying on the pattern of Christ's life of kenotic service unto death, to the glory of God the Father. Paul's explanation of the tradition amounts to an exhortation that the Christian community be more authentically what they are called to be or, as Augustine later put it, that they become the body that they receive.

The tradition of the gospel, the life of faith lived in the power of Christ's ever faithful Spirit, entails the struggle of the indicative and imperative. The tradition thus necessitates both the interpretation of how the gospel presently comes where threatened and the exhortation to receive and bring about the living reality of Christ's love in

---

[6] Murphy-O'Connor, "Eucharist and Community," 61.

[7] Ibid., 62.

the midst of the world. The key to Christian tradition, as is true for any tradition, is the living exercise of living memory. The exercise of memory is always purposeful; it is always performed with a view to reestablishing and confirming an identity in people that shapes their interpersonal and social actions.

The content, therefore, of what a tradition remembers through its narratives, symbols, and rituals is crucial. The content, moreover, is always threatened in the hermeneutical process whereby a given generation brings to the exercise of remembrance their own concerns, priorities, or even fears, which may very well take the upper hand in the interpretive and integrative process. The difficult task that tradition seeks to achieve is the conservation and assertion of some normative beliefs which, nonetheless, must be conveyed anew, that is, in a way that makes them formative of people's outlook and actions.

What we find at the origins of the Christian tradition, conserved in the normative texts of the New Testament, is both the essential content of its memory and the pattern whereby the rehearsal of that memory leads to exhortation for a way of life. The essential content of the tradition of faith is, of course, Jesus the Christ. As Scripture scholar Nihls Dahl has pointed out, however, the type of preaching needed within the Christian communities was not the evangelistic proclamation of the kerygma about Jesus, the announcement that in Christ has come the definitive revelation of God's saving wisdom for the world.[8] For those, rather, who have already heard the message and been initiated into the stories, ritual traditions, and ethical practices of the Christian way of life, the pastoral needs are different. The challenges and contradictions to the gospel that inevitably arise in society, as well as the life-crises and transitions in each person's life, can cause believers to forget the message of the gospel, or to misunderstand its content and implications, or to need new perspectives on its meaning. Believers' efforts to live the way of Christ, especially amidst suffering and sin, establish their need, time and again, to restore their memory of who this Jesus is to whom they belong and thus to gain insight, consolation, and encouragement into the mystery of his way.

[8] See Nihls Alstrup Dahl, *Jesus in the Memory of the Early Church* (Minneapolis: Augsburg, 1976) 19.

Dahl identifies in the preaching, hymns, and the Eucharistic account in the epistles of the New Testament a pattern of praising God by remembering the pattern of Jesus' life, death, and resurrection. This pattern of worship through remembrance, for which Christians are indebted to their Jewish ancestors, has the salvific purpose of forming their own thoughts and actions according to the memory of Jesus, that is, in imitation of him.

A stellar example of this pattern and impact of prayer is found in Philippians 2:5-11, in which Paul draws upon a liturgical hymn in order to instruct the community on how their attitude must be that of Christ. To pray in the name of Jesus is not merely a matter of tacking the phrase "We ask these things in Jesus' name" at the conclusion of the community's prayer. Prayer and worship, rather, are the pattern of giving praise and thanks to God by rehearsing what God has accomplished in Jesus' life unto death and asking God to continue to perform saving acts and to form the Church as participants in that action for the life of the world.[9] In their practice of the liturgy, to the extent that this practice is authentically Christian, authentically traditional, believers share a moment of realization, an experiential knowledge that bears its own compelling desire to know Christ more deeply, to be more fully one with Christ and all the many members of Christ.

Tradition has by its very nature a conserving function. People seek in traditions some measure of security in relation to the past that confirms their identity in the present. When one considers the message at the heart of Christian tradition, however, one discovers the ironic call to let go of the pursuit of security for its own sake, to empty oneself in the hope of knowing something of what Jesus knew about the kingdom of God, to trust that in believing that the actions of serving the lowly, of suffering for righteousness' sake, of striving to bring peace amidst conflict, one lives the tradition of Christ and his Church.

Christians do not face a simple alternative of either clinging to rituals that assure sacred boundaries for their own sake (mysticism in the narrow sense) or forging ahead in their lives, hoping that good intentions will sustain them in the effort to live good lives (unreflective ethics). The tradition of Christian faith cannot be reduced either to mysticism or ethics but, rather, can only thrive in what is often the

<hr>

[9] Ibid., 20–21.

strange and difficult meeting of the two. In the mystical practices of prayer, sacramental worship, and reflection upon Sacred Scripture, believers find the narratives and symbols that inspire, goad, and console them in their ongoing effort to live the gospel in their interpersonal, social, and political lives.

To articulate the practice of Christian tradition in terms of mysticism and ethics (or politics) is to approach the question of tradition from the perspective of liberation and political theologies. Among Northern theologians in this field, Johann Baptist Metz has given extensive thought to the question of religious tradition's viability in modern society. A brief look at Metz's work can provide confirmation and further insight into the dynamic notion of tradition I have pursued thus far. Metz has analyzed both the threatened situation of the practice of Christian tradition in modern society as well as the promise of renewed practices of the tradition in these conditions.

The concept of tradition, Metz observes, came to take on a pejorative connotation in modern society and the academy.[10] The fact that traditions are, in a variety of ways, historically mediated and, to varying extents, authoritatively mandated marks them as fetters to the freeing potential of autonomous human reason heralded by the Enlightenment. The social (political and economic) forms that Enlightenment came to take—the priority and pervasiveness of technical or instrumental reason and the market's principle of exchange—resulted in the marginalization of tradition as an authoritative source for decision and action.

In performing his analysis of the status of religion in late-modern society, Metz's purpose is to demonstrate how it is that the laudable and irreversible goals of the Enlightenment—the abolition of religiously sanctioned feudal and absolutist socioeconomic structures and, thus, the distinction between the public and private aspects of social life—have nonetheless resulted in the identification of social values with the exchange principle's values of production, trade, profit, and consumption. The result of this societal phenomenon for individuals has been the establishment of the middle-class citizen as not only the actual historical instantiation of the modern subject but, moreover, the very model for being an individual in society.

---

[10] See Johann Baptist Metz, *Faith in History and Society: Toward a Practical Fundamental Theology,* trans. David Smith (New York: Seabury, 1980) 32–48.

The grave challenge for Christianity in modern society, Metz insists, is grasped in the recognition that for middle-class Christians religion is a *private* affair. The Church (ironically, and at odds with its own most authentic tradition) has reinforced this tendency by providing liturgical services and pastoral approaches to the sacraments that effectively communicate to believers that the practice of these traditions is solely a matter of each individual's private connection with God and personal salvation. Now, it is certainly true that Christian tradition is about the salvation of each person and, moreover, that the Church, when truest to its gospel mission, has upheld the irreducible value of each woman and man as created by God and freely offered redemption in Christ. The difficulty, however, comes with the way in which this dignity and offer is received.

At this point in modern history, Metz implies that there are two poles framing the spectrum of Christians' understandings of how one is to receive and live the gift of faith.[11] On the one hand, there is the situation in which the values and priorities of the market and technology exercise the fundamental authority in people's lives such that they adapt the message and symbols of Christian faith as a "religious paraphrase" of how they already perceive the world and their place and purpose therein. What tends to happen to those who practice this form of Christianity is that over time the regular practice of worship becomes decreasingly necessary. At most, the Church's liturgical tradition decoratively embellishes the celebration of holidays.[12] On the other hand, there are those who, for various reasons, recognize the conflict that exists between the social processes of modernity and the content of the Christian faith and seek refuge in a "pure traditionalism," a rigid retrieval of past forms of religious practice that threatens the Church with sectarian isolation. Resis-

[11] Ibid., 95–98.

[12] Orthodox theologian Alexander Schmemann, in describing Christians' uncritical role in modern (technological and market-centered) society, offers an analysis strikingly similar to that of Metz: "the 'Christian year'—the sequence of liturgical commemorations and celebrations—ceased to be the generator of power, and is now looked upon as a more or less antiquated decoration of religion . . . it is neither a root of Christian life and action, nor a 'goal' toward which they are oriented."—Alexander Schmemann, *For the Life of the World: Sacraments and Orthodoxy*, 2nd ed. (Crestwood, N.Y.: St Vladimir's Seminary Press, 1973) 53.

tance to seeing how the gospel's promise and demands might arise in new circumstances for action in society results in a zealous and joyless preoccupation with defending certain interpretations of doctrine, patterns of ecclesial authority, and approaches to cultic ritual.

Somewhere between these two extremes Metz recognizes another approach, which critically recognizes the debilitating effects and strains that modern technocratic, capitalist society places upon its members and offers the Christian religion as relief and release from those pressures, for a while, in the practice of a "purely cultic spirituality." While this approach is laudable for its recognition that people hunger for different accesses to reality than the exhausting and relentless competitive and manipulative ways of exchange and technology, the problem is that the practice of such cultic spirituality provides only temporary relief or freedom from the strains of modern society. Its basic dynamic is not holistic or integrating but escapist.

Authentic Christian tradition, however, contains a different notion of freedom, one that does not merely salve the strains and sores that believers chronically suffer in a culture and society whose technology, despite ubiquitous promises to the contrary, seems to leave people more rushed, more tied to their workplace (now electronically), and more convinced that they are behind schedule, and whose marketing strategies make them feel endlessly inadequate, especially in their bodily images. The freedom offered by the gospel is not an intermittent relief from the constant conformity that a consumerist society and competitive workplace relentlessly demand of their participants. To interpret the gospel's freedom merely in those terms is to chain the Word of God and deprive people of its salvific content.

The Good News, rather, is an invitation to a life that is patterned on that of Jesus the Christ, a transformation in which one does not identify one's unique individuality with economic autonomy but, rather, with the use of one's gifts and talents and wisdom in service of others, especially those who are in need and suffering. In the pursuit of such a way of life, believers come to realize their own genuinely human and religious capacities for sorrow and joy, pain and play, mourning and expectation, generosity and gratitude, friendship and loyalty, solidarity and individuality. These capacities Metz calls "messianic virtues."[13] Practices of Christian prayer and liturgy (which, of course, include the reading and proclamation of Scripture) provide the images and motivation, consolation and goading on, of these virtues in the lives of believers. The ethical practices of believers in society and their "mystical" practices of individual prayer and ecclesial worship mutually influence each other and form a pattern of life that comprises the tradition of faith.

The reader may ask in light of these brief reflections: Can we not be more precise in defining what tradition is? The tradition of faith is the entire life-giving mission that God set in motion in Jesus and continues now through the work of the Holy Spirit. Far from being that which any individual or group of Christians can own or instrumentally control, the tradition is that which possesses us. With its origin in the teaching and healing ministry of Jesus, Christian tradition is far too radical for any individual or community of believers to think they have finally figured it out. For the human cannot encompass the divine, cannot control the reign of God inaugurated in Christ. The power of this reign is the "indicative," the free gift of God that mysteriously eludes the human grasp, thus establishing the "imperative" in our lives.

Thus, the struggle for tradition is for us today, just as it was for Paul's Corinthians in the middle of the first century, at the heart of what it means to be authentically Christian. We must keep constantly before ourselves the unsettling challenge of Paul's admonition, "It is not the Lord's supper that you eat," for if we eat without "discerning the body," we eat to our condemnation. One of the consequences of this teaching, to put it bluntly, is that being true to Christian tradition may have more to do with how we live with the other members of the Body of Christ (and, by extension, with all people) than how we

---

[13] See Johann Baptist Metz, *The Emergent Church: The Future of Christianity in a Postbourgeois World*, trans. Peter Mann (New York: Crossroad, 1987) 4–8. What Metz is arguing for with his concept of "messianic virtues" holds strong affinities with Saliers' conceptualization of the Christian moral life as constituted by affections and virtues whose source is the saving mystery of Christ and whose sustenance is found in practices of prayer and worship. In addition to the lead essay for this present book, see also Don E. Saliers, *The Soul in Paraphrase: Prayer and the Religious Affections* (New York: Seabury Press, 1980; reprint, Cleveland: OSL, 1991).

worship with them. This, at least, must be taught as a corrective to the ritual innovators and ritual traditionalists I described at the beginning of this essay, let alone to the "religious paraphrasers," "pure traditionalists," and "cultic spiritualists" described by Metz.

On the other hand, this is not to imply that the liturgy is unimportant. The celebration of the Eucharist remains central to the authentic living of the Christian tradition. Paul is absolutely clear on this point in his teaching to the Corinthians. His insistence that we look both to our liturgical practice and to our responsibilities in the community constitutes our earliest and most authentic Christian teaching on the meaning of tradition.

Paradoxically, then, liturgical practice contains both the symptoms of the illnesses that can afflict the Body of Christ as well as the medicine for the cure. Our various struggles at times to "own" tradition, to make tradition uncritically support our own personal and societal concerns, are symptoms of the malaise. The fact, however, that in these struggles we always claim to be celebrating the Lord's Supper also leaves us open to recognizing in the practice of its forms the authentic Body of Christ and, thus, to be more and more transformed into that Body and, thus, to imitate the one whose death we proclaim until he comes.

Henry H. Knight III and Steven J. Land

On Being a Witness: Worship and Holiness in the Wesleyan and Pentecostal Traditions

"But you will receive power when the Holy Spirit
has come upon you; and you will be my witnesses
in Jerusalem, in all Judea and Samaria, and to
the ends of the earth" (Acts 1:8 NRSV).

As a declaration of the calling of the Church to evangelism, this verse is certainly emphatic. The Holy Spirit *will* empower disciples, and as a result they *will* be witnesses. Like John Wesley, but even more literally, the world will be their parish. The Acts of the Apostles is an account of how this promise of the risen Jesus Christ is fulfilled in the early Church. There the Holy Spirit empowers an ever expanding circle of evangelistic activity that eventually encompasses much of the known world.

Witnessing is commonly understood as an activity—something we do. It involves bearing witness to the good news of Jesus Christ in both word and deed. If evangelism is defined as verbal, witnessing includes it; if evangelism is both verbal and visible, it is close to being identical with it.

We are struck, however, by the language of this verse. It doesn't simply say, as might be expected, that the disciples will witness; it says that they will "*be* my witnesses." More is involved here than evangelistic activity. The Holy Spirit seems to be not only empowering their ministry but forming their character, such that they not only engage in witnessing but *become* witnesses, some even through death. In the martyrdom of Stephen as recounted by Luke, Stephen's character enabled him to be a witness, giving credibility to his message.

Our thesis is that being a witness is necessarily fundamental to giving a witness, and being a witness is most appropriately understood in terms of holy affections, narratively shaped through participation in a worshiping community. We belong to two related traditions—the Wesleyan and the Pentecostal—which have traditionally understood being a witness as an essential expression of the Christian faith. We hope to show how persons in these two traditions are formed and shaped as witnesses through an examination of their pattern of worship practices.

With Saliers, we believe that "the Christian life can be characterized as a set of affections and virtues."[1] We find the terms "affections" especially useful for two reasons. First, it was used by Jonathan Edwards and John Wesley to describe the Christian life.[2] This roots it deeply in the same soil out of which the Wesleyan, Holiness, and Pentecostal movements emerged. Saliers has recovered this term and, while remaining faithful to Edwards' usage, redescribed it in light of contemporary theological and philosophical perspectives.[3]

Second, and most importantly, Saliers' understanding of the affections as simultaneously dispositional and relational is enormously helpful in articulating how Christian character (or, as our traditions would call it, holiness of heart and life) is formed and shaped over time. The affections do in fact characterize us because they are dispositions—they constitute our moral selves before God. Yet we cannot have or retain these affections apart from an ongoing relationship with God through Jesus Christ. Such a relationship is created and sustained by the Holy Spirit, particularly as we engage in the practices of worship and discipleship in the Christian community.

---

[1] Don E. Saliers, "Liturgy and Ethics: Some New Beginnings," *The Journal of Religious Ethics*, vol. 7, no. 2 (Fall 1979) 179; p. 22 above.

[2] A careful discussion of the use of the term "affections" and related terms such as "tempers" by John Wesley can be found in Randy L. Maddox, *Responsible Grace* (Nashville: Abingdon Press, 1994) 69. Detailed comparisons of Wesley and Edwards on the affections include Gregory S. Clapper, *John Wesley on Religious Affections* (Metuchen, N.J.: Scarecrow Press, 1989) and Richard B. Steele, *"Gracious Affection" and "True Virtue" According to Jonathan Edwards and John Wesley* (Metuchen, N.J.: Scarecrow Press, 1994).

[3] Saliers' reappropriation of Edwards' language of the affections is discussed in Don E. Saliers, *The Soul in Paraphrase: Prayer and the Religious Affections* (New York: Seabury Press, 1980; reprint, Cleveland: OSL, 1991) 8–20.

John Wesley called these practices "means of grace."[4] The means of grace included "acts of piety," which were practices related to God, and "acts of mercy," which were related to the neighbor. Early Methodism was not a Church but a renewal movement whose members were held accountable to a discipline involving regular engagement in these practices. Failure to take this discipline seriously would eventually lead to not being renewed as a member of the local Methodist society.

The structure of the Methodist societies facilitated adherence to the discipline. Every Methodist belonged to a class of ten to twelve persons that met weekly. The purpose of the class meeting was to inquire of the members how they had fared during the preceding week as they attempted to keep the discipline. The "constancy in season and out of season"[5] that Saliers says marks Christian prayer is encouraged by this discipline for the entire range of means of grace.

Wesley understood "discipline" to be the means to "doctrine," which designated not only conceptual but experiential reality. That is, "doctrine" involved the realities of justification, sanctification, and the witness of the Spirit as transforming experiences of God, at times instantaneous yet always gradual. Those "awakened" or convicted of sin would join a class meeting, in which they would undertake a relationship with God through participation in the means of grace. They would remain constant in prayer and other practices, often for months or even years, until they received, in an instant, the promised gift of justification and the new birth. The new birth initiated sanctification, a gradual growth in the knowledge and love of God that culminated in Christian perfection or entire sanctification, the wholehearted love of God and neighbor, again given in an instant. Should Christian perfection be received prior to the time of death, then one continued to grow in perfection through participation in means of grace.

---

[4] A comprehensive treatment of the means of grace in Wesley's theology and practice is Henry H. Knight III, *The Presence of God in the Christian Life: John Wesley and the Means of Grace* (Metuchen, N.J.: Scarecrow Press, 1992). Much of the discussion of Wesley that follows depends on the research and conclusions reached in this book.

[5] Saliers, "Liturgy and Ethics," p. 27 above.

This entire pattern of growth in the Christian life is understood as the acquiring, shaping, and deepening of holy affections, most especially love for God and neighbor. These affections are formed and shaped first and foremost in response to God's love for us, especially as mediated through the means of grace; as a result, they increasingly enable the Christian to reflect in his or her life the very life of God. Because God is love, Christian perfection is understood by Wesley as the restoration of the *imago Dei* in the believer. Or, as Charles Wesley put it, we become "transcripts of the Trinity."[6]

A cursory reading of Wesley might see his concern for holiness as anthropocentric. However, the relational nature of affections requires that the focus be on God, and most especially on loving God as God has loved us. The descriptive account of holiness as a restoration of the *imago Dei* requires God's nature and redemptive activity to be the framework within which holiness is understood.

That is why worship is so central to the means of grace. The very purpose of worship is to come into God's presence and remember who God is and what God has done, responding with thanksgiving and praise. Growing in sanctification requires our primary focus to remain not on ourselves but on God (and then on the neighbor). Worship is a "means of grace," if "grace" is understood not as something apart from God but as the gift of a relationship with God,[7] a means through which the Holy Spirit acts and, enabled by the Spirit, we then respond.

To illustrate this concretely, we can briefly examine Wesley's understanding of the Lord's Supper. Similar to Calvin, Wesley believed that Christ is present in the Lord's Supper by way of the Holy Spirit. The reality of this presence is known, at least to some degree, by all who come to this meal in faith. That is, faith is a "spiritual sense" given by God that enables us to know God.

---

[6] Charles Wesley, "Sinners, Turn: Why Will You Die." Hymn 7 in *A Collection of Hymns for the Use of the People Called Methodists*, vol. 7 of *The Works of John Wesley*, ed. Franz Hildebrandt and Oliver A. Beckerlegge (Oxford: Oxford University Press, 1983) 88.

[7] Maddox shows how Wesley adopts an Eastern Christian understanding of uncreated grace over the Western view of grace as a created substance. See *Responsible Grace*, 86.

But in the Lord's Supper, this knowing God's living reality comes in and through the words, actions, and signs that constitute the Eucharistic liturgy. These particularize our knowing God by enabling our remembrance of all that God has done and promised, as well as the character of God revealed in Jesus Christ. Wesley, following Daniel Brevint,[8] describes the experience of the communicant in three temporal dimensions of God's activity.

From the standpoint of the past, the participant in the Lord's Supper is brought experientially before the reality of the Cross. This is far more than a mere recalling to mind; rather, it is to "expose to all our senses, His suffering, as if they were present *now*."[9] Charles Wesley expresses this in one of his Eucharist hymns:

"Christ revives His suffering here,
    Still exposes them to view;
See the Crucified appear,
    Now believe He died for you."[10]

This deep experience of the Cross evoked at least two sets of affections. Because "our sins have done the deed" and "drove the nails that fix Him there,"[11] we experience repentance and grief. The Lord's Supper continually deepens the humility necessary to the Christian life and invites a critical examination of our lives before God to uncover remaining sin. This for Wesley is essential if we are to grow in sanctification.

At the same time, because this suffering and death was done for us by God out of love, it evokes and deepens affections of love and gratitude for God. Taken together, regular participation in the Lord's Supper in faith will enable one to be a living witness to the deep sacrificial love of God through becoming a person of humble and grateful love.

From the standpoint of the future, the participant in the Lord's Supper experiences in the present the eschatological reality to come. In the striking words of Charles Wesley,

[8] J. Ernest Rattenbury, *The Eucharistic Hymns of John and Charles Wesley* (London: The Epworth Press, 1948) contains Wesley's abridgement of Brevint.

[9] Ibid, 177.

[10] Ibid., 197.

[11] Ibid., 202.

"By faith and hope already there,
Even now the marriage-feast we share."[12]

Here the Eucharist evokes an expectant hope in the promise of God.
It is a firm hope because God is faithful, and it is expectant because
the sacrament not only is a pledge that one will participate in future
glory but conveys as an earnest something of that eschatological life
in the present. The one whose life manifests hope is a witness to
God's faithfulness in bringing about that which God has promised.

From the standpoint of the present, the participant in the Lord's
Supper partakes of the crucified and risen Christ. This is nothing less
than becoming one with Christ and, as a result, taking on the character of Christ. It is another way of speaking of the restoring of the
imago Dei in us, the heart of which is love.

"Now, Lord, on us Thy flesh bestow,
    And let us drink Thy blood,
Till all our souls are fill'd below
    With all the life of God."[13]

Through this present experience of Christ, descriptively presented
and enacted in terms of the biblical narratives, the participant responds to God's love and is conformed to God's image in Jesus
Christ. Thus he or she increasingly becomes a witness to the good
news of salvation through Christ. Put differently, as we participate in
this liturgy over time, the Holy Spirit transforms our character in
ways that reflect the moral nature of God.

If holiness of heart and life can be seen to constitute authentic witness, then certain alternative ways of life that Wesley warned against
exemplify inauthentic witness. These same dangers are descriptively
identified by Saliers in contrast to his own proposal. What they have
in common is they focus their attention on something other than God.

The first of these is formalism, which Wesley defines as having
"the form of godliness, but not the power."[14] Christianity, for Wesley,
is a matter of the heart renewed in love; it "does not consist . . . in

[12] Ibid., 225.

[13] Ibid., 205.

[14] John Wesley's Journal (Nov. 25, 1739) in *Journals and Diaries II*, ed. W. Reginald
Ward and Richard P. Heitzenrater, in *The Works of John Wesley*, vol. 19 (Nashville:
Abingdon Press, 1990) 124.

any ritual observances"[15] or right doctrine but in love ruling the heart and manifesting itself in how one lives one's life.

Formalism is a kind of going through the motions—it is the doing of Christian activities without being actually affected by God. Formalist worship for Wesley has nothing to do with the presence or absence of a written liturgy; it has to do with whether one is truly engaged relationally with God in and through that worship.

The reason why formalism is an inauthentic witness is that the focus of the formalist is not on God but on the Church as an institution or on a set of religious duties. Instead of coming into the presence of God to remember who God is and what God has done, worship becomes one more activity to accomplish. As Saliers says, "not all who participate in its language and actions are shaped by it."[16] Because the life is not changed—the holy affections have not taken root in the heart—the life that is lived bears witness to an empty and impotent faith.

A second form of inauthentic witness is enthusiasm, which is in many ways the opposite of formalism. Enthusiasts are defined by Wesley as "those who imagine they have such gifts from God as they have not" or "imagine themselves to be so influenced by the Spirit of God, as, in fact, they are not."[17] Another related variety of enthusiasm are "those who think to attain the end without using the means, by the immediate power of God."[18]

What these all have in common is a confusion of the intensity of experience with spiritual maturity. Wanting to avoid a dead formalism, they have opted for a religion grounded in having certain powerful feelings. They view these feelings as assurance that they are in relationship with God and identify true worship as that which elicits such feelings.

Wesley believed that the enthusiast had in effect an imaginary religion, in which the focus had shifted away from God to the self and its feelings. The danger was a self-deception in which God is removed from the biblical and liturgical contexts that narratively provide

---

[15] "The Way to the Kingdom,"in *Sermons I*, ed. Albert C. Outler, in *The Works of John Wesley*, vol. 1 (Nashville: Abingdon Press, 1984) 218.

[16] Saliers, "Liturgy and Ethics," p. 18 above.

[17] "The Nature of Enthusiasm," *Works* 2:53.

[18] Ibid., 56.

ascriptions and descriptions of God and is placed instead in the finite, ambiguous, and potentially sinful context of passing feeling.

Saliers shares Wesley's concern when he argues that "meaning what we pray requires more than the onset of lively emotions"; it entails "sharing a form of life in which the affections and dispositions are oriented toward God."[19] Thus "the love ingredient in the Christian story [is] not measured by episodic intensities, but by steadfast love."[20]

The Wesleyan discipline, by its emphasis on reading Scripture, hearing the proclaimed word, participating in the Lord's Supper, and praying the prayers of the Church, was designed to continually orient the Methodists to God's love as narrated in the Christian story. God was not whoever one felt God to be, but the God revealed in the story of Israel and in Jesus Christ. Thus the affections were formed and shaped as one worshiped over time, enabling one to grow in holiness and the knowledge and love of God.

Insofar as the lives of these early Methodists were consistent with the gospel they proclaimed, they were being witnesses to God's love. To be a witness required the forming and shaping of holy affections through participation in worship and other disciplines, resulting in a life oriented toward the active love of God and neighbor.

Wesley's eighteenth-century revival of personal and social holiness spilled over into the nineteenth century, affecting all of North American revivalism. John Wesley can rightly be considered the grandfather of the Pentecostal movement. His emphasis on a post-conversion crisis experience of entire sanctification or perfect love became in the nineteenth century the impetus for an enormously influential and denominationally diverse Holiness movement, which was the immediate seedbed of Pentecostalism. Without Wesley's teaching, there would have been no Pentecostal movement in the twentieth century.

There were changes in, as well as continuity with, Wesley's teaching in the Holiness movement. Perhaps most significant was the change in language from "entire sanctification" to "baptism in the Spirit" in the middle of the nineteenth century, most notably at Oberlin College, which, under the leadership of Asa Mahon and Charles Finney, had become a center of holiness revivalism and social radical-

[19] Saliers, "Liturgy and Ethics," pp. 25–26 above.
[20] Ibid., p. 26 above.

ism. By the end of the nineteenth century all the defining elements that characterize Pentecostalism today were in place. These included salvation as affective transformation, personal and social holiness, purity and power as two sides of the "second blessing," protracted meetings in order to "pray through," the correlation of holiness and healing, and an intense premillennial expectation.[21] But even with the doctrinal change that took place during the nineteenth century, the Pentecostalism that emerged in the twentieth was decidedly Wesleyan in its emphasis on holiness of heart and life and the centrality of being a witness.

Pentecostals today constellate around the two foci of worship and witness. These two central activities of the Pentecostal congregation are reciprocally conditioning and crucial in the formation of each Pentecostal believer. Preaching, teaching, listening, praising, shouting "Amen," sighs, groans, and testifying—all point to the intensively oral-narrative character of Pentecostal liturgy. Worship becomes a participatory democracy in which the Spirit moves sovereignly upon persons who perceive themselves to be liberated agents and no longer victims, in a salvation journey toward the soon coming day of the Lord. This helps to explain the fervency and expectation of Pentecostal worship.

The testimonies of Pentecostals indicate something of the crisis-development dialectic of the Christian life as they understand it.[22] The striking thing is that these testimonies center not in the Spirit but in Jesus. Christology as narrated by Pentecostals is a testimony to Jesus as savior, sanctifier, healer, Spirit baptizer, and coming King. Jesus' being is in his doing! And the Spirit bears witness to Jesus as persons are saved out of darkness into light, healed of their infirmities (whether spiritual, mental, emotional, etc.), brought into a moral

---

[21] The Wesleyan roots of Pentecostalism by way of the Holiness movement have been shown in Vinson Synan, *The Holiness-Pentecostal Movement in the United States* (Grand Rapids, Mich.: Eerdmans, 1971); Donald W. Dayton, *The Theological Roots of Pentecostalism* (Grand Rapids, Mich.: Zondervan, 1987) and D. William Faupel, *The Everlasting Gospel: The Significance of Eschatology in the Development of Pentecostal Thought* (Sheffield, England: Sheffield Academic Press, 1996).

[22] A more extensive discussion of the elements of Pentecostal spirituality and the resulting affective integration can be found in Steven J. Land, *Pentecostal Spirituality: A Passion for the Kingdom* (Sheffield, England: Sheffield Academic Press, 1993).

integration of love through the sanctifying grace of God, filled with the Spirit who displays signs and wonders, and filled with a longing for the soon coming King and his kingdom of righteousness, joy, and peace. The typical Pentecostal will testify, "I thank the Lord for saving, sanctifying, healing, filling me with the Spirit, and placing me on the way to heaven. Pray for me that I will be faithful unto the end."

Within the foregoing narrative context and in the presence of the Holy Spirit, Scripture becomes the living word of God. The Holy Spirit functions as a time machine so that believers may rehear the stories of Scripture and become primary witnesses of the Exodus, the resurrection, the day of Pentecost, etc. By the Spirit they already sit at the marriage supper of the Lamb. In this fusion of space and time, the already-not yet tension so central to Pentecostal existence is set against the apocalyptic horizon of expectation and vision.

Preaching, teaching, reading, and memorizing the Word, testifying, singing, praying for one another at the altar, as well as intercession—all these means of grace serve to instrument a discipleship that requires affective transformation. Prayers, testimonies, and witness shape and express Pentecostal Christian affections. There is gratitude for deliverance from darkness into light and from the world into the Church. There is a compassion born of a wounded love as believers intercede for a lost and dying world where so many suffer. Most Pentecostals are poor, urban, and third world. Identification with the poor, therefore, is no stretch, since Pentecostals are still mostly a Church of, and not simply for, the poor. Believers not only testify to the deliverance of salvation but pray for and anoint one another as they are moved by the compassion of Christ. The manifestation of gifts in the worshiping community encourages everyone and heightens the joyous expectation of the coming of the Lord.

But gratitude, compassion, and courage are also missionary affections that drive the mission of the Church. As the believer looks upon the world, she says, there but for the grace of God go I. The intense sense of being delivered from darkness into light compels Pentecostals to shine the light to every corner of the world. As Pentecostals tarry at the altar and crucify the affections and lusts that are unlike Christ, they come to testify to an infilling of love and moral integration. Compassion born of hours of intercession for the unloved around them moves Pentecostals to reach to their neighbors and to seek to enfold them into the community of love. In most of the third world there is a sharing of the gospel, food, and social services of the congregation.

Worship services naturally spill out into the streets, where the singing and testifying continue. Courage also becomes a missionary motivation. As persons who have so often been silent victims of their social and political system are filled with the Spirit, they are emboldened to speak up and to tell of the mighty acts of God. The gospel goes forth in word and power and demonstration of the Spirit. The gifts that have edified the body become missionary illustrations of the gospel that accompany the witness of every believer.

Since the Spirit bears witness to Christ, so do Spirit-filled believers. And this witness involves both the fruit and the gifts. In this way, character and personality are brought to bear in a holistic witness that is as concerned with being as it is with doing. The rehearing of the Christian story and worshiping in such a way as to reenact the events of salvation history become rehearsal for witness in the world. But then the effectual witness of the Spirit to Jesus Christ in the world drives the witnesses back into worship, along with the newly won converts. The worldly witness validates and deepens the corporate worship of the believers. As the congregation is disposed and thus characterized by gratitude, compassion, and courage, these very affections become reasons for worship and witness.

The goal of all worship and witness is the kingdom of God and ultimately God himself. If one believes that everything will one day be "holiness unto the Lord," then holiness becomes central to one's spirituality. This was true for Wesley, and it is also true for millions of Pentecostals in the twentieth century. This holiness has a structure of righteousness, a content of love, and a dynamic of power whereby the Spirit of God makes known and effectual God's will and care and all of creation. This righteousness, love, and power may be correlated respectively with gratitude, compassion, and courage—three characteristic and representative affections of Pentecostal believers.

The move toward a new integration of the affective life, one that seeks to incorporate new power, courage, and confidence into a life of active gratitude and compassion, can be seen in the following testimony, which is quoted at length from *The Apostolic Faith* paper in 1908. Miss Antoinette Moomean of Eustice, Nebraska, narrates her journey from the mission field of China to the Azusa Street Revival. This testimony conveys the ethos, affective tone, and something of the instrumented means used to effect affective transformation. It is clear from this account that baptism in the Spirit meant a strengthening of all that had gone before in her Christian development and a discovery of "the secret of the endurance of the martyrs." It is an interesting weaving together of doctrine, affect, gifts, practices, and self-disclosure. There were and are hundreds of thousands of testimonies like this one. Miss Moomean's testimony is an intriguing confluence of the Wesleyan and Pentecostal streams.

"On leaving China, October, 1906, I was asked to investigate the Apostolic Faith Movement in Los Angeles, where they claim to have manifested the same gifts of the Holy Ghost as of old (1 Cor. 12:8-10). I heard such contradictory reports that I kept away for some time, but praise God, He had His hand upon me for this wonderful gift, and I had no rest until I went and heard and saw for myself.

"It only took a short time after the beginning of the first meeting, to know it was of God. And when the altar call came, I went forward.

"Before this I had asked God to turn His great searchlight upon my heart and was astonished to find so much worldliness, spiritual pride, vanity, insincerity, lack of love, selfishness, and other things. When I had left for the foreign field seven years before this, I thought I had died to everything; but when the Spirit began to deal with me in preparing me for the fullness of the Spirit, I found I was very much alive, in fact had scarcely begun to die to self. Although the Lord had given me wonderful victories in my life and what I thought was the baptism of the Spirit, yet when God began to search me as never before, I had to confess that I had never even been sanctified.

"I had been taught the suppression theory and now and again the 'old man' would pop up in greater or less degree; sometimes harsh words did not escape, but I would feel them building up inside. But God showed me that His word meant just what it said, that provision was made in the atonement—not only for our sins but our sin, the Adamic nature (Rom. 6:6, 18, 22). How I did rejoice at the last, the longing of my heart to be rid of that which had kept me from being entirely free from sin, was to be satisfied. I had sought my baptism of the Spirit three times, when the Lord told me that I must be sanctified before the Spirit could take full possession of my body. Just so were the disciples sanctified before Christ left them (John 17:17, 19), that they might be ready for the baptism of the Spirit.

"After some of the saints had prayed for me, one of them asked me if I had the witness of the Spirit to my sanctification according to Heb. 10:14, 15. For some years back when I had been taught of the Spirit to keep 'short accounts' with the Lord, and there was nothing left to do in the way of restitution; and having laid all on the altar, I knew I had met the condition, and that God had fulfilled His promise; although there was no other feeling than the assurance that God had done the work because of His Word. I then began to praise God audibly, and in a few minutes I was flooded with billows of glory, and the Spirit sang through me praises unto God. Besides this witness of the Spirit, was the witness of the fruits; for under whatever provocation, there is no uprising, for there is nothing to rise up. Glory to Jesus.

"When sanctified, I was filled with such glory that I felt sure it must be the baptism, which did not come for three weeks. In the meantime, the power was upon me almost continually, sometimes lying under the power for hours, while I consecrated myself to God as never before.

"At last after a real dying out, as I never dreamed could be possible on earth, in the upper room Azusa Mission, the promise of the Father was made real to me, and I was charged with the power of God and my soul flooded with glory. The Spirit sang praises unto God. Glory to Jesus. He gave me the Bible experience, speaking through me in other tongues.

"The Lord showed me that the cross was going to mean to me what it had never meant before. One morning the Spirit dealt with me, singing through me—

Must Jesus bear the cross alone,
    And all the world go free;
No, there's a cross for everyone,
    And there is one for me.

"The last line He just seemed to burn into my soul by repeating it over and over again. Sometimes the Spirit would sing a line and then sob out a line. Although I wept and was in anguish of soul, it was all in the Spirit.

"The life of Jesus passed before me, and He asked me if I was willing to follow Jesus in living absolutely for Him in ministering unto others. I thought I had known something of what this meant in China; but now to preach the everlasting Gospel in the power and demonstration of the Spirit and to truly go out on the faith line and to minister day and night, sometimes unto the hungry multitudes in the face of fierce opposition, meant far more than ever before. But He enabled me to say, 'By Thy grace I will bear this cross.'

"The Garden scene came up before me next, as the Spirit again sang, 'Must Jesus bear the cross alone?' And He seemed to say, 'Your friends will forsake you, your own family will misunderstand you, you will be called a fanatic, crazy; are you willing to bear this cross?' Again I answered, 'By Thy grace, I will.'

"The crucifixion scene then came before me and it seemed as if my heart would break with sorrow, and I could only wait in silence. Then I said, 'Lord, if it was to be beheaded, I could, but—'I could go no further. Later in the day, the Lord spoke to me again as I was under the power. It seemed as if I would perish in soul anguish. I was unconscious of the workers all about me. It seemed as if Jesus Himself stood beside, looking down upon me. I could only say, 'Jesus, Jesus, Jesus, I will, I will, I will.' His promise came to me as distinctly as if audibly [and] said, 'My grace is sufficient for you.' And in a flash, He gave me to understand the secret of the endurance of the martyrs who were burned at the stake with the glory of heaven upon their faces, and seemingly free from pain. And He enabled me to say, 'Yes, Lord, your grace is sufficient.'

"Then the Spirit began to sing in a joyful strain, repeating over and over again the last line until I could almost see the crown:

> The consecrated cross I'll bear,
>   Till Christ has set me free;
> And then go home a crown to wear,
>   For there's a crown for me.

"To sum it up, the baptism of the Spirit means to me what I never dreamed it could this side of heaven; victory, glory in my soul, perfect peace, rest, liberty nearness to Christ, deadness to this old world, and power in witnessing. Glory to His name forever and forever!"[23]

---

[23] *The Apostolic Faith* 1:11 (October–January, 1908), p. 3, reprinted in F. T. Corum, ed., *Like As of Fire* (Wilmington, Mass.: 1981).

The outpouring and infilling of the Holy Spirit transforms the Church into an international house of prayer for the healing of nations. Through the integration of love, the world comes to know the Church as a congregation of witnesses unto the Lord Jesus Christ.

It was the vision of John Wesley to spread scriptural holiness throughout the land. In this postmodern age, in which we have come to be suspicious of all ruling metanarratives, Saliers and his disciples in the Wesleyan and Pentecostal traditions (and many others) have come to assert the crucial importance of construing the Christian life in terms of holy affections structured by the biblical narrative, grounded in the character of God, and directed by a vision of holiness and peace.

Stanley M. Hauerwas

Worship, Evangelism, Ethics:
On Eliminating the "And"

1. THE BACKGROUND OF THE "AND"

Tents—I think the problem began with tents. At least I know that tents created the problem for me. When I was a kid growing up in Texas, it never occurred to me that a revival could be had in the church building. You could only have a revival in a tent. You "went to church" in the church. You "got saved" in the tent. Worship was what you did in the church. Evangelism was what you did in the tent. Thus was created "the problem" of how to understand the relationship between worship, evangelism, and ethics.

I do not know if Don Saliers was a product of, or even participated in, tent evangelism, but I do know that, like me, he has benefited from but also suffered the American form of Christianity that tents produced. It is called Methodism. Moreover, like me, he has become "Catholic"—or at least our fellow Methodists often think that the importance that Saliers and I attribute to "liturgy" has made us Catholic. Saliers was trained to be a philosophical theologian and I am supposed to be an ethicist. How and why did we ever became so fascinated with liturgy, not only as something the Church does, but also as crucial for helping us better understand how theology should be done?

It would be presumptuous of me to speak for Saliers, but I suspect that he is as concerned about liturgy, and for the same reason, as I am—he is a Methodist. This may seem a strange confession, given the separation between worship and theology so often legitimated by current Methodist practice. Yet Saliers represents personally and intellectually the Methodist refusal to separate theology and piety. Indeed, Saliers' focus on worship becomes a way to explore how the "and" might be eliminated between theology and evangelism and/or ethics. Our difficulty, of course, is that we are members of a Church whose history, particularly in America, was shaped by the tent/sanctuary divide. Currently some Methodists are even suggesting, in the interest of Church growth (which has become synonymous in some circles with evangelism), that worship must be made more "user friendly." They thus assume that a tension exists between worship and evangelism.

I am not suggesting that the current tensions some feel between worship and evangelism is due to "the tents," but I think there are analogies between then and now. Certain pictures of worship and/or evangelism hold some Christians captive, leading them to think that there must be a deep difference between the Church at worship and the Church in its evangelistic mode. At least some seem to think that the only kind of worship consistent with effective evangelism cannot be identified, let alone associated, with what the Church understands as "traditional" Sunday morning worship.[1]

I would venture that those who have never experienced a tent revival, which includes many Methodists as well as Protestant evangelicals, associate evangelism with a Billy Graham crusade. Of course, Billy Graham just moved the venue to football stadiums, combined that move with media savvy, organizational sophistication, and got the same tent revival results, albeit on a larger scale. What some Methodists now want and have tried to do is to move the football stadium back into the church in an effort to attract the "unchurched."

---

[1] Of course, one of the ironies of this view is that the "Sunday morning worship service" that is often thought too "formal" for effective evangelism is the result of past evangelistic form. For example, it is not uncommon in Methodist services that the offering is taken up before the sermon. This order is the result of revivals in which it was assumed that following the sermon some would respond and be "saved." You would not want an offering intruding between the sermon and the response of the saved. Such an intrusion would mean that you might miss the emotional moment, thus letting the sinner escape. Edward Phillips notes that the revival had three distinct liturgical movements: (1) preliminaries, involving hymn singing, special music, testimonies, love offerings; (2) the message; and (3) the altar call. This pattern, he observes, "became embedded in the Protestant mind as the pattern of church meeting. The problem is that it became the pattern, not just for revivals, but for Sunday worship. Sunday morning was turned into an evangelistic service"—"Creative Worship: Rules, Patterns, and Guidelines," *Quarterly Review*, vol. 10, no. 2 (1990) 14.

The tents have become the church, which makes some worry that "traditional" Methodist worship is being watered down.

That is the context within which Saliers has tried to help us recover liturgy as the locus of the theologian's work. Of course, for him the very assumption that there may be a tension between worship and evangelism (or ethics) is indicative that something has gone terribly wrong. He rightly assumes that Christian worship has always been the way the Church has both evangelized and gone about its moral formation. "Go therefore and make disciples of all nations" is a command of Jesus, not a suggestion about which we might make up our minds. Making disciples is the legitimating activity that makes the Church the Church. As Julian Hartt, another good Methodist, notes, "Whenever the church is authentically Christian the conviction yet lives that its sole reason for existence is to preach the gospel of the kingdom in Christ."[2] There can be no such preaching without the Church at worship. The way the Church "wins converts," therefore, is by making us faithful worshipers of the God who alone is worthy of worship.

2. TRUTHFUL WORSHIP

Saliers has tried to help Methodists recover the way worship is evangelism and ethics by reminding us how worship is about the shaping of the affections. In what I hope has been a supportive move, I have tried to help Methodists recover the social and political significance of worship by claiming that the first task of the Church is not to make the world more just but to make the world the world. Such a claim is not, as is often alleged, designed to legitimate a withdrawal of the Church from the world, but just the opposite. If the Church's first task is to be the Church, it is so because without the Church the world would have no way to understand what justice entails. For as Augustine observed, "Justice is found where God, the one supreme God, rules an obedient City according to his grace, forbidding sacrifice to any being save himself alone."[3] That the "cities" in which we

---

[2] Julian Hartt, *Toward a Theology of Evangelism* (New York: Abingdon Press, 1955) 9. Hartt's book remains one of the finest accounts of evangelism we have. Hartt's influence at Yale Divinity School was everywhere during the years we studied there.

[3] Augustine, *The City of God*, trans. David Knowles (Harmondsworth, England: Penguin Books, 1972) 890 (19, 23).

now exist do not worship the one true God only indicates how important it is that the Church be truthful in its worship.

The Church's worship, therefore, is evangelism. That we Methodists thought we had to erect tents to evangelize should have suggested to us that something had gone wrong with our worship. The tents, to be sure, assumed a generalized Christian culture in which everyone—at least everyone in the South—assumed that sometime in their life they ought to be "saved."[4] This resulted in the further problem that many who "got saved" in the tent did not show up on Sunday morning with a regularity that might testify to the lasting effects of their being saved. Nonetheless, the same people got to claim the name "Christian," since they had been saved. That the saved did not act like someone who had been saved, moreover, was one of the reasons "ethics" became such a concern. Some hoped that if we just thought harder about something called ethics, we might find a way to make people live better lives. This was a deep mistake, as it turned out.

These problems are simply reproduced by those who are currently trying to make the Church the tent in order that they might reach the "seekers." They assume that what is important is that new people should come to church. As a result, they fail to see that the more important question should be: "Does the Church to which they are coming worship God truthfully?" As Saliers has insisted, in worship "form matters" for the truthful shaping of our emotions. The words we use matter.[5] It matters that the Word should be followed

---

[4] The reason I am a theologian is that I never was able to get "saved." I understood that I was a member of the Church, but I also knew that I was supposed to be saved at a Sunday night service (Sunday night services were what we did between summer tent events). I wanted to be saved, but it just never happened. I finally decided somewhere around age fourteen that if God was not going to save me, I would "dedicate my life to Christian service" by becoming a minister. So during the sixteenth singing of "I Surrender All"—a relatively short altar call as altar calls went on Sunday nights—I dedicated my life to God by declaring that I would become a minister. That never happened, but it did make me major in philosophy in college, go to seminary, do a Ph.D. in theology and, as they say, the rest is history.

[5] The effect of the loss of eloquence in worship is a moral loss. Our lives morally depend on our being able to describe that which we do and do not do truthfully. When the language used in worship is degraded, so are our lives. For example, consider the word "just." Often those who pray extemporaneously say,

by table if we are to be rightly formed as Christians. It matters what kind of music shapes our response to the psalms, since what the psalm declares is not separable from how we as the Church sing that declaration.[6]

In this respect, there is an interesting parallel between liturgy and ethics as disciplines. To think liturgically and ethically is to try to help the Church discover connections by developing historical analogies, exploring philosophical and theological implications, and in the process to make normative recommendations. That is why, hopefully, it is hard to distinguish the work done in liturgy and ethics.[7] After all, when all is said and done, liturgy and ethics are just ways to do

---

"Lord, we would ask you just to do X or Y." Not only is the use of "just" in that context ugly, but theologically it suggests, "Lord, we are really not asking for all that much, given your power." I realize that often the use of the "just" is meant to suggest humility, but such humility cannot help but sound like a pose. Eloquence, of course, is not achieved by using "archaic" language but by the constant attention necessary to put basic matters simply. [See Brian Wren's essay below, p. 181ff.—*Editor's note.*]

[6] I mention the psalms in particular because of Saliers' work to ensure their inclusion in the 1989 edition of the *United Methodist Hymnal*. It is my belief that this hymnal is the most important development in Methodism in the last fifty years. Theologians so often think that what is important is what other theologians think, but much more important is what the Church does. It is to Saliers' great credit that he has understood this. The time he has dedicated to help the Church sing is not wise if you want a successful academic career, but he has rightly understood that such a career is a very small thing indeed compared to the glory of praising God.

[7] This is particularly the case if you are, like me, a convinced Aristotelian. For Aristotle, what and how we "feel" when we do the virtuous thing is as important as our doing it. Aristotle says that moral virtue "is concerned with emotions and actions, and it is in emotions and actions that excess, deficiency, and the median are found. Thus we can experience fear, confidence, desire, anger, pity, and generally any kind of pleasure and pain either too much or too little, and in either case not properly. But to experience all this at the right time, toward the right objects, toward the right people, for the right reason, and in the right manner—that is the median and the best course, the course that is a mark of virtue."—*Nicomachean Ethics*, trans. Martin Ostwald (Indianapolis: Bobbs-Merrill, 1962) 1106b, 15-24. I take it that those concerned with helping us worship God rightly do so as Aristotelians—which is to say, it is not enough that we do what we do but that we do what we do rightly. It is, of course, crucial to remember that we do not worship alone, which means that sometimes I must rely on my fellow worshipers to feel rightly for me.

theology, and theology so understood might again be understood as worship.

The liturgist's concern to have the different parts of the liturgy "make sense" is quite similar to the ethicist's concern to help the Church understand the relation between certain kinds of behavior and moral judgment. Adultery means having sex with someone who is not your spouse, no matter how "loving" the extramarital encounter is or may have been. "In the Garden" is not an appropriate hymn for corporate worship, no matter how meaningful some people may find it.[8] Part of the difficulty is that Protestant Christians, evangelical and mainstream alike, have lost their ability to make such judgments. They have done so, moreover, because they debased their worship in the name of evangelism and moral uplift.

As Marva Dawn reminds us in her *Reaching Out Without Dumbing Down*, worship is "for" God, which is not the same thing as it being "meaningful for us."[9] Worship that is for God is, she argues, charac-

---

[8] For those from more liturgical traditions, "In the Garden" is a popular hymn written by C. Austin Miles in 1913. The problem with "In the Garden" is not, as is often suggested, the barely repressed sexual longing; there is nothing wrong with desire, even if it is confused. Rather, the problem with hymns like "In the Garden" is that their lyrics and music are shallow. A steady diet of worship formed by such hymns and prayers not only reflects a shallow Church but also produces a shallow people. I know this seems like a harsh judgment that can also betray a "high culture" arrogance that disdains "popular religion." I have nothing but profound respect for the "country churches" that thought that "In the Garden" was the best hymn they sang. The problem, however, is that hymn and the worship that was shaped by it proved incapable of preparing those who sang it to recognize, much less resist, the world that increasingly made their Christian commitments unintelligible. I am well aware, however, that many Churches whose hymns and prayers are richer are often equally unprepared to challenge the world. Yet hymns like "A Mighty Fortress" have the potential to help mount a resistance that "In the Garden" can never muster.

In a letter to me about this hymn, Ed Phillips, a Church historian and liturgist who teaches at Garrett Evangelical Theological Seminary, notes that "the last stanza subverts the entire text and makes it, actually, more interesting than you might at first notice: 'I'd stay in the garden with him / though the night around me be falling, / but he bids me go: / through the voice of woe / his voice to me is calling.' In other words, we *want* to remain 'in the garden' all day long, but Jesus says, 'Get out there where the suffering is!'"

[9] Marva Dawn, *Reaching Out Without Dumbing Down* (Grand Rapids, Mich.: Eerdmans, 1995) 75–104.

ter forming. That truthful worship of God requires that we proceed in "good order" is a reminder of the very God who alone is deserving of worship. For as the quote from Augustine reminds us, it is not any God that Christians worship but the God whose justice is to be found in Jesus' cross and resurrection. To learn to worship that God truthfully requires that our bodies be formed by truthful habits of speech and gesture. To be so habituated is to acquire a character befitting lives capable of worshiping God.

One of the ironies of our times is that many "conservative" Christians fail to understand the relation between truthful worship and truthful living. For example, many "conservatives" became upset at women and men allegedly worshiping Sophia in the name of making liturgy "meaningful for women." Yet too often the same people who criticize the worship of God as Sophia are more than ready to distort the proper order of Christian worship in the name of evangelism. They, of course, say they use the name of Jesus, but they fail to see that *how* Jesus' name is used makes all the difference. Without the Eucharist, for example, we lack the means to know the kind of presence Jesus' resurrection makes possible.

The Eucharist is usually not considered an essential aspect of Christian worship by those concerned with Church growth. Evangelism means getting people to church, because unless one goes to church, it is assumed that our lives are without moral compass. Thus the assumption that lack of attendance at church and our society's "moral decay" go hand in hand. What such people fail to see is that such decay begins with the assumption that worship is about "my" finding meaning for my life rather than the glorification of God. Such evangelism is but another name for narcissism. Christian worship requires that our bodies submit to a training otherwise unavailable if we are to be capable of discerning those who use the name of Jesus to tempt us to worship foreign gods. Without the Eucharist we lose the resource to discover how those gods rule our lives.

It is important to note that the problem is not whether our worship is "contemporary" or "traditional." Too often such an alternative is an attempt to make us choose hymns that were contemporary in the seventeenth century but sound "traditional" today because we no longer remember what seventeenth-century music sounded like. Nor is it a question of whether worship can be changed. Worship is always being "changed." To remain "the same" when everything around you is changing, whether you like it or not, is to be changed. That is why those who sometimes insist on the actual use of tents may think they are doing the same thing that was done in the past, but in fact the very consciousness required to use tents, when tents are no longer necessary, makes the use of these tents different.

The question, then, is not choosing between "contemporary" or "traditional," change or not changing, but rather the faithful character of our worship, insofar as such worship shapes the truthful witness of the Church to the world. The problem with churches that make "evangelism" (that is, the continuing acquisition of new members) the purpose of their worship is not whether the worship is contemporary. The question is whether they are worshiping the God of Jesus Christ. Moreover, it is not just the church-growth churches, the Willow Creeks, that have that problem, but "normal" mainstream churches.[10]

Consider, for example, this statement on the back of the bulletin of a very "successful" Methodist church (named changed to protect the guilty): "You are welcome, just as you are, at 'Pleasant City'! Everyone is welcome here. We particularly welcome those who have been away from church for a while, and those who are not members of any church. Whether you're married, single, divorced or in transition,

---

[10] I may have been among the last in this society to learn that Willow Creek is the paradigm of churches that use modern marketing methods to sustain church growth. The best way to think about such "churches" is to compare them to a shopping mall where periodically the customers are gathered for a common event. Such churches seek to be full-service institutions providing athletic activities, clubs, and child care. If such churches were more centered around determinative liturgies that were recognizably Christian, they might be usefully compared to medieval cathedrals. The latter were often centers for carnival, trade, and politics, and I see no reason to be critical. The problem with churches like Willow Creek is not that they are the center of so many activities, but that those activities do not require for their intelligibility the Mass. I realize that such a comment will invite the charge that I am romanticizing the medieval life, but I am more than willing to take that risk.

For an arresting account of the vitality of religious life in late medieval culture, see Eamon Duffy, *The Stripping of the Altars: Traditional Religion in England, c. 1400–1580* (New Haven: Yale University Press, 1992), as well as David Aers' criticism of Duffy for failing to provide an adequate account of the complex social, political, and military factors shaping "religion" in his "Altars of Power: Reflections on Eamon Duffy's *The Stripping of the Altars*," *Literature and History* 3/2 (Autumn 1994) 90–105.

you truly matter to us because you matter to God. We would be honored to have you become a member of Pleasant City Church. Check the box on the friendship pad if you wish to discuss church membership."[11]

Is that evangelism? What would worship in such a church look like? How would anyone in that church know which god it is that seems allegedly so concerned about them? It is easy to criticize Willow Creeks, but Willow Creeks merely exemplify the loss of the Christian worship of God in the name of "more members." The difficulty with worship intentionally shaped to entertain those who are "new" is not that it is entertaining, but that the god that is entertained in such worship cannot be the Trinity. For example, to worship the Trinity requires at the very least that we learn to say together the Apostles Creed. That such a discipline has, in the name of evangelism, become odd, even for Methodists, is but an indication of how distorted our worship has become.

The heart of Saliers' work has been to try to remind his Church, the Methodist Church, that faithful and truthful worship of the crucified God is evangelism. That he has done so has not won him universal acclaim among Methodists. That he insists that worship be done "right" is rightly seen by some as a threat to Church growth. I suspect that Saliers does not make that erroneous assumption. The fact that large numbers of people are attracted to a Church is not in itself a sign of false worship, but Saliers, like me, probably does think that if such is the case, it is an indication that a close examination of how

---

[11] That this invitation is particularly directed at a person's marital status is but an indication of the privatization of Christianity in liberal cultures. The church gets to claim its own peculiar jurisdiction, in this case something to do with the family, because the family is "private." Such an invitation would have been interesting if it had said, "Whether you are rich or poor, in debt or not, just out of prison or on the street, you are welcome." Such an invitation would have indicated some recognition of how class divides our churches, but to acknowledge class is even more threatening for most churches than the acknowledgment of homosexuality or racial divides. I have noticed the "higher" a church's liturgy, the more likely some recognition of class is possible. I have no strong evidence to support this generalization, nor am I sure, if it is true, why it is so. Of course, this is true mainly of Roman Catholic churches. That farm workers, for example, appear at Catholic Masses predominantly populated by middle-class people is open to many explanations. But such explanations surely must involve an account of how the liturgy offers some challenge to the power that class has over our lives.

that Church worships is a good idea.[12] That we, moreover, feel the need for such an examination is because we are Methodists who believe that the shaping of our lives in worship is inseparable from the moral shaping of our lives—a shaping that cannot help but make us appear quite odd, given the assumptions about what it means to be "morally normal" in American society.

3. HOLINESS

The name we Methodists have used to indicate the inseparability of worship, evangelism, and ethics is holiness. We believe that God's salvation is nothing less than participation in God's very life through word and sacrament. Worship is what we do for God, but in that doing we believe that our lives are made part of God's care of creation. To be made holy is to have our lives rendered unintelligible if the God that has claimed us in Jesus Christ is not the true God. To be made holy is to have our lives "exposed" to one another in the hope that we will become what we have been made.

From Wesley's perspective, Christian worship is evangelism, because worship is converting work.[13] Though this may sound Pelagian, the work that worship does is not something we do apart from God. Worship requires that our sins be named, confessed, forgiven.[14] In worship we discover sin is not something we do, but rather it is a power that holds us captive.[15] The good news of the gospel, the mes-

[12] To attract large numbers of people presupposes that they are coming to worship without that coming requiring fundamental change in their own lives. There is nothing wrong in itself with worship being entertaining, but the difficulty is the kind of entertainment necessary to attract large numbers. If worship must, as is often alleged, compete with TV, then TV will always win. Our only hope is that some will find the demanding character of the worship of God so enthralling that they will be drawn to it time and time again.

[13] For an account of Wesley's views on these matters, see Ole Borgen, *John Wesley on the Sacraments* (Grand Rapids, Mich.: Francis Asbury Press of Zondervan Publishing House, 1986).

[14] The worship service at Pleasant City had no confession of sin. Since the service from which I extracted the bulletin quote was a Fourth of July service, there were pledges made to the United States Flag, the Christian Flag, and a pledge to the Bible. Sin was mentioned in the last pledge, which went, "I pledge allegiance to the Bible, God's Holy Word, and will make it a lamp unto my feet, a light unto my path, and hide its words in my heart that I may not sin against God."

[15] Of course, that sin names the powers does not mean that we do not sin. We confess our sins as those who have willingly sinned, but our willingness names

sage proclaimed to the nations, is that we are freed from sin by the God who would be honored, who would be worshiped, before all else.

From a Wesleyan perspective, to be made holy, to be made capable of accepting forgiveness for our sins so that we might worthily worship God, is not just "personal holiness." As Augustine suggested above, nothing is more important for a society than to worship God justly. Without such worship, terrible sacrifices will be made to false gods. Contrary to the modern presumption that as enlightened people we are beyond sacrifice, few societies are more intent on sacrifice than those we call modern.[16] Societies that think they have left sacrifice behind end up basing their existence on the sacrifice of the poor in the name of human progress. Christians believe that we are the alternative to such sacrificial systems because we have been given the gift of offering our "sacrifice of thanksgiving" to the One who alone is worthy to receive such praise. That is what makes us a holy people, a people set apart, so that the world might know that there is an alternative to murder.

That I teach "ethics" through the liturgy and Saliers refuses to do theology as if prayer does not matter is, I hope, testimony to the fact that we are Methodist "perfectionists."[17] We have staked our work and our lives on the presumption that if, in some small way, we can help our Church recover liturgical integrity, we will not have to deal

---

complicity. I often think that the closest paradigm we have to what it means to confess our sin is the alcoholic's confession at AA meetings: "My name is X and I am an alcoholic." It may be that alcoholism is a power that possesses some persons in such a manner that they can never remember "choosing" to be an alcoholic. Only by confessing that alcoholism is "me" is there any hope of recovery. Sin may not always be something I have "done," but it is nonetheless mine.

[16] For an extraordinary account of our current sacrificial system we call America, see Gil Bailie, *Violence Unveiled: Humanity at the Crossroads* (New York: Crossroad Books, 1995). Bailie's analysis draws on the remarkable work of René Girard.

[17] For an account of the way I teach Christian ethics at Duke Divinity School, see my *In Good Company: The Church as Polis* (Notre Dame: University of Notre Dame Press, 1995) 153–168. I confess that I have no idea how much I have stolen over the years from Saliers' *The Soul in Paraphrase: Prayer and the Religious Affections* (New York: Seabury Press, 1980), but I know it has been more than I have acknowledged. For example, everything I have said in this essay could be and, hopefully, will be read as a commentary on his claim that "prayer is a logically required context for the utterance of theological truths" (82).

with a question about the relation between worship, evangelism, and ethics. Of course, it may still be useful to distinguish between worship, evangelism, and ethics as subjects of study, but hopefully such distinctions will be seen as part of the Church's ministry reflected in a diversity of gifts. Such gifts, however, cannot become separate disciplines or realms if they are to be of service.

Yet, neither of us can deny that if we do in fact worship God truthfully, we may well find the Church again worshiping in tents. For such worship creates a people who by necessity are on the move, forced to wander among the nations, home nowhere yet everywhere. Such a people are bound to attract followers, because the God who has called them from the nations is so beautifully compelling. That is, after all, why we believe that there is nothing more important in a world that does not believe it has the time to worship God to take time to worship God truthfully.[18]

[18] I am indebted to Kelly Johnson and Jim Fodor for their criticism of an earlier draft of this essay.

Part 3

Formation of Character:
Person, Practice, and Affection

Introduction

The previous section set the stage for a consideration of the relationships between liturgical practices and the formation of Christian persons. In this section we give our attention more specifically to the particular practices of hymnsinging, contemplative and intercessory prayer, and the Reproaches of Good Friday. Each essay of this section addresses the question of what it means to "gesture the self" before God and how this gesture, while expressive of Christian faith and belief, is a constituting activity for Christian belief and ethical action.

E. Byron Anderson explores the implications of the performance of a hymn by Charles Wesley as such a gesture of the self. He argues that singing the hymn is a bodily engagement at once personal and communal, situating believers in the transformative stream of tradition, wherein connection to the past provides direction for the future.

Peter Fink and Mary Stamps explore the Ignatian and Benedictine traditions of contemplative and communal prayer, respectively. Fink takes up the classic contrast between contemplation and action, considering more closely Saliers' description of Jesus' life as one of "active prayer and prayerful action." For Fink, the task of exploring the unity of contemplation and action requires examination of the lifelong journey of "conversion and transformation that leads to communion with Christ." He unfolds the map for this journey through the Spiritual Exercises of Ignatius Loyola, wherein contemplation turns out to be not a way of looking but rather a way of loving.

Stamps turns to the Rule of St. Benedict, arguing that the christocentrism in the Rule fosters a christomorphism in the monks who practice it. The communal practice of the daily Offices, the *opus Dei*, or "Work of God," encodes over time the Word of God in the lives of the monks, while also building trust and mutual reliance among them. The praying of the texts comes to practical life in the monks' living of Christlike virtues that, in turn, contributes to the integrity of the monastery's prayer.

Through a reflective analysis of her experience of praying the Lord's Prayer, Roberta Bondi demonstrates how the authenticity of communal worship and intercessory prayer depends upon the members of the community doing the work of introspective, interior prayer in their individual lives. Leading us through the parables and actions of Jesus, instruction from teachers of the early Church, and autobiographical narrative, she opens ways of perceiving deep connections between God, self, and neighbor in praying "Our Father in heaven."

As Bondi leads us from the prayer for "me" to prayer for "us," so, too, Gail Ramshaw identifies how Christian communities can both misappropriate a particular prayer text as well as recover its original intention "to pry us open." Through a study of the Reproaches of Good Friday, Ramshaw demonstrates how Christian prayer draws self-preoccupied individuals out of their shells and into the Body of Christ, whose arms extend to embrace all of humanity, with all its Otherness.

E. Byron Anderson

"O for a heart to praise my God": Hymning the Self Before God

In the midst of the current divisions, skirmishes, and even battles about "traditional" and "contemporary" worship, it could appear to be either sheer boldness or outright foolishness to make any claims about the function of hymnody in the life and practice of Christian communities that reach beyond understandings of song as personal or communal expression. We sing because it expresses who we are. Yet both sides of the traditional/contemporary debate do make claims that exceed those of mere expressiveness. We know, too, that if the issues were only that of expression, there would be no cause for the present debate. Whether traditional or contemporary, both argue, at least implicitly, that the shape, context, and style of Christian song are normative and constitutive— normative in that it provides rules about personal and communal life in faith and constitutive in that it provides a means through which persons come to faith and by which communities are nurtured in faith.

Regardless of which side one chooses in these conflicts, we know that Christian song is powerful. We also know that the singing of hymns is more than making music:

"The hymns that I have sung often and memorized are ones that I quote to myself in times of spiritual need or in times of rejoicing. I can remember the words, and if not the exact words, I can remember the spirit and the general message of the hymn. So hymns continue to minister to me just like the scripture does. Which [sic] is one good argument for repeating certain hymns in liturgy with some frequency, so people have a chance to recall them."[1]

---

[1] Interview elicited as part of the study "The Faith and Practices of Christian Congregations" (Thomas E. Frank, Candler School of Theology, project director)

Or, as Fred Pratt Green states in one of his well-known hymns:

"How often, making music, we have found
a new dimension in the world of sound,
as worship moved us to a more profound
Alleluia!"[2]

And, in his preface to *A Collection of Hymns for the use of the People called Methodist* of 1780, John Wesley commends its hymns and the hymnal to the reader "as a means of raising or quickening the spirit of devotion, of confirming his [sic] faith, of enlivening his hope, and of kindling or increasing his love to God and man. When poetry thus keeps its place, as the handmaid of piety, it shall attain, not a poor perishable wreath, but a crown that fadeth not away."[3]

The poetry of which Wesley speaks is presented for the purpose of congregational song and personal devotion. His reserve about its place as the "handmaid of piety" echoes Augustine, who was himself of divided opinion about song in Christian worship. In the *Confessions*, Augustine remembers the hold that music exercised upon his spirit, finding in it not only the "pleasures of the ear" but a "sense of restful contentment" as well. He resisted pure emotional expressiveness, arguing that it was not the music but the words or "thoughts which give [it] life" that granted music a place of honor in Christian worship. Fluctuating "between the danger of pleasure and the experience of the beneficent effect," Augustine settled for the latter, permitting music in worship that "through the delights of the ear the weaker mind may rise up towards the devotion of worship."[4] The handmaid of piety, indeed.

In the midst of debate about Christian song, each of the examples suggests that the singing of a hymn is more than making music,

---

on the reception and use of *The United Methodist Hymnal* undertaken by Don Saliers. Used by permission.

[2] "When in Our Music God Is Glorified," *The United Methodist Hymnal* (Nashville: The United Methodist Publishing House, 1989) 68.

[3] *A Collection of Hymns for the Use of the People Called Methodists*, vol. 7 of *The Works of John Wesley*, ed. Franz Hildebrandt and Oliver A. Beckerlegge (Oxford: Oxford University Press, 1983) 75.

[4] Augustine, *Confessions*, trans. Henry Chadwick, bk. 10, chap. 33 (New York: Oxford University Press, 1991) 207–208.

more than a nice song filling dead space in a liturgy, more than an aesthetic act, more than an act of self-expression. It is also an act of pastoral care in times of need and rejoicing. It provides, or at least offers the potential to provide, a dimension of depth in our worship of God. It has a place as "the handmaid of piety" and directs us to worship. It is all of these things, and more still. As Don Saliers has argued in his essay "Liturgy and Ethics," "to thank God, to praise God, to confess, to intercede—all these are ways of gesturing the self in and through words."[5]

While Saliers' concern is to describe how we "gesture the self" in and through the words and actions of the liturgy, I wonder how the singing of a hymn might be such a gesture. What does it mean to "hymn the self before God"? In addressing these questions, I want to argue that to sing a hymn is to "gesture the self before God." I also want to argue that this gesture of the self, while expressive of who we are as Christian people, in some way also norms and constitutes us as Christian people.

Rather than speaking about hymns in general, I propose one hymn, Charles Wesley's "O for a heart to praise my God,"[6] as the instantiation of a particular gesture. The 1780 version of this text reads:

"O for a heart to praise my God,
A heart from sin set free!
A heart that always feels thy blood,
So freely spilt for me!

A heart resigned, submissive, meek,
My great Redeemer's throne,
Where only Christ is heard to speak,
Where Jesus reigns alone.

O for a lowly, contrite heart[7]
Believing, true, and clean,

---

[5] See above, p. 19.

[6] A Collection of Hymns, hymn 334, pp. 490–491. This hymn first appeared in the Wesleys' collection Hymns and Sacred Poems of 1742. It has appeared with regularity in the major Methodist hymnals since then.

[7] The 1742, 1765, and twentieth-century versions read "A [or An] humble, lowly, contrite heart."

Which neither life nor death can part
From him that dwells within!

A heart in every thought renewed,
And full of love divine,
Perfect, and right, and pure, and good—
A copy, Lord, of thine!

[Thy tender heart is still the same,
And melts at human woe;
Jesu, for thee distressed I am—
I want thy love to know.

My heart, thou know'st, can never rest
Till thou create my peace,
Till, of my Eden repossessed,
From every sin I cease.

Fruit of thy gracious lips, on me
Bestow that peace unknown,
The hidden manna, and the tree
Of life, and the white stone.][8]

Thy nature, gracious Lord, impart;
Come quickly from above;
Write thy new name upon my heart,
Thy new, best name of love!"

Four questions will guide this conversation: First, what does this text say or do? Second, what does the context of the text do with or to the text? Third, how does the practice of this text become a gesture of the self before God? Finally, how is the practice of singing a hymn a liturgical gesture of the Christian self?

What does this hymn say or do? As a devotional text, the hymn comes from Wesley as a form of self-expression, commentary, and reflection on Psalm 51:10: "Create in me a clean heart, O God, and renew a right spirit within me." S T Kimbrough describes Wesley's work as biblical interpreter, in part, as reenacting "the initial experience of Scripture," personalizing "the text so that the text becomes

---

[8] All the North American Methodist hymnals of this century omit these three stanzas.

his own," and "transforming the imagery of Scripture into categories of contemporaneous experience."[9] While we do not have access to Wesley's state of mind or heart when he wrote this text, placing his hymns in chronological order does provide the closest we have to a spiritual autobiography. As an expressive act, Wesley wrote this hymn some three years after his evangelical awakening. In the context of this awakening, it reflects Wesley's hope for a new heart as well as a new life.

The psalm itself is a statement of unwavering honesty about the depth of human sinfulness. The psalm verse to which Wesley responds (v. 10) follows a confession of sinfulness and a prayer for the forgiveness of this sin. Verse 10 begins a prayer for renewal only possible following forgiveness. This renewal leads the psalmist to end the psalm with an act of praise.[10] Rather than paraphrasing the psalm text or Christianizing it, as we find in English hymnwriters before Wesley (such as Thomas Sternhold, Nahum Tate, or Isaac Watts), Wesley appropriates David's experience of a ruptured relationship with God as his own, interprets that experience through the heart and mind of Christian faith, and sets out an expectation of the new and perfected life that comes from the healing of the relationship through the transformation of the heart.[11] The way in which Wesley states this expectation reflects his reliance on Matthew Henry's commentary. In Henry's comments on verses 7-13 of the psalm, he names the concerns of the psalmist as seeking an assurance of pardon, an assurance of restoration to God's favor, of seeking sanctifying grace that his nature, his heart, might be changed.[12]

---

[9] S T Kimbrough, Jr., "Charles Wesley and Biblical Interpretation" in *Charles Wesley: Poet and Theologian*, S T Kimbrough, Jr., ed., (Nashville: Abingdon, 1992) 114, 118.

[10] Artur Weiser, *The Psalms* (Philadelphia: Westminster Press, 1952) 401–407.

[11] Teresa Berger writes: "For Charles Wesley, the creation of a new heart is the essence of the 'new creation.' Wesley's preference for this image of a new heart is a good example of his interiorization of the larger image of the new creation. Those hymns devoted to the theme of Christian perfection repeatedly offer prayers for a new heart as a precondition for the life of perfection. . . . The heart, which longs for re-creation, is to be a copy of the heart of Jesus, and the *imago Dei*, which is to be restored is the *imago Christi*. . . ."—*Theology in Hymns?* (Nashville: Abingdon, 1995) 147–148.

[12] Matthew Henry, *Commentary on the Bible* (New York: Revell, 1935) 3:432–433. It is worth considering another influence on Wesley's language at this point. One

Wesley's first four stanzas focus on the present imperfect character or heart of the individual Christian. The heart is not completely free from sin, even as it is not solely the dwelling place or throne of Christ. It is a heart renewed but not yet perfect in thought and love. It is a heart aware of its imperfection and of what it yet requires to bring it to completion. The perfect heart will be "believing, true, and clean," "perfect, and right, and pure, and good," a heart fashioned in the *imago Christi*. However, it is not until the end of the fourth stanza that we discover that the hymn is not only a vehicle for the expression of the singer's self-awareness of imperfection but a prayer directed to Christ in the form of a comparison between the heart of the singer and that of Christ. The editorial decisions to delete stanzas 5-7 in later Methodist hymnals undercut this comparison.

At the end of the fourth stanza and in the succeeding stanzas, we come to realize that the hymn is a petition—as is the psalm verse on which it builds. This petition, even as it expresses a certain self-awareness, enacts a relationship between God in Christ and the singer, thereby constituting the person in relationship with God. The petition also intends a transformation of that relationship, thereby indicating a set of norms for that relationship. The goal of the text, as petition, is named at the end of stanzas five and eight: "I want thy love to know" and "Write thy new name upon my heart, Thy new, best name of love!" The heart fashioned in the *imago Christi* is the heart enabled to praise God through an experience of the love of God for the singer. The heart upon which the "name of love" is written is the heart brought to Christian perfection.

In answering the second question, What does the context of the text do with or to the text? we must acknowledge that there is more than one context shaping the reception of this hymn. The first is the context of Charles Wesley's work in the early years after his conversion of 1738. In reading his journal from this period, we find a man

---

of the concluding prayers in the Great Litany of the Book of Common Prayer, which John Wesley commended to the Methodists to read each Wednesday and Friday, reads: "O God, merciful Father, that despiseth not the sighing of a contrite heart, nor the desire of such as be sorrowful; mercifully assist our prayers that we make before thee, in all our troubles and adversities whensoever they oppress us . . . ." (The prayer text is that found in John Wesley's abbreviation of the Book of Common Prayer for the Methodist societies in North America, generally known as the "Sunday Service" of 1784.)

filled with evangelical fervor, traveling the countryside, preaching as often as five times a day, visiting and praying with the sick and imprisoned, in active conflict with "predestinarians," and successfully winning hearts and minds to the way of Jesus Christ. This was a time filled with new hope and new life for Wesley.

The hymn also has a particular theological context within the Methodist movement itself. Charles and John were in agreement upon the ideal of Christian perfection, but they were not of one mind on its attainability in this life. While John remained cautiously convinced that perfection was attainable in this life, Charles believed that it was only likely to be attained at the end of the Christian's life. He believed that while the Christian person longs for perfection of the heart throughout life, life is characterized less by the attainment of perfection than by the ongoing striving toward perfection.

This theological context provides the framework for the context of the hymn within the 1780 hymnal itself. The Wesleys intended the hymnal to function as a theological document as well as a "manual for public worship and private devotion" for the Methodist people, what John Wesley called "a little body of experimental and practical divinity."[13] As editor, John Wesley gave the hymnal a specific theological shape, much as we find explicitly or implicitly in any contemporary hymnal. But he also gave it an experiential shape. For the Wesleys, this shape is determined by what they understood to be the pattern of the Christian life, from an initial exhortation to return to God to its culmination in the life of glory, a life that is simultaneously individual and communal.

One might expect a text petitioning Christ for "a heart to praise my God" to address the concerns of the "mourner convinced of sin" or the "mourner brought to new birth"—the concerns of those awakening in faith for the first time and the categories of the hymns in the early part of the hymnal. While this text does help with these concerns, its position in the hymnal functions as a resource for those presumably mature Christians "groaning for full redemption." It is concerned with the ongoing growth of the Christian person toward and in perfection. This context of the hymn within the hymnal also positions it to address the teleology of life with God in perfect love. In this regard, it echoes the final stanza of the familiar "Love Divine,

13 Berger, *Theology in Hymns?* 1.

All Loves Excelling": "Finish, then, thy new creation; pure and spotless let us be."

There are two performative contexts, that of private devotion and that of corporate song, that also require our attention. It is from the former that the text seems to develop at the first. In personal reflection on the psalm text, Wesley engages the psalm text as if it named his own experience, as described earlier. What we discover in his hymn is that this engagement is no longer an "as if"; it is a naming of Wesley's personal experience in and with God in Christ. As such, it becomes a personal petition for the ongoing transformation of Wesley's heart and a statement of personal relationship with God. The personal character of this hymn is clear throughout: "O for a heart to praise *my* God," "*My* great Redeemer's praise," "*My* heart, thou know'st, can never rest / Till thou create *my* peace." This personal devotion and experience were central to the Wesleys' conversion experiences and to the work of evangelical revival that followed from it. It was out of concern for the personal appropriation of this experience that the Wesleys engaged in their work.

The more difficult question, I think, is what happens when this form of personal petition is sung corporately. Does its corporate performance make it any less personal? Here it is helpful to make a distinction between personal and private. What is personal is of and about me but not "owned" by me, whereas what is private is mine alone. By placing this hymn in the 1780 *Collection* and in the hymnals that preceded it, John and Charles Wesley offer a personal, rather than private, language and teleology of relatedness to individuals and a people "called Methodist." As the language of a people rather than a person, the hymn establishes a framework within which Methodist people join in the song of all creation as, together, it groans for full redemption. In this form, it becomes a petition for a corporate heart with which to praise God. It takes the individual experience of a broken relationship with God, as described above, and claims that experience for the evangelical society. It claims for that society a vision of the new and perfected life that comes through the healing of the relationship by the transformation of the heart. It is the heart of the Body of Christ yearning to be shaped in and united with the perfect love manifest in the "tender heart" of Jesus. It is the heart yearning in new life and new hope for the completion of God's sanctifying work.

Teresa Berger describes the expressive-constitutive work of doxology through hymnody this way:

". . . doxology is the bearer of a very specific and unique worldview (or more concretely, of a particular interpretation of religious existence), which, in the final analysis, only has meaning for those who make doxological speech their own. Specifically, the doxological interpretation of existence has meaning for those who understand and commit themselves to 'a sacrifice of praise to God, that is, the fruit of lips that confess his name' (Heb. 13.15)."[14]

What was a personal expression of faith becomes a communal expression that also begins to constitute person and community. The singing of the hymn provides not only the means for person and community to express their faith but also the means by which it proposes to person and community a way of meaning and being in the world. Singing the hymn commits person and community to a vision of relatedness to God and community no longer marked by rupture. Singing the hymn commits self and community to a stance of love and desire before God. It is to commit oneself and the community with which one sings to the doxological life that seeks perfect praise and perfect love of God. In doing so, we have gone beyond self-expression. Our singing of the hymn results, in a fashion, in the hymn "singing" us, naming us, identifying us as people of faith.

We know that the act of singing identifies us as singers. But in singing a hymn, we identify ourselves also with a particular text and tune, even if only momentarily. To sing requires the full engagement of body and mind in a commitment to act. It engages us in an intention to form sound at a particular pitch and in a particular rhythm not otherwise defined by the habits of speech. In this we are reminded that we have to do with a text and tune, with something printed on a page and something to be realized in performance. While we may read the text silently or listen to someone else sing it, our performance of the hymn results in our apprehension of the hymn "being registered integrally, by body and mind together."[15]

---

[14] Ibid., 162.
[15] Frank Burch Brown, *Religious Aesthetics* (Princeton: Princeton University Press, 1989) 93.

The images, themes, and claims of the text are realized not as text but as a "writing on the body" in performance.

To the extent that the hymn is sung by a corporate body, it not only requires our engagement in mind and body but requires a bodily engagement that is simultaneously individual and communal. The strophic and rhythmic character of the hymn requires that if we are to sing, we must sing and breathe together. What is registered integrally is registered communally. As the images, themes, and claims of a hymn are appropriated through performance and repetition, the hymn begins, so to speak, to take on a life of its own and to have its way with us. Writing in body and mind, the hymn is no longer only the expressive statement "This is who I am" but a constituting statement, "This is who you are coming to be."

This leads to my third and fourth questions and, more specifically, to the question of this essay: How does the practice of this text, the singing of a hymn, become a gesture, a "practice" of the self before God?[16] As I have tried to suggest in the preceding paragraphs, the liturgical gesture of the self is more than a form of self-expression, more than a mode of private action by which the autonomous person stands in solitude, even if with a community, before God. As a practice by which persons express personal and communal faith, hymnsinging physically and mentally situates the person in a context of relatedness to the whole of a community whose voice is united in song and to God. In this, the hymn offers an experience of related-

---

[16] While I may be accused of a sleight of hand in equating *gesture* and *practice*, there is a meeting point for the two terms that justifies this. Generally, we think of gestures as physical acts to assist in expressing a thought or emphasizing a speech act. Gestures also function as signs of intention or attitude. It is this latter usage which I believe Saliers intends and which suggests my use of practice. Here I want *practice* to function in two ways. First, in its more familiar form we speak about the rehearsal of something intended for future, more polished performance. Second, in the technical sense now shaped by the retrieval of an Aristotelian understanding of praxis, practices are "socially shared forms of behavior that mediate between what are often called subjective and objective dimensions. A practice is a pattern of meaning and action that is both culturally constructed and individually instantiated."—Rebecca Chopp, *Saving Work* (Philadelphia: Westminster John Knox, 1995) 15. It is the "sign of intention or attitude" and the "individually instantiated pattern of meaning and action" that describe equal human actions.

ness that is ours to appropriate. At the same time, it offers a language with which we may name and interpret that experience.

As I indicated above, our appropriation of this experience and its interpretation suggest that in singing a hymn we engage in a ritual practice that makes claims upon us individually and in community. That is, in at least a small way, the singing of the hymn helps us as Christian persons and communities to mark, contain, and direct the flow of our lives in relationship to God and the world. Here we need only recall the pastoral function of hymnsinging described in the opening quote. We also know that ritual events variously reveal, convey, and enact the power and permanence of a group. They break the individual out of isolation and define the boundaries of the community in which we are situated. They attend to the human needs for the affirmation and maintenance of the values and beliefs that ground the unity of a group. Here we need only think of the power conveyed by the playing and singing of a national anthem.

Judith Kubicki, in her discussion of music as ritual symbol, argues that such a symbol is "a mediation of recognition which evokes participation and allows an individual or a social group to orientate themselves, that is, to discover their identity and their place within their world."[17] Our hearing of a tune, repeatedly associated with texts and other events, recalls not only our physical act of singing but particular emotional states and experiences. It recalls in us an engagement of mind and heart with an event, a text, an image, a relationship. Its symbolic effectiveness, Kubicki argues, is not our rational apprehension of what we are doing but the "insight and interaction" determined by participation.[18]

It is tempting, especially in contexts that treat tradition as that which is only of the past, to treat hymnsinging as the dull repetition of past poetic, musical, and theological languages. But if our singing is a form of participative knowing through which we come to know ourselves and our place in the world, then our singing is a context in which past and present encounter one another, meaning and self-understanding are transformed, and tradition engages the future. We may understand ourselves to be only singing a hymn, but this

[17] Judith Marie Kubicki, "The Role of Music as Ritual Symbol in Roman Catholic Liturgy," *Worship* 69:5 (September 1995) 431.
[18] Ibid., 437.

ongoing practice results in the writing of a variety of poetic, musical, rhythmic, and theological languages on the body and in the mind and heart of the singer. We "are moved to a more profound alleluia"; we are moved to more perfect praise. As a ritual practice, the singing of the hymn expresses the faith of persons in community even as it defines the terms by which person and community are constituted. In singing and praying for a new heart with which to praise God, we begin that for which we ask.

It is relatively easy, perhaps even commonplace, to understand ritual practice as involving person and community in a statement of their past and present identity, the story of a people in a particular relationship. In this sense, the singing of Wesley's hymn manifests and presents a confession of personal and communal identity in imperfect relationship with God, unable to fully praise God due to the binding power of sin. But if we are also beginning that for which we ask, if we are singing the hymn in the knowledge and expectation of God's transforming power, in the possibility of a transformed heart, then our gesture is about the future as much as it is about the past and present. In beginning that for which we ask—"a heart to praise my God"—we begin to gesture ourselves into the future of our relationship with God.

The self that we sing in this hymn is a self living in expectation of the life that is yet to be, a self emerging in time and in relationship to God. As an act of petition—as is the psalm verse on which it builds— the hymn enacts an unfolding relationship between God in Christ and the singer and prays for the ongoing transformation of that relationship. Walter Brueggemann makes a similar argument: "Praise is not a response to a world already fixed and settled, but it is a responsive and obedient participation in a world yet to be decreed and in process of being decreed through this liturgical act."[19] Even as person and community name a present state in which the heart is not yet free, not yet resigned, submissive, or meek, not yet believing, true, and clean, it names and begins a future in which this is the case, in which the love, peace, and nature of Christ are bestowed. In singing and petitioning for a heart with which to praise God, we open ourselves to and engage in the transformation of our heart because we

[19] *Israel's Praise: Doxology Against Idolatry and Ideology* (Philadelphia: Fortress Press, 1988) 11.

are praising God. In our hymnic gesture we sing our future into being.

The practice of singing the future into being is not to suggest that our future as Christian people is unconditionally open, that there are no expectations for the shape of that future. Were unconditional openness the case, we would have no reason to sing. Our lives would be marked, to the extent that they could be, by aimless wandering or indifference to the condition of our future. The theological and experiential shape of the *Collection* of 1780 suggests, as does the Christian story, that there is a normative horizon for that future that yields neither aimlessness nor indifference. As Brueggemann argues, "It is the act of praise, the corporate, regularized, intentional, verbalized, and enacted act of praise, through which the community of faith creates, orders, shapes, imagines, and patterns the world of God, the world of faith, the world of life, in which we are to act in joy and obedience."[20] The future that we sing into being is already the world of God, faith, and life. It is undetermined in that our participation shapes the future. But it is conditioned, it has direction. Our singing directs us toward relatedness to God and transformation by God, a direction that in turn invites concern and commitment.

In singing "for a heart to praise God," our expectation of a new and perfected life in Christ defines a normative horizon. The inbreaking future is a heart fashioned in the *imago Christi,* a heart that is right, pure, and good. Yet, as a practice in which past, present, and future meet, the hymn becomes an instantiation of that for which it asks. For a moment we seem to transcend our present imperfection and are united in that "love divine" and "peace unknown." In our hymnic gesture, we manifest our openness to God's future for us, practice our intention to act in and with God, and reveal "the reality of God's intention to act toward us in accordance with God's unfailing promise."[21] In this we are constituted in a particular vision and practice of the Christian life.

It is perhaps in this sense that we can speak about the liturgical practice of hymnsinging as a gesture of ourselves by which we participate in the divine life of the Triune God. That is, our gesture not

[20] Ibid., 25–26.
[21] Don Saliers, *Worship as Theology: Foretaste of Glory Divine* (Nashville: Abingdon, 1995) 78.

only identifies our stance before God but engages us in the life and practice of God. The openness we express permits God's work of liberation, healing, and transformation. Our expression permits our participation in God's constituting work of grace and normative future.

In this vein John Thornburg suggests that hymns do more than remind us of God's work of grace: "Hymns also provide saving moments by placing us face to face with the glories and blemishes of our inherited faith tradition. They push us into places we might not otherwise go."[22] Our expressive gesture constitutes and defines a pattern of relatedness to God. We also find that as this relationship develops, we develop an awareness of and ability to be in relationship to other persons and to the world. The conclusion that this leads us to is that the practice of singing the hymn, while a gesture of the self, is instantiation of the rule of prayer determining not only belief but our life in the world. *Lex orandi, lex credendi, lex vivendi?*

Within the larger complex of liturgical sacramental practices defined by the rites of Christian initiation and the Eucharist, Wesley's hymn provides a specific example, perhaps a "micro-practice," of the liturgical gesture of the self. In our hymnic gesture, we practice what is already and not yet in our Christian lives. What is already is a pattern of relatedness in and with the Triune God. This prompts our song in the first place. What is not yet is the completion of our "being made perfect in love." This prompts the particular gesture of this song, the petition for "a heart to praise God."

While our singing requires conscious action on our part, the transformation and participation in God that it enacts is less overtly conscious. It is simultaneously something done to us, with us, and by us in God's name. It is simultaneously a gesture of ourselves before God and God's constituting and normative action with us in and for the world. It is a way of writing God's way on our bodies and in our hearts and minds. In our sung prayer for a heart that is "a copy, Lord, of Thine!" it is a way of cooperating with God's redeeming work to fulfill human identity in the image and likeness of God. It is a way of practicing ourselves in relationship to one another and to the relational God revealed to us in God's own practices of exodus,

---

[22] "Saved by Singing: Hymns as a Means of Grace," *The Hymn* 47:2 (April 1996) 7.

lawgiving, covenanting, incarnating, dying and rising, and inspirit-
ing. With Wesley, we hymn ourselves before God:

"Thy nature, gracious Lord impart;
Come quickly from above;
Write thy new name upon my heart,
Thy new, best name of love!"

Peter E. Fink, S.J.

Life as Prayer: Contemplation and Action

My task is to explore contemplation and action as these two are related within the unity of Christian life and prayer. The keynote is set by the man we honor, Don Saliers, who has questioned the classic contrast between them and suggested instead that the two are interwoven. He says of Christ's life: it is "active prayer and prayerful action."[1] And since Christ's life is generally offered as the model for all Christian life, I assume that Saliers intends as well the life and vocation of all who are baptized into Christ.

There is, however, a question we must ask at the outset. Is this claim for Jesus' life true? It is certainly an elegant play on words. But is it profound theological insight or mere poetic fancy? The Gospel records make no such claim for Jesus but show him rather in the same conflicting dynamic that the classic distinction upholds. At times he withdraws to pray, to a mountain, a desert, a garden, where he finds intimate union with God and the claim of God on his life. At other times he is quite occupied, preaching, teaching, healing, or simply going about the busy-ness of life. Whatever it is that uncovers the unity of prayer and action in Jesus' life, it does not exempt him from the distractions of life or the need to withdraw into the Silence of God.

On a deeper level, however, Scripture does affirm an interplay of prayer and action in Jesus' life. His withdrawal is always for the sake of his mission, never a retreat from its demands. He withdraws to listen, to find guidance and strength, and to let God's claim be forceful in his life. Moreover, it is the very stuff of life that he brings, and that brings him, into the Silence of God. Conversely, as this claim of God unfolds in action, God is never far away, not now as Silence but as

[1] "Liturgy and Ethics," p. 30 above.

127

Passion, a driving force arising from within him. He sees what God sees; he desires what God desires; he does what God summons forth from within him. Jesus' life is portrayed as *communion with God*, and in that communion God is both Silence and Passion.

The question posed about Jesus' life yields a different answer depending on whether you look to "what Jesus does" or go beneath the surface to "who Jesus is." On the surface, prayer and action remain quite distinct even for Jesus. Their unity and interplay remain obscured in apparent opposition. It is only beneath the surface, in the communion with God that Jesus both has and is, that what otherwise might seem mere poetic fancy becomes profound theological insight. The Silence and Passion of God accompany Jesus whether he is withdrawn in prayer or engaged in work for the kingdom. Indeed, the Silence and Passion of God constitute Jesus to be who he is, for he is God's Silence and Passion incarnate. For this reason his life is "active prayer," prayer alive with the Passion of God. For this reason, his life is "prayerful action," action imbued with the Silence of God.

The question yields the same twofold answer when asked of the Christian life. On the level of "what Christians do," prayer and action will always remain distinct, often in conflict. In prayer the vector of one's attention and affection is toward God, wherever God is imagined to be. In action, it is the action itself and those to whom it is directed that claim one's energy and one's heart. It is only on the level of "who Christians are," baptized into Christ, that the truth of Jesus' communion with God emerges as our truth as well. It is not our truth by nature, for we are not ourselves the incarnation of God. But by baptism into Christ we are united to Christ, established as heirs with him, and set in that same communion with Abba that by right is his alone (Gal 4:5).

For Christian men and women, communion with Christ is established in sacrament, but its full truth must unfold in human life. It is a matter of vocation. Christians are called to see as Jesus sees, to desire what Jesus desires, to know and become one with the person of Jesus himself, and in communion to know with him the Silence and Passion of God. For Christians really to enter the communion with Christ that is signed and established in baptism requires a journey of conversion and transformation of heart, the post-baptismal mystagogy at whatever age it begins. At first God's Silence and Passion are engaged separately, the one drawing us into itself and the other sending us out to do the work of Christ. But along the way, as the heart is transformed more and more into Christ, the unity and interplay between Silence and Passion will become manifest. Prayer in the Silence of God will come alive with God's Passion, and one's everyday life will reveal within itself the alluring voice of God's loving Silence.

The task of exploring the unity of contemplation and action requires that we examine the journey of conversion and transformation that leads to communion with Christ. There are, of course, many ways to explore the journey: the range of spiritual traditions with which the Church is blessed. I will proceed along the one path I know best, namely, that mapped out in the Spiritual Exercises of Ignatius Loyola.[2] My hope is that others will find here helpful insight as well.

THE JOURNEY OF THE SPIRITUAL EXERCISES

Let me begin at the end of the journey, for it is at journey's end that prayer and action become as one. The horizon and goal of Ignatian prayer is to become *contemplative in action* and to seek and find the presence of God *in all things.* I begin, not with a theoretical description, but with the witness of three people who capture for me what the outcome of this journey looks like in life.   *Teilhard de C.*

The first is Teilhard de Chardin and the freedom he exudes at the close of his *Divine Milieu.*[3] Having proclaimed his conviction that "the progress of the universe, and in particular of the human universe, does not take place in competition with God" (153), he concludes with a wonder and a proclamation:

"The temptations of too large a world, the seductions of too beautiful a world—where are these now? They do not exist. Now the earth can

---

[2] The Spiritual Exercises of Ignatius Loyola emerged first from his personal journey of conversion. They were later presented to others and form the spiritual backbone of the Society of Jesus, which Ignatius founded. They belong to the Church and have served countless women and men on their own spiritual journeys. They are readily available in numerous editions. The reader may consult, e.g., *The Spiritual Exercises of St. Ignatius,* trans. A. Mottola (Garden City, N.Y.: Image Books, 1964). Helpful companion references: D. Stanley, *A Modern Scriptural Approach to the Spiritual Exercises* (St. Louis: Institute of Jesuit Sources, 1971); W. Barry, *Finding God in All Things* (Notre Dame: Ave Maria Press, 1991).

[3] New York, Harper & Row, 1960.

certainly clasp me in her giant arms. She can swell me with her life, or take me back into her dust. She can deck herself out for me with every charm, every horror, every mystery. . . . But her enchantments can no longer do me harm, since she has become for me, over and above herself, the body of him who is and of him who is coming" (154–155).

The second witness is a Jesuit priest from my novitiate days, whose life could aptly be described as "constant expectation." Whenever anything happened to him, whether it was a sudden assignment, a chance meeting on a train, or just the ordinary rounds of life, he was always alive with wonder at what God might have in store for him. Nothing was taken as a matter of course; everything held out the promise of a great adventure with God.

My third witness is Paul to the Romans, a good reminder that the vision is not restricted to Ignatius nor to those who follow his Spiritual Exercises, but is available to all who follow Christ. In answer to his own question, "What shall separate us from the love of Christ," Paul proclaims his bold conviction: "I am sure that neither death, nor life, nor angels, nor principalities, nor things present, nor things to come, nor powers, nor height, nor depth, nor anything else in all creation, will be able to separate us from the love of God in Christ Jesus our Lord" (RSV: Rom 8:38-39).

These are three very different witnesses, but together they capture what the pursuit of God in all things means, and what it is to be contemplative in action. The contemplative in action is a person of vision, of expectation and wonder, and of profound inner freedom. The contemplative in action consciously lives in the abiding and vibrant presence of God.

But let's step back from journey's end and look at the journey itself. In the structure of the Spiritual Exercises, there are four "weeks"[4] to the journey, each with its own task to perform along the way. The first week begins with withdrawal into God's Silence,

---

[4] The term "week" is a technical term referring to a unit of prayer with its own spiritual theme and grace, as will be explained in the text. As a concentrated retreat, the full Exercises contain four such units and take about thirty days to complete. The length of each week varies with the needs and progress of each retreatant. Beyond the concentrated retreat, the term can also serve to identify stages along the spiritual journey. Its primary use in this essay is this second sense.

where one is invited to learn, first of all, the truth about one's self. Alone before the cross, which sets God's redeeming love as a beacon to shed light on the darkness of one's sin, the mind is illuminated and the heart is tugged toward conversion. The mind learns the destructiveness of sin and the heart yearns for sin's undoing. The grace that offers itself as the fruit of this first week requires that it be born of a struggle: the desire, on the one hand, to be rid of one's sin and the harsh realization, on the other, that such is not ours to bring about. The grace, which is given *as grace,* is offered in the form of a freedom: to know that *even as sinner* one is loved by God, and that it is only God's love that can lead one from sin. This is a grace entered into, never fully achieved. It is a grace which, as Ignatius himself affirms, could occupy one fruitfully for the whole of one's life and to which those who move beyond it must return frequently during life.

The second week of the journey emerges from the first, but movement into the second week is not automatic. It requires a spark, a desire, a movement of the heart in response to the movement of God toward us. Without this spark one may engage the texts presented for the second week without necessarily engaging the prayer of the second week. This second week material consists of contemplations on the life of Christ and some special meditations designed to awaken, guide, and strengthen the call to discipleship. One could stay with this material as continuing to present the unfailing love of God for sinners, and the material would serve this well. But the spark that will make second-week prayer of these meditations and contemplations is a happening in the heart beyond the grace of living as a loved sinner. It is an overwhelming gratitude for God's loving embrace and a profound desire to join Christ in his mission for the world. It is, in other words, a desire to give something back to God.

The prelude of the second week has Christ issue an invitation to disciples:

"It is my will to conquer all infidel lands (i.e., the whole world). Whoever wishes to come with me must be content to eat as I eat, drink as I drink, dress as I dress, etc. He (she) must also be willing to work with me by day and watch with me by night. He (she) will then share with me in the victory as he (she) has shared in the toils."[5]

[5] *The Spiritual Exercises* (see footnote 2) 67.

The recipient of this invitation is urged to respond:

"It is my wish and desire, and my deliberate choice, provided only that it be for Thy greater service and praise, to imitate Thee. . . ."[6]

The spark that allows the second week to begin is the desire to labor with Christ and embrace as one's own his mission, his desires, and his total way of life.

This leg of the journey likewise has its struggles and its challenge to conversion of heart. Two elements in particular give shape to second-week prayer. The first is a focus, subtle at first, less so as the journey goes on, on the "cost" of discipleship. The Christ whom one is invited to join is the Christ who has been rejected and crucified. The second is a focus on vocation and choice. To what specific way of life does Christ summon *me*? Both require a measure of inner freedom, and this freedom is ultimately the grace that is sought.

The first is freedom to be faithful to the gift of God and the claim of Christ on one's life. It requires that a loving relationship with the person of Christ be formed and strengthened. The invitation to be a disciple of Christ is an invitation of love, and only a response of love is worthy of its summons. Indeed, only a profound and committed love relationship with Christ will provide the resources needed to be faithful to his call.

The second freedom is to discover in one's own life what Christ is summoning one to be and do. Discipleship is not generic; it always lays particular claim on, and gives particular shape to, one's life. This is freedom from abstract demands and unreal ideals, even those born of religious ideology. It is freedom from one's own illusions and from the expectations of others. It is freedom to take a wager on one's own life before God, based only on the conviction that *this* is what Christ is calling me to be, and *this* is what fidelity to Christ and myself demands.

Entrance into the third week is more subtle, and often nothing like what one expects. At this third stage of the journey, Christ is no longer in clear focus as a dialogue partner in prayer. Christ himself becomes the prayer uttered into the Silence of God. The biblical focus of the third week is the passion of Christ, but it is not the passion ob-

[6] Ibid., 68.

served in the manner of second-week prayer or the cross displayed in the manner of first-week prayer. In the third week the passion of Christ is entered into, felt in both body and spirit. In the prayer of the third week one comes to know from within the pain and desolation of the suffering Christ. One cries out with his own voice, "My God, my God, why have you forsaken me," and, far more important, comes to know the God into whose hands Jesus surrenders himself. In the first week one is stripped of all self-illusion; in the third week it is God who is stripped of all illusion and made manifest to experience only as faithful, loving embrace.

If the journey of the second week is a journey of discipleship, with eyes fixed firmly on the person of Jesus, the journey of the third week is a journey into *Abba,* the One who *is* the life of Christ, who is known only through the eyes and heart of Jesus himself. "All things have been delivered to me by my Father . . . no one knows the Father except the Son and any one to whom the Son chooses to reveal him" (Matt 11:27). In the prayer of the second week one attends to Jesus as he speaks about *Abba* and engages himself in the work of God's kingdom. In the prayer of the third week one is drawn into such intimate communion with Christ that one addresses *Abba* directly with Christ's own voice and learns in communion with Christ the art of surrender into God.

It is only from a position of surrender into God that the vision and freedom of the fourth week can open up. The God into whom one surrenders is the God who raised Jesus from death, the God who in Christ is committed to bringing all creation into that same victorious realm. "And I, when I am lifted up from the earth, will draw all to myself" (John 12:32). It is thus the God who is actively engaged in bringing creation to its completion. It is only from a position of surrender into God that Paul's conviction that "nothing can separate me from the love of God" can be born, that Teilhard could frame his ecstatic cry "You, O earth, are the body of Christ," and that a simple priest could embrace the possibilities of life in wondrous expectation. Entrance into the prayer of the fourth week requires surrender into God, and such surrender transforms all of life and makes all things new.

Surrender into God with Christ completes the transformation of the heart and seals the communion between Christian and Christ. In this full communion with the Risen Christ, reality becomes as it is for

Christ. One begins to see as Christ sees. One begins to love as Christ loves. One comes to know both the Silence and Passion of God as Christ embodied and proclaimed them. This full communion with Christ born of surrender establishes the Christian within Christ's own prayer and opens him/her to all that Christ perceives from his place of final victory. From that place there can be no separation between contemplation and action, for all of life is pervaded by the Passion and Silence of God.

THE FOURTH WEEK: CONTEMPLATION IN ACTION

The prayer of the fourth week as journey's end is by no means the end of the journey. Contemplation in action is a way of living and praying, not an end point in any static sense. At journey's end one discovers oneself in living dialogue with the mystery of God. The Ignatian phrase "pursuit of God in all things" is one way of naming the dialogue. "Contemplation in action" is another. "Active prayer and prayerful action" is yet a third. At journey's end we discover that we are able to pursue God in all things because God is pursuing us. At journey's end we discover that God can be loved in all things, because everything that exists is the act of God loving us. The prayer of the fourth week sets us firmly in an ongoing journey of mutual love.

At the heart of the fourth week in the Ignatian Exercises lies the "Contemplation for Obtaining Divine Love." Its first principle is that love ought to be manifested in deeds rather than words. Its second is that love is a mutual interchange between two parties, lover and beloved sharing all they have and are. Ignatius considers these not simply principles for love among humans; he offers them also to name the love God has for us and which God invites from us. The "Contemplation for Obtaining Divine Love" is exactly that: a focus of the imagination and affections on God's self-sharing with us, in the hope of evoking from the human heart a like sharing in return.

The contemplation begins with God's presence in creation and considers how all creation is a gift from God. It considers further how God gives God's own self in and through all that is. God is present as lover, and the gift of creation carries within itself not only the love that God *offers* but indeed the love that God *is*. The aim of this contemplation is to train the imagination and school the affections to recognize and respond to the omnipresence of God. In this contemplation one is invited to move from gratitude for the gifts that have been given, through a gradual embrace of everything that happens in life as gift, toward a deep and abiding love of God, who is himself the gift. This contemplation teaches the secret of contemplation in action. What is contemplated and engaged in action is the manifest, all-pervading love of God.

To see the journey into God as a journey of love is to gain further insight into the prayer that constitutes the contemplative in action. Love has many faces. It involves humans with each other in a mixture of give and take, of desire from and desire for, of intimacy with and distancing from, where the primary rules to be observed are mutual respect, reverence for each other's freedom, and delight in each other for the mystery that each one is. For Christians who proclaim that "God is love," the many faces of love are likewise the many faces of God.

In Christian life, love is a religious as well as a human journey. Christians are admonished by Jesus to "love one another as I have loved you" (John 15:12). They are also invited to "love the Lord your God with all your heart, and with all your soul, and with all your mind" (Matt 22:37). Indeed, a link is drawn between the two: "those who love God must love their brothers and sisters also" (1 John 4:21). God is named *Love*. And Jesus, the incarnation of God, is proclaimed both as humanity's love for God and as God's love for all men and women. The ways of love among humans are the only guide to their relationship with God.

Of course, love among humans is not identical with love between humans and God. As Karl Rahner would insist in his theological anthropology, God is not an object of love alongside other objects of love nor a loving subject alongside other subjects who love. God is the condition for the possibility of love, its ground, its horizon, and its own true substance. God sustains human love along its complex journey and guides it to its proper shape and form. Love is the work of God within the human heart. At a point of advanced theological and spiritual insight, God neither loves nor is loved. Rather, "God *is* love" (1 John 4:8).

At the beginning, however, and throughout the human journey into God, it is humanly necessary to engage God as both lover and beloved, to discover and express the human affections that are proper to loving God and being loved by God. It is perfectly proper to address God as personal Other, to hear oneself addressed by God as by One who loves, and to understand our relationship with God through the language and experience of human love. The language must be used analogously to be sure, but it must be used. The reality of God's love cannot be given *sui generis* content such that it bears no relationship to the dynamics of love among humans. Nor can it be reduced to those dynamics alone. It is once again the theological paradox. The ways of human love are the privileged human ways we have to explore and understand the mystery of God's love. Yet in the end these human ways can only point us toward, and open us to, God's love. God must reach out to us and draw us the rest of the way.

There is at least one important point in the analogous relation between human love and divine love that I would like to include in this essay. Human love is not negated or suspended when divine love is set in motion. When God reaches out, it is into human love that the reach is made. Human love is brought to completion in the love of God.

This simple point is at the heart of one important work that explores the intersection of human and divine love. In his noted work *The Four Loves*,[7] C. S. Lewis examines the human loves of affection, friendship and eros, and illustrates why and how each is and must be brought to completion in charity, which is God's love. These human loves are wonderful, but in themselves they are not enough.

Lewis does not mean to imply, and in fact rejects, any sense of conflict between human love and the love of God. The conflict in love arises within human love itself. Neither affection nor friendship nor eros has within itself the resources unambiguously to succeed. Each is vulnerable to distortion. Affection is distorted when it is imposed on someone who does not wish it or when it demands response from one who does not wish to respond. Friendship is distorted when it does not rest on mutual respect and affection. And eros is distorted when it violates or utilizes another. Charity opposes these distortions and provides the resources to overcome them. At the intersection between human love and the love between humans and God, it is the action of God to offer human love the resources it needs to be true. Affection, friendship and eros are drawn into, not replaced by, charity, and in charity each is fulfilled. In Lewis's own words: "Divine

[7] New York: Harcourt, Brace, Jovanovich, 1960, 133.

love does not *substitute* itself for the natural—as if we had to throw away our silver to make room for the gold. The natural loves are summoned to become modes of Charity while also retaining the natural loves they were."

Lewis offers a way to understand God's action in the affairs of human life. His work, which is worth a much fuller treatment than is possible here, sheds important light on our own question of prayer and action and the pursuit of God in all things. God's presence in all things is a presence-in-action. And God's action is nothing less than God's own love working within the ways of human love, bringing human love to its proper completion in the Love that is God.

A CONCLUDING REMARK

Lewis also provides the language for a retrospect on the Ignatian journey. The prayer of the first week intends to shape affection: for Christ on the cross, surely, and for the God whose love he embodies. But even more, it shapes affection for oneself, against the negative of one's sin that would deny that affection. The grace of being a "loved sinner" is affection for oneself drawn into charity, the power to love oneself, not because one is worthy of that love but because God who is Love freely chooses to bestow it.

The prayer of the second week establishes friendship between Christ and the one who prays. The spark that allows passage into the second week is the desire for friendship with Christ, and the enduring grace of the second week is a deepening of that friendship. As human love, friendship with Christ is always a fragile venture. When drawn into the charity of God, however, it becomes God's own power to love.

The third week is a time of eros, the intimate communion with Christ in which Christ and Christian become as one. It is a fearful thing to be summoned into the love of eros with Christ, for it must be encountered first in its human face, which is union with Christ in his darkest human hour. The incarnate Christ could not achieve full communion with the human race until he surrendered himself to its darkest truth. Nor can men and women achieve full communion with Christ until they embrace him in his darkest hour. It is only in that hour of darkness that light breaks through, the light of God that "shines in darkness" (John 1:5). Human eros needs to be drawn into charity to discover beyond the anguish of surrender the ecstatic delight of mutual embrace. Charity is the ecstasy of light that is the fourth week.

When each human love is drawn into charity, one knows the omnipresence of God. It is not a static "being there." It is the God of creation within creation bringing creation to its completion by giving full and final shape to the way creation loves. Contemplation in action is not in the end a way of looking but a way of loving. A life that is "active prayer and prayerful action" is not in the end a way of "doing things" but a way of loving. It is the many faces of love itself that interweave and intermix and constitute the complex unity of Christian life and prayer. It is God's draw of the many faces of love into God's own love that brings to completion what Christ in his life, a life that is "active prayer and prayerful action," set in motion for us all.

Mary Ewing Stamps

Epis.

Lives of Living Prayer:
Christomorphism and the Priority of Prayer
in the Rule of St. Benedict

INTRODUCTION

In his hagiographical accounts of notable holy women and men, St. Gregory the Great remarks of St. Benedict that "anyone who wishes to know more about his life and character can discover in his *Rule* exactly what he was like as an abbot, for his life could not have differed from his teaching."[1] We know nothing of Benedict except what we learn from his one extant writing—a rule for monasteries—and Gregory's short biography. This sparsity of material reveals little if anything about his personal life, his family and friends, his personality, or even his hopes and dreams for the monasteries that arose under his guidance. Yet, if it is true that Benedict's manner of living was in absolute continuity with his regulation of the cenobium, then we do know that the whole of the saint's life must surely have been prayer, for both his *Rule* and Gregory's *Dialogues* testify to the primacy of this activity above all others.

Why Benedict though? There are many saints for whom prayer was of first importance and about whose lives we have more detail, from themselves as well as their biographers, and from whom we have more extant writings. Unlike Benedict, there are a multitude of saints whose thoughts and feelings and circumstances have been recorded at great length. Yet it is easily argued that few recognized saints have had greater influence upon the Christian Church (and

---

[1] Gregory the Great, *Life and Miracles of St. Benedict,* trans. Odo J. Zimmermann, O.S.B., and Benedict R. Avery, O.S.B. (Collegeville, Minn.: The Liturgical Press, 1987) 74. See J.-P. Migne, *Patrologia Latina* 66 (Paris, 1866) 200 for Latin translation.

upon the world) than has Benedict. The long history of his progeny—Benedictines, Cistercians, Trappists, Camoldolese, and other religious movements that either follow the *Rule of St. Benedict (RB)*[2] or whose founders have been significantly shaped by it, and the legacy of their influence upon contemporary spiritual writers—gives witness to the continuing power of the document to mold lives into living prayer.[3] This essay, then, will explore Benedict's *Rule* in order to uncover something of the formative effect of prayer upon the character of the one who prays and the expressive nature of prayer as a mark of sanctification.

CHRISTOMORPHISM IN THE RULE OF ST. BENEDICT

The *RB* is a thoroughly christocentric document. This singular fact must be understood before anything else about the work. To know who Christ is for the monks is to know much about the chief monastic virtues. According to Benedict, Christ makes his will known to human beings without regard for their earthly stature (3.3). He is the one before whom all are equal and in whom all are united (2.20). He was obedient even to the point of death, just as the monks are called to obediently follow the teachings of the Lord in the monastery until their death (Prol. 50). Christ, in his self-emptying, affords the monks the supreme example of humility before God, yet he is more than a model of great virtue. Christ aids the monks in difficult tasks of obedience and good works so that they may gain everlasting life in their heavenly home (68.5; 72.12). Above all, he desires that they seek his assistance and promises that he will hear the prayers of those who do good (Prol. 18).

Throughout the *RB*, emphasis is placed on loving Christ by obeying and serving him. Regard for Christ is not a matter of losing oneself in ecstatic reverie or pious sentiment; rather, he is to be honored in the monks' goodness of life and wise judgment. The accent on ex-

Chief virtues

---

[2] All references to the *RB* are taken from Timothy Fry, O.S.B., ed., *RB 1980: The Rule of St. Benedict in Latin and English with Notes* (Collegeville, Minn.: The Liturgical Press, 1981).

[3] Benedict's influence has not been limited to the Roman Catholic Church. Notable leaders within the reformed tradition, such as Methodism's John Wesley and Br. Roger Schutz of the Taizé Community, have also been formed by Benedictine precepts. Contemporary authors join this company, as well, for example, Esther de Waal and Kathleen Norris.

terior manifestations of reverence for God, though, should not obscure the underlying motivation for monasticism, that is, love of Christ embodied in community. Without this foundation cenobitic discipline would rely on nothing more than raw self-will or external compulsion. As Benedict admonished the hermit Martin: "If you are a servant of God, attach yourself with the chain of Christ, not one of iron" (*Dial.* III.16).

Christ stands at the center of all monastic thought and activity. It is this christo*centrism* of the *Rule* that engenders the christo*morphism* of the monks. They strive to make Christ the focal point of their existence and are transformed in the process. The *RB* seeks to accomplish this task by offering concrete guidelines for following the Gospel mandates to love God and neighbor, to pray, to care for the sick, the poor, the stranger, etc. In this way, the monk is formed in Christlike dispositions, that is, patterns of intention and action by which the disciple begins to assume the shape of Christ's own life. Every practice detailed in the *Rule* is designed to bring the monk closer to God in Christ.

The consequent sanctification of the human being develops a mentality wherein God is sought in all things. There is neither time nor place in which Christ is incapable of presenting himself for recognition by the monk. Furthermore, since Benedict believed that God is watching at every moment (4.48-49), there can be no action that does not have its spiritual consequence. This state of affairs demands a receptivity to the will of God through constant communion with the mind of God. Prayer cannot be compartmentalized and restricted to certain hours of the day; it must comprehend and infuse the whole of life. The "inward" practices of prayer and spiritual discipline will thereby be made manifest in "outward" concern for others in whom God is present.

Benedict's *Rule* offers no formal description of the wholly sanctified monk modeled after Christ.[4] He is a legislator rather than a theorizer, and is concerned to organize a life wherein the love of Christ is foremost and prayer becomes possible. Nowhere does he give a direct

---

[4] The abbot and cellarer may be considered exemplary, however, and some clues regarding Benedict's "ideal" may be garnered from a close study of the chapters he devoted to these two figures. See *RB* 2, 31, 64. A review of *RB* 4, "The Tools for Good Works," might also be instructive on this point.

compendium of virtues or characteristics by which it can be plainly known that when the monk possesses "these" qualities in "this" order of importance, then that person will have attained monastic perfection. Instead, Benedict gives the reader mostly hints and glimmers, at sometimes unexpected and inconspicuous moments. For the most part, his portrait of the faithful monk is painted in tiny strokes against a broad background of presupposition regarding the ubiquity of prayer; or better, the *pentimento,* the underlying image of seeking God in prayer, can be found in every aspect of monastic life as detailed by the *RB.*

THE VIRTUES OF A MONK

Fear of the Lord

There are a few qualities, however, that are fundamental to the monastic endeavor as interpreted by Benedict.[5] First among these virtues is the fear of the Lord. It is a genuine, tremorous fear inasmuch as the monk's eternal well-being is at stake,[6] but more than this understandable concern, it is "fear" in the biblical sense of reverential awe, deepest respect, and love.

Love of God and neighbor is the *telos* of all ascetic striving (4.1, 21; 5.2; 72.11). Each practice, even the most seemingly inconsequential, is designed to craft the monk into one whose every thought and deed tends toward charity. The monastery is seen as a workshop in which the monastic dispositions and patterns of behavior—the monks' spiritual tools—are to be wrought and employed (4.78). By loving one another, seeing Christ in one another, the monks learn to love and "prefer nothing whatever to Christ" (72.11) in order that he may bring them *all together* to everlasting life" (72.12). When the novice is received into the community, he importunes God, saying, "Receive me, Lord" (58.21), and his plea is repeated three times by the community, which then adds, "Glory be to the Father" (v. 22). Thus, the gathered assembly expresses in its fullness the cenobitic intent: the monk is to die and rise again in Christ in the company of believers for their common sanctification and the glorification of God. The dis-

---

[5] Those principal virtues that are addressed in their own chapters are: obedience (5; 71), restraint of speech (6), humility (7), reverence in prayer (20), and good zeal (72). Fear of the Lord surfaces at various points in the *RB,* for example, Prol. 12; 3.11; 5.9; 7.10; 66.4.

[6] See, for example, 2.10; 4.44-49; 5.3; 7.10ff.; 72.1-2.

position of love keeps them faithful to the task and accomplishes this end in those who truly seek God and fear the Lord.

Humility

Benedict places special emphasis on the virtue of humility, not as self-denigration or the rejection of one's personhood, but as a lively awareness of one's true identity before God. Humility, therefore, is a relational virtue inasmuch as it marks right relation between God and monk (20.2), with visitors to the monastery (53.24), and among the community of monks themselves (e.g., 60.5).

The seventh chapter of the *Rule* outlines twelve "steps" by which this humility is demonstrated. The humble person fears God (vv. 10f.), rejects self-will (vv. 31f.), is obedient (v. 34), quietly endures suffering (vv. 35f.), confesses all of his sins to the abbot (vv. 44f.), is content with low position (vv. 49f.), regards others as superior to self (vv. 51f.), follows the *Rule* and directions of superiors (v. 55), values silence (vv. 56f.), does not readily laugh (v. 59), speaks in a manner becoming a monk (vv. 60f.), and manifests humility both in bearing and in the heart (vv. 62f.). In a footnote to 7.10, the *RB 1980* suggests that the order of these steps "seems to have been intended to indicate a progression from the internal cultivation of humility to its external manifestations." The monk begins at the beginning with proper regard for God and gradually extends the effect of that primary relationship to encompass all other associations.

Humility is above all else a matter of christomorphic identity, of being who one was created to be in and through Christ. Since Christians understand their identity to be with God, we can say that there is no true humility in isolation from God and those persons whom God has created to be in relation with one another. The christomorphic monk cultivates the virtue of humility in order to know and be known by the divine Source of all that is or, as Benedict says, in order to attain the "perfect love of God" (7.67). This quality is not intended merely for personal religious advancement, though. It is only through growth in love, in proper regard for others, that humility and the other virtues are wrested from the grip of narcissistic spiritual self-interest and placed rightly within the context of community.

Communal prayer sustains each monk in the long struggle to learn love by taking individual weaknesses up into the strength of the gathered assembly. It promotes humility by bringing the individual to an understanding of the mutuality involved in the spiritual life.[7] In times of personal insufficiency, doubt, or even weariness, the monk is carried in faith by the prayers, example, and encouragement of the community. Pride is out of place in this context. The monk must rely upon grace with humble acceptance. During the *opus Dei*, the monks model for one another the expected stance before God: reverence for the holy and concern for the human.[8]

Obedience

Obedience is perhaps the most misunderstood of all monastic qualities. It is neither unthinking nor unreflective.[9] In fact, it is etymologically tied to "listening."[10] This linguistic connection implies that the obedient monk is a listening monk, one who is always prepared for the thoughtful reception of a command from God. Obedience is neither a burden to be borne grudgingly nor a curse upon the underlings of the power structure; rather, it "comes naturally to those who cherish Christ above all" and are in tune with his will (5.2). It is a "blessing" rather than a curse and is "to be shown by all," even those of higher rank, as a token of their familial bonds (71.1). The emphasis here is upon love and upon right relationships to God and to one's fellow monks.[11]

The model for monastic obedience is found in Philippians 2:8. Benedict cites this passage in his chapter on humility, saying: "The third step of humility is that a man submits to his superior in all obedience for the love of God, imitating the Lord of whom the Apostle says: 'He became obedient even to death'" (7.34). The obedience that the monk renders to those of greater rank in the monastery is moti-

---

[7] "On rising for the Work of God, they will quietly encourage each other, for the sleepy like to make excuses" (22.8).

[8] Along with respect, sincere devotion, compunction, brevity, and purity, humility is a hallmark of appropriate reverence at prayer (*RB* 20).

[9] The term "blind obedience" has nothing whatever to do with Benedict's notion of the virtue. Benedict is sufficiently concerned to impress upon the monks a correct understanding of obedience and of its role in monastic life that it is the only virtue to which he devotes two full chapters—5 and 71.

[10] Obedience (Latin: *obaudio* > *oboedio*); listening (Latin: *audio*). Note: Listening is so important to Benedict that he departs from his primary source, the *Rule of the Master*, and inserts it as the very first word of the Prologue to his *Rule*.

[11] ". . . younger monks should obey their seniors with all love and concern" (71.4).

vated by love for God and is an imitation of the submission that Christ showed to his heavenly Father. The particular configuration of Christ's relationship with God is meant to shape the monk's relationship with those of higher ranks in the monastery as well as his confreres (*RB* 71). Those concrete relations, in turn, become the *means* of obedience and humility inasmuch as they provide the immediate context for serving Christ.

In his first chapter on obedience (*RB* 5), Benedict describes the obedient (listening) monk as follows: "Almost at the same moment [or: "even as one motion"], then, as the master gives the instruction the disciple quickly puts it into practice in the fear of God; and both actions together are swiftly completed as one" (v. 9). The passage indicates that there is no true obedience without a response to the word that one hears. The model of Christ's obedience even to the point of death removes every limit from the command. Benedict, however, having keen insight into the human condition, modifies this demand somewhat by adding a chapter on "Assignment of Impossible Tasks to a Brother" (*RB* 68) for those who feel that they have been given a duty that is beyond their capabilities. The monk and the superior must listen to one another (v. 4) and trust God for the proper response in loving obedience (v. 5).[12]

Trust is an important prerequisite for obedience. There may be times when the self-sacrifice involved in carrying out an assigned task necessitates an extraordinary amount of confidence that the command given is indeed within the will of God. Such assurance is not restricted to the more heroic domain of the saint. It is a call issued to every person—not to abandon one's own skill and competence but to rely wholly upon the Source of one's abilities, trusting that Source to meet the day's needs, whether by prayerful use of one's own skills or by the contribution of others. As Benedict enjoins, "What is not possible to us by nature, let us ask the Lord to supply by the help of his grace" (Prol. 41).

---

[12] Nowhere is the concept of "trust beyond one's own highest capacity" (Saliers) more evident in the *Rule* than in this chapter. The *RB 1980* translation of its title is rather tame. The verb *iniungantur,* which has been rendered simply as "assignment," conveys more the sense of having an impossible task "inflicted upon" one. This alternate translation bears the added dimension of odiousness or, in the language of chapter 58, *opprobria.* From this perspective one would have all the more reason to pray for divine assistance!

It should be of consolation to the would-be monks among us that candidates for the monastery are not expected to come already equipped with the perfection of the aforementioned virtues. When persons arrive at the monastery doors seeking entrance into the community, Benedict requires, rather, that their desire for God be tested, specifying these three points: whether they are eager for the *opus Dei* (the "Work of God," that is, the daily prayer offices), for obedience, and for *opprobria* (variously translated as trials, difficult things, humble service).[13] It is not clear whether these criteria are somehow representative of the essence of cenobitism or were arbitrarily selected from among a number of possible qualifications, but they no doubt offer an indication of cenobitic priorities. These three elements of monasticism—prayer, obedience, and humility—are exemplary of the monk's commitment to the *communal* christomorphic endeavor. They do not entirely comprehend the monk's promise, yet they are central to the common life.

First among the qualities sought in a novice is "eagerness for the Work of God"; in other words, the monk must have a desire to seek God in communal prayer. This is the chief identifying characteristic of the monastic temperament. It is interesting to note that some of Benedict's most important legislative predecessors do not list eagerness for the *opus Dei* as part of their criteria for membership. Both Basil's *Long Rules* 10 and the *Rule of the Master* 88.1 give "stability" as the criterion for membership in a community, while Cassian's concern is to test the potential monk's perseverance, will, humility, and patience (*De institutis coenobiorum* IV.3.1). Perhaps Benedict understood community prayer as such a vital part of the christomorphic endeavor that he dared not leave it unspoken but put it at the forefront of all considerations.

The proximity of the *RB's* liturgical code (chs. 8–20) to the spiritual chapters (1–7), and to the beginning of the *Rule* itself, makes a strong statement about the importance given to prayer in Benedictine cenobitism. Purposeful communion with God holds first place in the life of the monk. The point is amplified in *RB* 43.3: "Indeed, nothing is to

---

[13] Contrast these prerequisites with the lifestyle of the sarabaites, who live without either rule, abbot, or experience, who do whatever they please in the name of holiness, and whom Benedict has therefore dubbed "the most detestable kind of monks" (*RB* 1.6-9).

be preferred to the Work of God" *(Ergo nihil operi Dei praeponatur).*
This is the same phrase that is later used (72.11) concerning the
monk's regard for Christ: "Let them prefer nothing whatever to
Christ" *(Christo omnino nihil praeponant).* Connection is made here between the source of and reason for monastic life, Christ, and that activity which draws the monk most closely to him, prayer. To prefer
one is to prefer the other. Thus, prayer is identified as an intrinsic
part of the christomorphic endeavor in that it structures the dialogue
between community and Christ by exposing the prayer assembly to
the mind and will of Christ on a regular basis.

The urgency of Benedict's call to prayer is undeniable: "On hearing the signal for an hour of the divine office, the monk will immediately set aside what he has in hand and go with utmost speed"
(43.1).[14] The monks are even directed to sleep fully clothed so that no
delay will be made in their response to the call to prayer (22.6). This
demand for preparedness also extends to monks who are away from
the enclosure, whether on a journey or at work in the fields; they are
to keep the hours of prayer regardless of their physical location (*RB*
50). No work takes priority over the Work of God.(prayer)

The ambiguity of naming communal prayer the "Work of God" is
quite appropriate.[15] It is both God's working in and through those
who pray and the monks' labor in service of the divine.[16] Yet it is unlike any other form of enterprise that the monks undertake, because
it is the privileged place of colloquy with the divine: Community
prayer encodes the revealed Word into the heart of the hearer, re-
asserts the trustworthiness of God, and reaffirms the monks' hope
through their progressive assimilation of biblical history and of the
promises set forth in Scripture.

In an article entitled "Prière et communauté dans la règle de saint
Benoît," Phillipe Rouillard refers to the divine office as a "crucible"
wherein the gradual transformation of each monk occurs through the
joint effort of praying the same texts and through a growing sense of

[14] This theme is taken up from Cassian and modified by the Master and by
Benedict. The first rule urges the monks to immediately respond when summoned to *any* community activity (*Inst.* IV.12), while the latter two narrow this
manner of response only for the call to the *opus Dei* (*RM* 54; *RB* 43.1-3).

[15] Curiously, common prayer is not referred to in the *RB*'s liturgical code (chs.
8–20) as the *opus Dei.*

[16] See 16.2; 18.24; 19.3; 50.4.

themselves as "'collaborators' in the same labor."[17] As Rouillard notes, though, this growth is always a mutual one: "If the daily office nourishes and forms each monk, it also has the function and effect of constructing, of nourishing, of protecting the community, as such."[18] The individual members become one body through bonds that are established in listening together for the word of God. Community prayer is, among other things, a vehicle for mutual support and cohesion.

It makes sense, then, that the *opus Dei* is found together with obedience at the outset of monastic life (58.7). In addition to deep listening, obedience also involves the promise to be at prayers, to make oneself available for formation, and to support the formation of those with whom one prays. Commitment to the Work of God day in and day out recognizes that the process takes place over time. This effort demands not only lifelong persistence but intentional vulnerability as well. Common prayer necessitates a willingness to open oneself to the Word and to those persons in whose company one listens for the Word. Such radical vulnerability is impossible to mandate. We do not easily stand naked before the living God—even the God who has knit us together in our mother's womb (Ps 139:13b)—much less before one another. Each person must freely, if sometimes reluctantly, choose to expose the inner being to a transformative power beyond human control.

It is natural that frail humanity would require a measure of encouragement in order to face the rigors of such a discipline, the unromantic grind of daily faithfulness to their commitment. For this reason, the task is not undertaken alone. The community is both journey companion and source of nourishment on the way because it manifests the christomorphic embodiment of divine love. In their collaboration and attentiveness to one another, the monks become increasingly christomorphic not only as individuals but as a collective whole as well. Community prayer is a token of mutuality in the shared encounter with God through prayer.

The *opus Dei* does not simply gather the monks for a period of corporate worship; it promises a genuine encounter with the holy. As it immerses the one who prays in the mystery of Christ's life, his dying and his rising, a foundation is laid for interior transformation. This experience of encounter is literally "taken to heart" in its preparation

[17] *Notitiae* 16 (June 1980) 314.
[18] Ibid., 312.

148

and execution. Four times in the liturgical code of the *RB*, Benedict instructs that the Scripture be recited "by heart" (9.10; 12.4) or "from memory" (10.2; 13.11).

There are no parallels for these particular formulations either in the Master or in any other likely source of the *Rule*. This is not to say that the Master did not require his monks to spend time memorizing biblical texts, as was common in a day when printed materials were not readily available. Indeed, it may well have been the case that his monks also recited Scripture by heart during the offices; he does not make this explicit.

It is difficult to say why Benedict might have thought it important to stress the memorization of readings. Perhaps he wanted to emphasize the indwelling word as a naturally flowing font of monastic prayer. As a practice that touches the core of one's being, Scripture recitation requires a reconfiguration of the heart, a change of shape to accommodate the new word that has entered in. The monastic experience of God is bound to this process of formation.

Two additional forms of prayer in the *RB* deserve mention here: *lectio divina*, or spiritual reading,[19] and personal prayer. *Lectio divina* is the prayerful reading of a text—either Scripture or some other spiritual work—for the purpose of receiving a word from God and of continuing the transformation begun in the *opus Dei*. It is intended for the advancement of the soul rather than for intellectual achievement.[20] The monk does not shun knowledge as inherently evil but seeks it only inasmuch as it pertains to spiritual ends. If it does not further one's relationship with God, it is not to be pursued.

Personal or *private prayer* receives only scant mention in the *Rule*. We can assume, however, that Benedict encourages the practice. Other than the *opus Dei* and key moments of episodic prayer, such as rites of initiation, reconciliation, and commissioning, the only act that is explicitly sanctioned to occur in the all-important oratory is private prayer (52.3). Along with *lectio*, compunction, and self-denial, prayer

---

[19] It is interesting to note that Benedict addresses the subject of *lectio* in his chapter "The Daily Manual Labor" (48). At this period in history, reading was thought to be a physical event involving the whole person and on a par with other forms of strenuous exercise.

[20] Benedict himself, while still a student in Rome, turned away from worldly knowledge in favor of divine wisdom. "He took this step, fully aware of his ignorance; yet he was truly wise, uneducated though he may have been" (*Dial.* II.1).

is a recommended Lenten discipline (49.4). It is connected with avoidance of sin and amendment of behavior (4.55-58). Through *lectio* and private prayer, the monk strives in obedience and with the aid of the Holy Spirit to relinquish self-will in favor of the divine will (Prol. 3), thereby emulating the humility of Christ.

John Chrysostom, writing nearly two centuries before Benedict, claims that "if you have deprived yourself of prayer you have acted as though you had taken a fish out of water; for as water is life to the fish, so prayer is to you" (*De precatione*, Oratio 2, col. 781). The author of the *Rule* understood this sentiment and fashioned the cenobium around prayer as the living idiom of the community. He framed the day with the divine offices, filled it with the meditative discipline of spiritual reading, and adorned it with private prayer. These offerings are all of a piece, each supporting the other in a harmony of interdependent interactions with the holy.

MONASTIC ETHICS: APPLIED TRUST

To make the whole of one's life prayer implies that prayerfulness cannot be limited to designated times or places of converse with God. Rather, the prayerful person must maintain a continuity of perspective, to see with God's eyes, to follow God's bidding in every circumstance. As prayer deepens the virtues deepen. As the one who prays becomes increasingly attuned to the mind of Christ, a heightened sensitivity toward those whom Christ loves is fostered in that person. Private epiphanies of God spill over into relationships within the created order.

The text encountered in prayer must come alive in the attitudes and behavior of the monk toward other persons; the community is to embody the word it receives in the way it acts. The fear of the Lord must be translated into Christlike humility, responsive obedience, and an abiding trust in the goodness of God. As a guide for following the Scripture received at times of prayer, the *Rule* assists the formation in these virtues through its practical commands. For instance, the "natural" inclination to show preferential treatment to the wealthy and powerful is tempered by the cultivation of christomorphic dispositions that attend with equal care and dignity to the poor and outcast as particular bearers of Christ.[21] When Christ is cherished above all,

---

[21] See, for example, *RB* 53.15: "Great care and concern are to be shown in receiving poor people and pilgrims, because in them more particularly Christ is received; our very awe of the rich guarantees them special respect."

the love that the monks have for him carries over into a love of those persons who are made in his image, and the difficult service sometimes required by life together is then performed naturally and without complaint (7.68). In meeting the Word enfleshed, fresh insight is brought back to the word intoned. Thus, prayer and life are one within the framework of the monastic world-view.

It is evident that for Benedict prayer matters, ethics matter. The two are intertwined and inseparable. For the Benedictine, this concept might best be described by expanding the ancient dictum "The rule of praying is the rule of believing" with a further step: *Lex orandi, lex credendi, lex faciendi*. Prayer and belief must show themselves in action. Had Benedict been at all interested in presenting theological explications, he might well have said that the former two are complete only when the latter is held to be consistent with them. Thus, efficacious prayer is inextricably tied to ethical behavior.

Transformation of the individual through prayer requires persistence and intentional vulnerability because it pertains to a whole way of being, feeling, thinking, and acting. The relationship is a reciprocal one: quality of life affects quality of prayer, and vice versa. For Christians, this means that one's affections must be trained to comply with the mind of Christ. While prayer accustoms a person to acting in concert with Christ, the christomorphism of one's capacity for virtue as exercised in the world influences the integrity of one's prayer. A lifetime of commitment to spiritual discipline and the conviction of God's abiding presence and loving concern are necessary in order for sanctification to become a reality. The nature of transformation to a closer likeness of Christ demands integrity within a lived theology, that is, a holding together of prayer (what is said) and ethics (what is done). In this way, the whole of the believer's life—"saint" or not—becomes a living prayer to God.[22]

[22] I would like to offer grateful acknowledgment of the Benedictine Sisters of Perpetual Adoration, Clyde, Missouri, for the gracious hospitality and invaluable insights they so generously extended to me during my research of this essay.

Roberta Bondi

Praying the Lord's Prayer:
Truthfulness, Intercessory Prayer, and
Formation in Love[1]

My dear friend,

I was so glad to get your letter last week. I know that apart from Advent and Christmas the period between the beginning of Lent and the end of Easter is the busiest time of year in the life of a pastor. Still, I've missed our correspondence, and I've wondered how you were doing in your new church.

I'm sorry, however, to hear that your congregation is being torn up by a dispute over the use of the Lord's Prayer in worship. The first group, you say, is largely made up of women, but also of some men, who object to praying it because they believe that both in its use of "father" language for God and in its language of kingdom and kingship, it is making a political statement about male dominance and authority. You report that this is not an abstract problem for them. Being aware of the way we are unconsciously shaped by the language we use, they are concerned about the long-term psychological and social effects of what seem to them to be the oppressive images carried in the words of this prayer.

---

[1] In his essay "Liturgy and Ethics: Some New Beginnings," Don Saliers says that in intercessory prayer "we encounter dimensions of ourselves as praying with and for others," and he notes that "a truthfulness about who we are in relation to others as well as a vulnerability born of empathy" is necessary to such an encounter (p. 29 above). The following paper is a response to the editors' request that I explore this topic. Please note that, given the nature and difficulty of the topic, it has seemed to me to be more useful to try to illustrate and reflect on how a small part of this process actually works rather than simply to weave abstract theories about it.

As you describe it, the second group, made up of men and women equally, is outraged by these objections. Everybody has to pray this prayer, they say, whether they want to or not, because Jesus commands us to pray it. As far as they are concerned, what our job is as Christians is "to be obedient to the will of God" as Jesus lays it out in Scripture, not to get entangled in all that soul-searching, psychological stuff that is destroying not only the Church but the whole of modern society.

You say in your letter that at this point you are so confused, exhausted, and battered by the acrimony of the whole debate that you can hardly bear it, but you know that there is no way your congregation is going to let you just turn your back and walk away from all this, even if you wanted to (which, if you have any sense, you surely do!). For this reason you wonder hesitantly if I would be willing to answer two rather complicated questions to help you regroup and think through all this. First, you ask me how I would reply to the objections of the two groups in your church, and second, you ask me to tell you a little of how I personally pray the opening phrase of this prayer that is causing so much trouble in your church.

My friend, I am glad to answer your questions as best I can, not only because I want to help you but also because I think the various issues you and your church are dealing with are so important.

Let me begin with your first question. Of course, the women and men who are objecting to the use of the Lord's Prayer are right that the language and content of the prayer are making political statements about power, authority, and social order that are intended to shape our social relationships as well as our relationship with God at a very deep level. If we look at the rest of what Jesus says in the Gospels, it seems clear that this is just what Jesus intended.

They are also undeniably correct in their claims that the Church over the centuries has used male, and particularly father, language for God, coupled with language about God's ruling authority to dominate and oppress women (and men, too) in the name of God. Those who object are doing exactly what they ought to be doing in bringing their own personal experience of this up against what they believe the prayer is teaching and challenging it.

I differ from them, however, at the point where they give up on the whole thing. For reasons I don't fully understand, they accept a status quo reading of Jesus rather than trusting that, because God intends our life and not our death, Jesus couldn't possibly be intending to make the political statement they think Jesus is making. Thus, they neither allow this prayer to challenge what is most oppressive in the Church and in the larger culture nor to begin to heal all the oppressed and suffering parts of themselves.

Of course, they are right that the prayer uses kingdom language to talk about God's governance of the world, but it seems to me to be of enormous significance that in his very use of it, Jesus subverts every ordinary notion of kings and kingship we might have. Did I ever warn you, by the way, never to invite Jesus to come to your church to speak on family values? Whatever else we can say about Jesus, one thing was certain: both in his understanding of the way God governs the world and in his vision of the way human beings are to relate to one another in God's presence, Jesus was radical in a way the most radical of us can never hope to be.

Jesus never told women, or men either, much less poor or oppressed people, to knuckle under and accept the status quo as God's powerful "will" for them, nor does he describe God as an ordinary, benevolently just ruler. On the contrary, he teaches that the folk who will have the highest place in a society of God's ordering are not the rich and successful or even the good and the religious, but rather the poor, the widows and orphans, the not-so-religious, and those who are social outcasts because of the unsavoriness of their jobs. Telling his listeners in the Gospels to abandon the idea that the world as they know it has a cosmic rightness to it, he challenges them (us) to take the risks necessary to live in this oppression-free, upside-down world right now.

As I read it, Jesus' teaching about God's fatherhood is just as subversive. Jesus certainly doesn't use God's fatherhood to shore up human male authority, including the authority of our own fathers over us, or he would never have said "call no one father save God alone."[2] As for how God does act as father toward us, I get a tremendous amount of help from the conversation Jesus has with Philip

---

[2] Matt 23:9. Please notice that the context in which this saying is preserved makes it very clear that what Jesus is about here is not the shoring up of the authority of God at the expense of "puny" human beings; it is the dismantling of the everyday structures of authority and respect in order to allow us to stand next to each other in a radical equality of love.

after telling his disciples that he is about to go to his and their Father. "Who is this Father?" Philip wants to know. "Just show him to us and we'll be all right about it." "Look," says Jesus, "after all this time, do you still not know that you have already seen what the Father is like if you've seen me?"[3] But if it is true that looking at Jesus tells us what God's fatherhood is like, then we have to pay attention to the people—women like Mary and Martha, for example—with whom Jesus, acting like God the Father, spends his time and the respectful, loving, non-authoritarian, non-bullying way he actually treats them.

Now, let me say a thing or two about the position of those in your congregation who hate what they call the "psychological approach" and insist on praying the Lord's Prayer because "God said it; I believe it; that settles it." First, they are undoubtedly right in insisting that Jesus has given us the Lord's Prayer with the expectation that we pray it. On the other hand, it is extremely important to remember that Jesus gave this prayer to his disciples not as a command (pray this way, or else), but, if we can trust the Gospel of Luke,[4] he gave it to them as a gift, as the answer to a request that he teach them how to pray. Here, as we just said, we must notice that while Jesus frequently describes and challenges us in what we are called to in our life in God, he is not at all in the habit of laying down the law for those who would follow him or telling people to do what he says without thinking about it or questioning it.

Now, let me try to answer their objections to what they call the "psychological approach," which, of course, in the form to which they object, does not simply address interior, private issues but also wrestles with the way the norms and expectations of the larger culture shape us interiorly and keep us from being the loving people Jesus invites us into the kingdom to be.

I want to start by stating clearly that I, and many other very "traditional" Christians from the time of the early Church onward, believe that the goal and the point of the Christian life Jesus summons us to in the Gospels is nothing more or less than the love of God, which we are to exercise with all our heart, strength, mind, and soul, and the love of our neighbor as ourselves. To put it on other terms, I think what Jesus is asking is no more and no less than a total trans-

[3] John 14:8ff.
[4] Luke 11:1ff.

156

formation into the love of God and neighbor of our entire persons, interior and exterior, public and private, social and personal, hearts, minds, strength, and souls.

But Jesus did not just command us to love in this radical way and then expect us to be able to grit our teeth and do it by an exercise of massive, blind obedience that bypasses interior reflection. In fact, just the opposite. A huge number of Jesus' parables, like the workers in the vineyard, the prodigal son, the good Samaritan, and the unforgiving servant, seem to me to be clearly designed to help his listeners radically open their hearts to a deep examination of their own internal as well as external family experience, their perceptions, motives, desires, and the religious, social, and personal expectations that govern them. In this way, Jesus pushes harder than the most aggressive and probing therapist.

As for the charge that such a psychological approach is not traditional, I want to point out that not only did John Wesley, the founder of the Church to which your objectors belong, regard it as essential, but so did the great and wonderful ancient teachers of the early Church from the fourth through the sixth centuries, the field in which I work.

Did I ever tell you the story from the Sayings of the Fathers on this subject? Once there was a foreign anchorite who made a long trip to the Egyptian desert to look for Abba Poemen and listen to his wisdom. The visitor was so happy when he finally found Poemen that as soon as he arrived, he began "to speak of the Scriptures, of spiritual and heavenly things."[5]

Poemen, however, who was normally a friendly man, unexpectedly refused to answer him. The poor bruised visitor requested that the brother who had originally introduced him to Poemen find out why he wouldn't talk to him. When the brother asked Poemen directly why he simply seemed to be ignoring this famous holy man, his reply was unequivocal: "He is great and speaks of heavenly things and I am lowly and speak of lowly things. If he had spoken of the passions of the soul, I should have replied, but he speaks to me of spiritual things and I know nothing of that."

---

[5] Poemen 8, *The Sayings of the Desert Fathers,* trans. Benedicta Ward (London and Oxford: Mowbray, 1981) 167.

Upon receiving this report, the visitor understood his mistake. As far as Abba Poemen was concerned, lofty spiritual talk about the demands of God and even about Scripture is only a distraction from the real business of the Christian life, which is the transformation and healing of what destroys our ability to love God and neighbor with all our hearts, souls, strength, and mind, and our neighbors as ourselves—what the ancient teachers and theologians called the passions:[6] exactly those deep, long-term attitudes of heart, mind, feeling, and perception that Jesus addresses in the Gospels.

Having learned this lesson, the visitor went back again to Poemen and tried again, saying, "What should I do, Abba, for the passions of the soul master me?" This time the abba received him happily and talked to him willingly about the actual stuff of their own lives. If we assume that that conversation was like so many others depicted in the Sayings of the Fathers, they would have discussed such topics as their struggle against, among other things, anger, envy, self-righteousness, consumerism, judgmentalism, and obsessive needs to be liked.

This tradition that stresses the importance of such introspective work is one that I find entirely useful in our own times. However much we might like to tell ourselves otherwise, there just isn't any way we can love one another or give true worship to the one true God if we can't even see God or our actual neighbors because of our various combinations of misperceptions, self-deceptions, and psychic and spiritual injuries to the image of God in us.

As for the place of this work in our common worship, this is what I believe: Worship not only depends upon us individually doing the interior work and seeking the healing we need to be able to hear what God asks of us and respond to it; real worship itself forms us into who we are individually and as the people of God. This formation, whether we are aware of it or not, takes place as we are attentive to Scripture, as we hear sermons, as we participate in

---

[6] For an ancient description and classification of the passions, see Evagrius Ponticus, *The Praktikos: Chapters on Prayer*, trans. John Eudes Bamberger, O.C.S.O. (Kalamazoo, Mich.: Cistercian Publications, 1981). For a modern discussion, see "The Passions" in my book *To Love as God Loves: Conversations with the Early Church* (Minneapolis: Augsburg Fortress, 1987). For why I believe it is important that we recover this tradition of understanding the passions, see the first chapter of my *In Ordinary Time: Healing the Wounds of the Heart* (Nashville: Abingdon Press, 1996).

intercessory prayers in addition to the Lord's Prayer, and as we share in the Eucharist.

Now, my friend, having responded as best I could to your first question, I come to your second, which is that I tell you a little about why and how I myself pray the Lord's Prayer.

As for the why, I pray it, first, as a basic and deliberate part of my own formation as a Christian in the ways of love. I need it; it is one of the major places I can bring for healing both my short term convictions, feelings, confusions and prejudices, and my whole long-term autobiographical self, including personal and cultural memories of my childhood and adult experiences and expectations that have formed me and fight in me still against the patterns of love.

At the same time, in the context of this daily self-examination, I also need this prayer as a guide and corrector for my intercessory prayer. I need it to help me remember who to pray for, and I need it for something else besides. I don't know about you, but I somehow learned in my growing-up years that when it comes to praying for other people, I must set aside my own "selfish" needs and desires. But I have to keep learning over and over that there is a fundamental connection between how much actual compassion and empathy I can feel for the needs of others and my ability to accept that what I need is valid too. What does it say I really think about others people's needs if I consider it somehow morally superior for me to "rise above" my own? I must pray this prayer, therefore, for myself, not only to teach me what to pray for the people with whom I share my life and my world, but to train me in an ever growing vulnerability and empathy for them as well.

As for the mechanics of how I pray this prayer, it is probably obvious to you by now that when I am praying alone, I don't go straight through it as we recite it in church. Instead, I use it as a guide for my prayer. I begin by speaking the words of the first phrase. Then I meditate briefly, or at length if I need to, on what I believe that part of the prayer is guiding me toward. Finally, in a short sentence or two, I rephrase what I am asking God for on that particular day. Needless to say, what I ask for varies considerably, depending upon what is going on in both my interior and my exterior life.

But let me stop explaining and simply show you what I mean by going through the first words of the Lord's Prayer for you as I have sometimes prayed it in the past and as I actually pray it each day now.

I begin each morning with the phrase that as often as not is now the most important part of my prayer: *Our Father in heaven.* You will probably not be surprised to know that for many years the word in this phrase that I responded to the fastest was "Father," and my response was one of pain and anger.[7] Part of my difficulty lay, as it does for the people in your congregation, with my inability to escape the way God's fatherhood had been used to support a status quo in the Church and in the culture that hurts women and had hurt me.

In addition, in terms of my own particular experience, I had grown up in the forties and fifties with a loving but authoritarian, perfectionistic father who left the family when I was eleven. Like many other people, having transferred to God the Father all the pain I felt around my human father, I simply couldn't get past the "father" language of the prayer to reach God.

Though I was aware of all this at the time, I was hurting so much and so mistrustful of God that I simply couldn't face trying to work through these issues in my prayer. During this period I found that when I prayed it helped me to substitute a name, like mother or friend, that actually would allow me to approach God rather than turn me away.

A long time passed after that in which through my everyday prayer I actually began to learn a little something firsthand about the trustworthiness of the God I couldn't address as Father. Then several things happened in my life that allowed me to become both desperate enough as well as brave and trusting enough to do the work of prayer I needed to do around the issue of what Jesus might have meant when he tried to teach us to call God "Father." I pored over Scripture for help, and in God's presence I began to be able to understand in my own heart what I just told you I have come to believe about the radical implications of Jesus' teaching about God's fatherhood when he said to Philip, "The one who has seen me has seen the Father."

---

[7] For a fuller discussion of what I consider to be the problems around the language of God's fatherhood and the solutions to those problems, see chapter 1 of my *Memories of God: Theological Reflections on a Life* (Nashville: Abingdon Press, 1995).

As I continued to bring my own past and present experience into painful, direct conversation with God through the help of this and other passages of Scripture, I found myself increasingly freed from my secret belief that the way my father had been with me as a child was somehow a normative description not just of God but of the power men exercise over women in the world.

But remember, I said that prayer is about formation in love as much as it is about anything else. Now, let me give you an example of what I mean in regard to the whole question of God's fatherhood. Once having stopped confusing my father with God, I was able to forgive my father for his failures toward me and let my father simply be who he was—not God, but simply an ordinary human being with ordinary weaknesses. At last, as his fully adult child, I could be reconciled with him and learn to love him, enjoy him for the actual man he was, and care for him in a way appropriate to him.

These days, when those old scars begin to ache and I begin to feel internally trapped by the sexism all of us still encounter, I nearly always get help at once by praying, "Our Father, who art in heaven," followed immediately by "God, I know your fatherhood is not underwriting and supporting this stuff that hurts me; rather, your fatherhood calls me into life and fills me with energy. Help me repudiate the hold these things have on me."

Still, my wounds associated with God's fatherhood are fairly well healed for the most part now, and so I don't often find myself needing to pray this way anymore, unless I am praying for other people— or for the Church—who are struggling with their own injuries around fallen notions of God's fatherhood.

Oddly, now the part of the phrase "Our Father in heaven" that daily grips me instead is the seemingly much less difficult word "our." "Our" is a tough word for me in prayer and I'm working hard at it.

"Oh, no," I can hear you saying to yourself, "are you losing your mind? In the light of all the difficulties around praying to God the Father, what on earth could make praying the perfectly ordinary word 'our' an issue for you?"

Well, I'll start by reminding you of what we acknowledge all the time, which is that we in twentieth-century Protestant America are almost fatally individualistic in every area of our lives, and this includes our religion. Christian or not, I am still a product of my own culture, and so I continue to fall into the trap of thinking of *my* spirituality and *my* prayer as a private matter involving nobody but myself and God.

As if this were not enough to fight against in myself as I try to learn to love, like everybody else, I also have to deal with my own temperament and the way I have been formed by the things that happened to me both in my growing-up years and in my adult years, which have made me who I am.

Let me show you what I mean. I've already mentioned that I grew up with a difficult father. One of the things that was difficult about him was that he was an elitist; he did what he could to make sure that I thought of myself as superiorly different from the other perfectly nice, smart children I went to school with. Nothing would make him madder, for example, than my request for a particular item of clothing that "everybody else" wore or for a toy everybody else played with, unless it was my use of the slang they spoke in.

Predictably enough, his plan to make me superior and independent backfired. Being a very shy child who was overly aware of all my faults, I found it impossible to think of myself as superior to anybody. At the same time, because I couldn't find a way to fit in with the other children, they really didn't like me. I suppose it was inevitable that I should have experienced myself as being not only excruciatingly different but as an actual outcast from human society.

The Baptist religion of the Kentucky relatives I visited in the summer didn't make things easier for me, either. My assumption that God the Father was like my human father, coupled with what I thought of as my criminal inability to "believe God loved me and accept Jesus as my Lord and Savior," told me that I was as much an outcast in God's kingdom as I was in the world of school.

Now you begin to see, I hope, why when I prayed the first words of the Lord's Prayer as a child, what I said was "*Our* Father, who art in heaven," but what I meant was "*Their* Father, who art in heaven," the Father of the good, deserving children who belong in the society of other children or adults in a way I never found I could.

Even in my early adult years I couldn't escape this sense of isolation and abandonment. You know already how much guilt and hopelessness I suffered as a woman violating the status quo by going to graduate school and taking up teaching back in the sixties and seventies. It probably won't surprise you to hear, therefore, that during the whole of that time I continued to experience God as I had as a child, not as "my Father" who supported my socially unacceptable desires and ambitions, but rather as the Father of those who were considered "good" in the terms of that culture.

My adult life wasn't all hard, of course, and I made some progress against my sense of being an outcast in a world I hadn't been able to live in comfortably over the years. The birth of my children, the presence of my second husband in my life, and my teaching all helped me enormously. The words of the great desert teachers I study began to give me saving help as soon as I met them. Still, even having made such progress, about fifteen years ago I realized I wanted to move much further out from what had become by then a mostly interior isolation from other people and God.

I began with God. At that time, under the influence of my teachers from the early Church, I began a discipline of prayer that enabled me to learn firsthand, face to face, how different God is from the rejecting, hypercritical God I had imagined. Ultimately, it was here in my daily prayer, as I brought my own experience into conversation with the tradition of early monasticism I study and with Scripture, particularly the psalms and the Gospels, that I began to know what it meant to me personally to say that God is the God of the despised, the socially outcast, and the rejected.

This was real progress. At last I was able to pray the Lord's Prayer as my own prayer, to pray "*Our* Father in heaven" and mean by these words not *their* Father but *my own* Father. It was wonderful. For the first time in my life it did not seem to me that God was on one side of the universe attending to everybody else while I was all alone on the other. God was with me. I knew God both as the safe place I could turn to when I felt alone or afraid and as the one who supported me in my desire to do the work I felt called to do. When I found myself under the pressures of living and working with another real live person or persons who had hurt or angered me, or whose expectations I felt unable to meet, or who just plain wore me out, I could withdraw into the safe space of my prayer and pray, "*My* Father in heaven . . . give *me* this day *my* daily bread . . . lead *me* not into temptation."

For a while it was enough. Then the day came when I could no longer let myself forget that in this particular prayer, what Jesus is teaching us is not how to pray "*My* Father, who art in heaven," but rather "*Our* Father." Neither finding a safe space nor being supported by God is the goal of the Christian life; it is love of God, but it is love of neighbor too.

For help in learning how to pray "*Our* Father" and mean it, I began to meditate frequently on what I first read in the commentary on the Lord's Prayer by the third-century North African Cyprian.[8] At some level it doesn't matter whether I think I am praying this prayer alone or whether I consciously acknowledge my basic identity as a member of the Body of Christ when I pray it. At some deep level, my unity with other Christians doesn't have to be something I make happen myself. Whether I want it or not, the fact is that whenever I speak these words, "*Our* Father . . . give *us* . . . *our* daily bread," by virtue of my very baptism I am praying it as part of the people of God, and in return they are praying with me.

Of even more help to me now, however, is a way of praying the first words of the Lord's Prayer that only came to me about a year ago. Over a period of weeks I had been unsuccessfully struggling to forgive what I had experienced as a significant betrayal by a close friend I'll call Jane Anne. I was fairly sure she was unaware of what she had done, and I had no intention of talking with her about it. Some days I told myself that trying to discuss it would only make things worse; other days I told myself that my feelings would go away if I just didn't pay any attention to them.

Neither strategy worked, nor were my prayers for help in forgiveness successful. Though I had days when my anger and hurt receded a little, for no apparent reason, on other days my pain and rage were as new and sharp as they had been in the beginning. One part of me—the smaller part in which God's grace is always calling me to truthfulness and vulnerability—knew that love is too valuable ever to be thrown away and that I still valued my friend. The larger part of me, however—the old, wounded, isolated part—felt that the very ground had fallen away under my feet. All I wanted to do was

[8] "Before all things the Teacher of peace and Master of unity is unwilling for prayer to be made single and individually, teaching that he [or she] who prays is not to pray for himself [or herself] alone. For we do not say, *My Father Who art in heaven,* nor *Give me this day my bread* . . . . Prayer with us is public and common; and when we pray we do not pray for one but for the whole people, because we the whole people are one."—*St. Cyprian on the Lord's Prayer,* trans. T. Herbert Bindley (London: SPCK, 1914) 32–33.

simply follow my familiar patterns of safety by praying for myself and going away never to see her again.

I struggled on with my prayer, nonetheless, and one morning when I was feeling really hopeless, as I began to pray Jesus' prayer I heard myself praying the opening words in a new way. "*Our* Father, who art in heaven," I heard myself say, and then immediately after that, "*My* Father and *the Father of Jane Anne.* . . ."

My friend, I hardly know how to tell what happened next. It was entirely undramatic, but all at once I realized that as I said these words, "My Father and the Father of Jane Anne," I knew that I was no longer alone in a private world in which I was blinded and isolated by my own mental anguish. Rather, I found myself in the presence of God, Jane Anne beside me, in the bright and open space of God's mysterious love for the two of us. Immediately my grief and anger began to lift. For the first time since what I had thought of as her original betrayal, I understood that the issue I had been wrestling with was not so much my specific need to forgive Jane Anne for what she had done as it was my old need to keep my footing on what I thought of as my hard-earned place in the universe in which everybody else lived.

By speaking the words "My Father and the Father of Jane Anne," I had prayed for her and myself together. Somehow, in that moment when I was given the gift of praying "*Our* Father" and really meaning it, I knew I had a place I didn't have to fight for or defend; it was a place in the family of God to which I belonged simply because I was a human being. Finally, set free of my blinding fear, I was set loose to begin to see and love Jane Anne with empathy and compassion.

Still, there was the shadow of the original betrayal lying between us. What was I to do? In the days that followed I continued to pray for myself and Jane Anne together as I had been doing. Finally, it became clear to me that I must tell her my feelings and give her a chance to respond. The conversation wasn't easy, but it helped each of us to see in a new light what had happened, to repair what had been broken, and to grow together toward the future.

What I have learned from all this for dealing with my long-term struggles to pray "Our Father" and my ongoing desire to grow in love through my prayer has been enormously important to me. Each morning now I begin to pray the Lord's Prayer by saying the words "Our Father." After that I visualize the face or faces of the people I must be with that day with whom I am angry, or whom I would avoid because they have hurt me or sap my energy, or who exercise internal or external destructive power over me. Then I paraphrase the words "Our Father" and repeat them as a prayer for myself and a prayer for the other person or persons together, "my Father and the Father of my student Stephen"; "my Father and the Father of the church group I am on my way to speak to"; "my Father and the Father of my uncle."

If I am angry enough at someone, I have to prod and push myself to pray it, knowing that this is a necessary way for me to pray. Mysteriously, as it once happened with my prayer for myself and Jane Anne together, what nearly always comes along with the words of the prayer is an immediate, intimate awareness of being equally loved members of God's family. This awareness seems to take away my own defensiveness and self-protection, and lets me be more present with the other person or persons on that day in the way they—and I too—need.

Why praying in this way should be helpful in this way, I don't know for sure. I suspect that it is connected with what Dorotheos of Gaza told the brothers of his quarreling sixth-century monastery. How can you fight this way? he said to them. "Pray instead, 'O God, help my brother and me through his prayers.'"[9]

Perhaps whenever we stand before God and pray at the same time for ourselves and for someone else from whom we feel separated, we are stepping into a place of humility that lets us admit to ourselves the way our own lives depend not only on the prayers of strangers but even on the prayers of our enemies. I don't know whether other people's lives will be saved by such an admission, but I have come to believe that mine is being saved in this way at this very moment.

No matter, perhaps, that I can't explain this mysterious process of learning to pray the word "our" better than I have. Whatever our capacity to explain, the healing of our ability to love is never something that we do ourselves; healing always finally comes as a gift of God.

At any rate, I'm sorry for your troubles, my friend, and I hope you are able to find something in this very long letter that will help you with the tough situation in your church. Don't give up. As you can

---

[9] *Dorotheos of Gaza: Discourses and Sayings,* trans. Eric P. Wheeler (Kalamazoo, Mich.: Cistercian Publications, 1977) 154.

see, I believe that the conversation you are in is terribly important. Perhaps, if you aren't already doing it, you might try praying the Lord's Prayer for yourself and your congregation together in the way we have been talking about. Whether you do or not, I'll keep you in my prayers, and you keep me in yours too.

Yours in Christ,
Roberta

Gail Ramshaw

Pried Open by Prayer

What we have is one pea per pod, one lone voice droning on from inside a jar, the Cartesian I trying valiantly to stand up straight. Stick to yourself, for the Other is unknowable. On the city streets, the Other is dangerous, and even the Bible salesman is out to steal my peg leg. How much did the Reformation accelerate this isolation of the individual? Here, Heidi, is a Bible. Learn to read it, for you alone are responsible for taking it into yourself.

Religion does not necessarily pry us open. Religion can even encourage us to keep our eyes tightly shut. In much religion the I-idea is enshrined. My religion may tell me that God likes me and only those people who are like me. Only we do the sacrifices correctly, so we'd better beware of all the others who do not. My religion might even assure me that I am God. Nothing is finally more divine than I, and I must be careful not to contaminate my holiness. Religion can be the ultimately closed system, the safe I lock myself in. I feel protected by some truth, now and at the hour of my death. Even when religion puts lots of us peas into one pot, the I-idea pervades. The pot is now the I, and we need only our own peas. Aren't we all happy here, singing ditties and laughing together? All the rest can go to hell.

Teachers like Don Saliers tell us that, quite to the contrary, Christian prayer pries us open. The words of prayer put God and the neighbor into our mouths and, it is hoped, into our hearts. As petitions proceed from our mouths, loving action is to proceed from our hands. Christian prayer is profoundly countercultural. The I is not me; the I is not even the we that I know and respect. The I is rather the Body of Christ throughout time and around the globe, filled with folk I don't know and wouldn't like; and the Body of Christ calls into its arms all those not yet in the Body. The Body seeks to embrace all the unbaptized, perhaps even all the animals and all the trees. We do not know nearly as much as we wish we did about Jesus of Nazareth. But the sparse records agree that in most surprising ways he extended his hands to the Other, finally becoming one of the Other himself.

Remember Augustine's *Confessions*? Many scholars claim that Augustine invented the Western introspective autobiography. Ironic, isn't it, that this father of orthodox Christian doctrine was obsessively examining himself. In Book 9, after pages of fruitless endeavors and paragraphs of bifurcated will, Augustine writes simply, "We were baptized."[1] That's it. But I want to know, What was Augustine feeling? Is it true that he and Ambrose began improvising the *Te Deum* right then and there in that great round pool? Was there a party afterward? Not only are we given few such details, but Augustine speaks in the plural: "*We* were baptized." The old I is already transformed. Augustine the pear-stealer and the career-climber has been immersed in the ancient story of the faithful people. These metaphors have drawn him out of himself and sent him out into a life lived for others.

So ought to be all Christian prayer. I come to the liturgy bound up in myself. But the prayer of the liturgy inserts me into a narrative older and deeper than myself, giving me language for myself that I would not have discovered looking at myself in the mirror. In so doing I meet other people and seek yet more. After we say "We were baptized," the next logical line is "Let us pray for the whole people of God in Christ Jesus and for all people according to their needs." An example of how Christian prayer pries us open can be seen in an unlikely place: the Reproaches, as rendered in the United Methodist Book of Worship.[2]

Unlikely? I should say! The story goes that the religion editor of the *New York Times* was hard up for his annual first-page story for the Good Friday paper and decided to interview some Jewish rabbis about the traditional Reproaches. Their understandable concern, even alarm, over the words of this litany induced many Christians to dump the tenth-century text as at least abstruse but probably anti-Semitic.

[1] *The Confessions of St. Augustine*, bk. 9, chap. 6, par. 14.
[2] *The United Methodist Book of Worship* (Nashville: The United Methodist Publishing House, 1992) 363–364.

That a text arising from the Christian Church of medieval France might be anti-Semitic is unfortunately not surprising. Look, for example, at the thirteenth-century *Bible Moralisée*,[3] a massive picture book in which the stories of the Hebrew Bible are paired with what the designers decided was their contemporaneous meaning. One picture shows Moses at the burning bush, and the paired picture shows thirteenth-century Jews turning away from the fire of God (33Bb). God keeps the Egyptians from eating the Passover lamb, just as God keeps the Jews from tasting the Eucharistic host (39Bb). Israelites watch the angel slaying the first-born; Christians watch the angel slaying demons and Jews (39Dd). The Israelites cross the Red Sea, and in the parallel picture a bishop protects naked catechumens from mermaids and Jews (41Aa). But enough of this unpleasantness.

Although many people find in the Reproaches this medieval mindset, even the traditional text hoped to use the story of the Exodus, not against the Jews, but against the perpetually sinning Church. As with much liturgical language, the Reproaches attempted to pry us open by employing metaphor, pulling us out of what some fantasize is a better way—a falsely simplified world of white and black—into the real complex world of shades and tones, overlaps and blendings. Words can mean many things; words have their meaning specific to the context; and the totality of the mind of God cannot be rendered in first-grade English. By using metaphor, liturgical prayer hopes to acquaint our minds with the ambiguity of our life and God's grace.

However, not everyone in church on Good Friday got an A in Metaphoric Thinking, and so the medieval text, as with so many artifacts with which the Church worships, needed some overhaul. Several noble Methodist souls, who understood what Christian prayer means to do, offered the version now in Methodist hands. They retained the metaphor of the Church being the people of Israel saved from slavery and brought to the Promised Land, but they made the metaphoric meaning explicit: the Sea is called "the waters of baptism." They both kept the ancient references and brought the litany up to the present. They included both more obscure references, as in "the royal scepter," and easily recognizable ones, such as "the least of your brothers and sisters." This text is worth our study.

[3] *Bible Moralisée*, Codex Vindobonensis 2554, Vol. 40 Reihe Codices Selecti.

1. O my people, O my Church,
     what have I done to you, or in what have I offended you?
   I led you forth from the land of Egypt
     and delivered you by the waters of baptism,
   but you have prepared a cross for your Savior.

2. I led you through the desert forty years
     and fed you with manna;
   I brought you through times of persecution and of renewal
     and gave you my body, the bread of heaven;
   but you have prepared a cross for your Savior.

3. I made you branches of my vineyard
     and gave you the water of salvation,
   but when I was thirsty you gave me vinegar and gall
     and pierced with a spear the side of your Savior.

4. I went before you in a pillar of cloud,
     but you led me to the judgment hall of Pilate.
   I brought you to a land of freedom and prosperity,
     but you have scourged, mocked and beaten me.

5. I gave you a royal scepter,
     and bestowed the keys to the kingdom,
     but you have given me a crown of thorns.
   I raised you on high with great power,
     but you have hanged me on the cross.

. . . .

9. I grafted you into the tree of my chosen people Israel,
     but you turned on them with persecution and mass murder.
   I made you joint heirs with them of my covenants,
     but you made them scapegoats for your own guilt.

10. I came to you as the least of your brothers and sisters.
    I was hungry but you gave me no food,
      thirsty but you gave me no drink.
    I was a stranger but you did not welcome me,
      naked but you did not clothe me,
      sick and in prison but you did not visit me.

The backbone of the Reproaches is the refrain of the Eastern Trisagion. The praying I stands before the Triune God. Not only am I before the living God, but I am not standing alone. I pray with others: "Have mercy upon us." We were baptized; now, have mercy on us. God is the holy One, the mighty One (I'm glad it's not *al*mighty), the immortal One. Even God the Three-in-One is not a great lonely I, the super clamshell in the sky. Rather, the Trinity is the one in whom community originates.

The first step that Christian prayer takes in prying us open is to tell us someone else's story. (My story, my story—aren't we getting sick of "my story"? By the number of personal memoirs being published, I guess not. To all the clergy who begin their sermons with their own story: remember C. G. Jung chiding us that the common characteristic of autobiographers is self-delusion.) The story in the Reproaches is the preeminent narrative we Christians inherit from the Hebrew people, the story of their symbolic death in the sea and eventual salvation in the Promised Land. As the Reproaches review for us, the Israelites were brought out of Egypt and led across the sea, fed in the wilderness, guided by the pillar of cloud, granted a kingdom in the new land. Each stanza of the Reproaches reinserts us into that mighty tale of God's salvation.

No better time, of course, for this retelling than the Triduum. Good Friday can be for Christians another exercise of the I. I am unworthy. I will die. I had better meditate on Jesus, another loner. I am walled up in my grief over the past year's deaths. I am alone on my knees. And into my solitary confinement flows the water of the Red Sea. We are swept into that story of other people's death and life, their suffering and God's mercy to them. Ha, says the Reproaches! Today is not only about you and the dying Jesus. Today is about all the world's people: listen to Moses cry, hear Miriam sing.

The second technique of Christian prayer in prying us open is to employ the metaphors to enlarge us. We appropriate the metaphors into ourselves and as a result grow too big for our shells. I am not any longer only I. I am also the whole people of Israel, making it across to the shore, receiving the keys of the kingdom.

The metaphors in the Reproaches call me beyond both the best and the worst in myself. What, do you think the worst thing you've done is cheat on your income taxes? You, I, we, prepared Jesus' cross, pierced his side, murdered others in his name, quarreled among ourselves, persecuted his people, and ignored the hungry and the poor. Both the splendor of the ancient narrative and the magnitude of our offenses are greater than I had known. Neither all this adventure nor all this evil can squeeze into my outhouse with me. I must come out into God's air.

In fact the Reproaches make clear: in the liturgy, "you" is not a singular word. "You" is always "you-all." You think you are alone in your pew. No, you are the entire Church. "The body of Christ for you" means "for you-all." The words should be proclaimed loudly over the communal distribution, not privately mumbled in through the crack of our clamshells.

Finally, Christian prayer, having given me a self far greater than myself, sends us out to get to know that self, to be one with all its parts, to clothe all its limbs, to visit its edges in prison. The metaphor takes on life by remaking our life. We get connected to all and everyone before God. We meet all the creatures without whose health we are sick, without whose life even we are dead. Here, Heidi, is a Bible. Read in it that God's mercy comes to you-all.

Could all our prayer do such as these Reproaches? Would that our liturgy set us into God's great story of redemption, dancing alongside Miriam at the sea, accompanying Mary Magdalene in the garden. Would that these metaphors become ours, so that I am not merely me but mythically more. Would that this metaphoric transubstantiation could release me from the prison of my own making and propel me out to welcome the stranger. That's the hope. Let's see if it works.

In closing, let's hear one of us who is part of I, the certifiable Christian poet Christopher Smart. He got beyond his crazy self into his cat:[4]

For I will consider my Cat Jeoffry.
For he is the servant of the Living God duly and daily
    serving him. . .
For having consider'd God and himself he will consider
    his neighbor. . .
For if he meets another cat he will kiss her in
    kindness. . .
For he purrs in thankfulness, when God tells him he's a
    good Cat. . .

[4] Christopher Smart, "Rejoice in the Lamb," in *Poems*, ed. Robert Brittain (Princeton: Princeton University Press, 1950) 118–120.

For the Lord commanded Moses concerning the cats at the
    departure of the Children of Israel from Egypt. . .
For he knows that God is his Saviour. . .
For the divine spirit comes about his body to sustain it
    in complete cat. . .

I do not know how Jeoffry knew all of that. But my hope is that we
can learn it: daily to serve the living God, to hear the story of the escape from Egypt, to purr in thankfulness, and to kiss one another in
kindness. "Complete cat": a marvelous metaphor for the Body of
Christ. May we practice it in prayer.

Part 4

Word and Music:
Forming a Liturgical Aesthetic

Introduction

In this final section we turn to the tension between the arts *in* worship and the art *of* worship. This art patterns the deep and durable affections of the Christian life. Gail Ramshaw's attention to the transformative power in the narrative and metaphorical qualities of liturgical prayer in the previous essay prepares the way for Brian Wren's and Paul Westermeyer's reflections on the words and music of Christian prayer. Wren and Westermeyer challenge us to consider what the Church requires in the creation and performance of text and tune to provide the aesthetic and imaginative power, spiritual depth, and metaphoric range that sustain Christian life and witness in the world.

Wren wonders if shapeless prayers yield a shapeless spirituality. Does our fumbling with liturgical texts lead us to our stumbling in works of justice and mercy? In response to this question, he offers five interrelated proposals about the language of public prayer. In light of these proposals, he then subjects a "model" prayer text to a series of scrutinizing theses that both illuminate good and bad qualities of congregational prayers and articulate issues their authors and choosers should take into account.

Westermeyer reminds us, perhaps more so than the preceding essays, of the initial intent of this book—to honor Don Saliers—and spins a word of praise that points us beyond the book to our shared work in praise of God, *soli Deo gloria*. Westermeyer's questions about the function of liturgical music and, by implication, of worship itself return us to the themes of the opening section of the book. He asks if worship and its music are properly considered means to certain ends, such as Church growth, evangelism, or aesthetics. More specifically, does liturgical music have a utilitarian purpose? Should the music in worship be a tool for converting people? Or is liturgical music the means of empowering believers? Westermeyer finds the typical approaches to these questions wanting. He proposes that we consider liturgical music, far from a means of manipulating or converting people, as serving in the humble capacity of accompanying, expressing, and participating in the entire action of worshiping God, the God revealed through the cross of Christ.

These essays, as with those that precede them, invite us "to pray into a new way of living and to live into a new way of praying." We are invited to an encounter with Jesus Christ in the power of the Spirit that, as our true worship, leads us to life with one another "at full stretch before God."

Brian Wren

Clunky Prayers and Christian Living: Reflections on Writing, Prayer, and Practice

With careful solemnity, the eight-year-old acolyte lights the last candle on the communion table and walks down the aisle. The organ prelude ends and the service begins: Welcome—Notices—Call to worship—Hymn (all stand, some sing, then all sit)—Prayer: "Let us confess our sins to God as we say together the prayer printed in the bulletin." We park our hymnals, fumble for our bulletins, find our place, and speak:

"Loving and merciful God, we confess before you and before each other that we are a people who have failed to be the kind of people you call us to be, or to live the kind of life you call us to live in the world of today. We confess that we cannot see beyond our own horizons, and that we often lose our sense of your presence in our individual lives and in the world around us. . . ."

Mumbling and stumbling, we trudge through the prayer as if walking through sand, perking up only at the liberating word "Amen."

Do they matter, these clunky prayers that spill out Sunday by Sunday onto worship bulletins in so many mainstream Protestant churches?[1] If we deplore their arrhythmic verbosity, is our objection "merely" aesthetic? If worship shapes our spirituality, do shapeless prayers render it shapeless? If their theology is inadequate, how far can we ignore it or mentally "translate" it? If we fumble the liturgy, will we stumble in our work for justice, peace, and kindness? Or do we bemoan their linguistic tedium, wishing we could be touched by

---

[1] As a paleface man in the Reformed tradition, I write from that context and experience, hoping that others will glean from it.

holiness, yet secretly relieved when tedium insulates us from transformation?

As one who writes for public worship, I live with these questions, as do many who publish prayerbooks and hymnals, or choose words to be spoken, heard, and sung in worship services. With brushstrokes of discernment, Don Saliers has illuminated the formative power of liturgy and sketched the elusive relationship between what is said and done within worship and outside it.[2] Building on his insights, I shall make five overlapping proposals about the language of public prayer and then explore the responsibilities of worship-writers and word-choosers.[3]

1. *The language of public prayer has formative and performative functions.* Prayer language presumes a commitment to God—accepted, ignored, or resisted—by those who pray. If we give ourselves to God through the prayer, its language helps to enact and confirm our commitment. "To thank God, to praise God, to confess, to intercede—all these are ways of gesturing the self in and through words. What is done with the words is part of the meaning of what is said."[4] "What is done" invites us to look at what the praying person does before and after prayer, and how the prayer is used in the liturgy and the liturgical community. The "gesturing" metaphor suggests that the formative power of prayer language is neither simple nor guaranteed. Gestures are bodily movements expressing meaning, mood, or intent. Because body and spirit are one, posture and gesture can also shape and reinforce mood and intent. Yet, we can distance ourselves from our gestures, or gesture with intent to deceive.

2. *Because the language of public prayer is formative, it can be liberating and respectful or manipulative and oppressive. Its formative function is covert though not coercive.*

In showing the conceptual link between liturgy and ethics, Don Saliers brings insights needing to be qualified by other parts of his discussion. Although "those who say they love God but who are not

---

[2] Don E. Saliers, "Liturgy and Ethics: Some New Beginnings," pp. 15–35 above. I am glad to write for Don's birthday Festschrift and thereby celebrate, as best I can, the scholarship, artistry, and friendship of this spirited and spiritual man.

[3] Similar questions apply to other words spoken, heard, and sung, and to music, movement, preaching, and ritual, including sacraments.

[4] Saliers, "Liturgy and Ethics," p. 19 above.

disposed to love and serve the neighbor are *misunderstanding* the words and actions of worship,"[5] neither their "mistake" nor the function of the prayers they pray is merely cognitive. As Saliers also observes, whenever prayer uses words, to pray means more than just saying the words of the prayer. Prayer requires the orientation of the whole self to God.[6]

Because one of the functions of verbal prayer is to enact self-commitment to the One most worthy of adoration and trust, the invitation "Let us pray" invites us to suspend our critical faculties and "go with the flow," vulnerable to the language that follows. That is why, in public prayer, "people are often more relaxed, receptive, less on guard, and hence more susceptible to the variety of messages being conveyed."[7] Focusing on the logic of how Christian prayer Christianly forms us should not make us starry-eyed about liturgical language. Formation quite often degenerates into malformation, as when beautiful words have oppressive meanings:

"We cannot be beguiled by pleasant sounds.
The cadences of Cranmer and King James
caress the palate, smooth as ancient wine,
yet clothe the humble power of love divine
in Tudor pomp, and absolutist claims,
while soaring plainsong from a thousand tongues
sent Inquisition victims to the flames.
We cannot be beguiled by pleasant sounds."[8]

(Brian Wren, © 1996, Hope Publishing Co. Reproduced by permission.)

---

[5] Ibid., 18, emphasis mine.

[6] "Regarded from a human point of view, prayer is the activity in which human beings explore their life 'unto God.' It is much more than words. In uttering the words of prayer, we are doing something, performing an act. . . . The meaning of praying is not a simple matter of saying the words. To pray is to become a living text before God."—Ibid., 19 and 25.

[7] Janet Schaffran and Pat Kozak, *More Than Words: Prayer and Ritual for Inclusive Communities* (New York: Crossroad, 1986) 5.

[8] Brian Wren, *Piece Together Praise: A Theological Journey—Poems and Collected Hymns Thematically Arranged* (Carol Stream, Ill.: Hope Publishing Co, 1996) p. 185, no. 201. The opening line is quoted from Carolyn Jennings' article "Why Are You Walking Away," *Creator* magazine, November-December 1991.

The formative power of the invitation "Let us pray" is covert, because the entailed invitation to suspend critique and "go with the flow" is not openly stated. Yet, however persuasive the language that follows, it can neither coerce our acquiescence nor predetermine our response. Except for technical language, linguistic communication has an inbuilt indeterminacy. It is not a matter of my putting thoughts into word canisters that you unpack exactly as I packed them. I cannot prescribe the meanings nor control the associations that my prayer-language will arouse in your mind, nor should I try or want to. The fact that your experience and preconceptions shape and filter what you hear me say is essential to human freedom.[9]

The necessary imprecision of linguistic communication, combined with the community-building function of liturgy, may explain why it is not always essential to get the words right. In September 1988 I visited Pitt Street Uniting Church in downtown Sydney, Australia. In a large, old building on a main street was a small yet vibrant congregation. The language was crisp, clear, and imaginative, the singing strong and committed, and the sharing of stories, joys, and concerns honest, deep, and caring. Asking for the congregation's history, I was told that revitalization had been spurred by its decision to welcome gays and lesbians and to advocate Aboriginal land rights. These and other moves had brought intimidating phone calls, swastikas and abusive slogans daubed on the church door, notoriety, admiration, hostility—and new members.

"How has all this affected your worship?" I asked. "The first thing we did under pressure" (paraphrasing the reply) "was to sing the old hymns we knew and loved. We sang our hearts out. They brought us together, even when the language was out of date and not really relevant to us. As time went on, we began to create new liturgies that better express who we are." This suggests that the bonding function of familiar words can override their semantic inadequacies (especially when sung to beloved tunes) until experience creates more adequate language.

3. *Prayer language should form us to perceive that our service to God is completed by what we do outside public worship.* As Don Saliers observes,

[9] For the background and backing to this analysis, see Brian Wren, *What Language Shall I Borrow?—God-Talk in Worship: A Male Response to Feminist Theology* (New York: Crossroad, 1989) 70–75.

184

"Worship ascribes glory to God alone; but unless the glorification is shown in works of justice, mercy and love faithful to God's commands, Christ's liturgy is not fully enacted." Not all who say liturgical prayers are shaped by them, and liturgy cannot guarantee how honestly we confront the suffering and gladness of the world.[10] Nonetheless, without a prayer language that longs for the completion of liturgy in works of justice and love, either such enactment will be hindered or we will miss seeing its liturgical meaning and perpetuate false and dispiriting disjunctions between "worship" and "life" or "prayer" and "action."

The distinction between public worship and what happens outside it should be modeled, not as separate realms, but as concentric circles. Within the widest circle—the political, social, and economic macrocosms of which we are a part—is a smaller circle, the total life of each particular faith-community. Within this mesocosm is the smallest circle, that faith-community's services of public worship. When it assembles for worship, its liturgy is not "mere ritual" or "mere words." To do justice, kindness, and truth in the words and actions of the liturgy is to do in microcosm what we are called to live out in the mesocosm, and what we struggle, hope, and pray for in the macrocosms we inhabit. Our freedom of action is limited. Sometimes the best that an oppressed, beleaguered, or outcast Christian community can do is celebrate, enact, and anticipate in its worship and community life the freedom, justice, peace, and love that a hostile world crushes and denies.

4. *Liturgical prayer is Christianly formative only when nourished by its leaders' and participants' immersion in "the world" through solidarity, service, prayer, and kindness.* "Where encountering the reality of human need is not part of the experiential background in intercessory prayer no amount of lovely text—said or sung—will suffice."[11] Don Saliers' comment suggests that the relation between words and actions inside and outside worship is not one-way but interactive and dialectical. Liberation theologies have long been aware of this. From 1970s apartheid South Africa, Cosmas Desmond called on his readers to ask, not "What does the gospel tell us about an unjust situation?" but "What does that situation tell us about our understanding and practice

[10] "Liturgy and Ethics," 25 and 24 above.
[11] Ibid., 30.

185

of the gospel?" The gospel bids us love our neighbor, and we pray for strength and discernment to do so. But Bible and liturgy cannot completely tell us *how* to love here and now. "We can only learn that from the people we are supposed to be loving."[12] Vital prayer needs such learning experiences. Contrary to many hymns, prayers, and exhortations, the traffic between "liturgy" and "life" is not one-way and does not flow along a Platonic Boulevard, from ideas through words into actions.[13] To suggest that we pray ourselves into a new way of living is a half-truth, completed only if we are also living ourselves into a new way of praying.[14]

5. *Writers and choosers of public prayer have a professional duty to learn its genre and critique its language.*[15] Because its formative function is covert and persuasive, the language of public prayer should be scrutinized and critiqued before it is embraced. Desirable for all worshipers, such scrutiny and critique are for writers and word-choosers a professional duty, so that other worshipers can trust the language of our prayers.

Let me exemplify my own scrutiny by presenting, then analyzing, the complete text of the prayer through which we were invited to trudge at the beginning of this discussion. Because it would be invidious (and possibly expensive!) to single out published examples, the prayer is a constructed composite, albeit longer than life. Its smaller siblings populate the bulletins of innumerable Protestant churches. Worlds apart from the sparseness of Episco-Luthera-Catholic liturgies, it raises issues to which they too should attend:

"Loving and merciful God, we confess before you and before each other that we are a people who have failed to be the kind of people

---

[12] Cosmas Desmond, *Christians or Capitalists?* (London: Bowerdean Press, 1978) 25 and 26.

[13] See, for example, the "Prayer for True Singing" in the *United Methodist Hymnal* (Nashville: United Methodist Publishing House, 1989), no. 69, which asks that the words we sing "on our lips" may be believed and then lived.

[14] A member of a Christian community in Brisbane, Australia, described to me how they had learned from experience that "we do not so much think ourselves into a new way of acting as act ourselves into a new way of thinking."

[15] Compare Don Saliers: "Part of our mutual task as liturgical theologians and as Christian ethicists is to keep the language and rites of Christian worship clear and resilient with respect to the moral life."—"Liturgy and Ethics," p. 34 above.

you call us to be or to live the kind of life you call us to live in the world of today. We confess that we cannot see beyond our own horizons and that we often lose our sense of your presence in our individual lives and in the world around us. And yes, we confess with shame our pride and selfishness, our apathy and indifference, in the face of the sin and the suffering of our war-torn world, and the ease with which we are distracted by manufactured needs, material comforts, and meaningless activities. Yet as we come into your presence, we are also emboldened by the realization that we stand before the Ruler of the nations, in whose hands are all the corners of the earth. We pray that your Spirit may water the wasteland of our hope, set us on fire with faith, and breathe into us the breath of love, so that with intentionality and empowerment and inspiration we may live according to the manner of Jesus the Christ. Help us to remember that justice, peace, truth, and love are not just words in the Bible but the blueprint for the life we are called to live as your community of faith. Amen."

Here is my analysis of this prayer, as a model for critiquing others like it.[16]

1. *The prayer was written without being spoken.* The writer is unaware of the difference between writing and speech, between words designed to be read silently off the page (for example, an essay or magazine article) and words crafted to be read aloud to an audience. As my preaching professor used to say, liturgists need to learn the difference between "talk stuff" and "write stuff." Though a skillful worship leader might speak this prayer in such a way that the congregation could follow it, a congregation cannot read its rambling phrases without stumbling.

2. *The writer has not listened to a congregation reading prayers and does not know the rhythms of corporate speech or the formats that express and enable them.* To read well, a congregation needs short phrases with

---

[16] Because what is done with the words of prayer goes beyond saying or hearing them, worship leaders also need to ask how a given prayer is used in worship. For example, what should precede and follow it? How is it prepared for and introduced? Are worshipers given enough time to get ready for it, pray, and make the transition to what follows? Does the worship leader act and speak as one who is in the presence of God?

clear typographical cues, cast in sense lines in lowercase type,[17] as in this, from St. Francis:

"Where there is hatred
let me sow love;
where there is injury, pardon;
where there is doubt, faith;
where there is despair, hope. . . ."[18]

or this, from St. Paul:

"And now, sisters and brothers,
all that is true,
all that is noble,
all that is just and pure,
all that is lovable and gracious,
whatever is excellent and admirable
fill your thoughts
with these things."[19]

Both prayers use short, crisp phrases, preserved in translation. I don't know about Francis, but Paul expected his letters to be read aloud to the receiving congregation. He dictated "talk stuff," using the skills of Greek rhetoric. Even when cast in paragraphs, such language is easy for a congregation to read. When cast in short lines, as above, the congregation's voice becomes stronger, rhythmic, alert, and corporate. In company with others, I call them "sense lines," because, whether punctuated or not, each line is a building block of

[17] Words in lowercase type have distinctive shapes, formed by the interplay of stems rising above the line (ascenders: b, d, f, h, k, l), tails below it (descenders: g, p, q, y), both (j), and partial ascenders (i, t). For most readers, the resultant "contours" greatly aid recognition. WHEN TEXT IS PRINTED IN CAPITAL LETTERS, WORDS LOSE THEIR DISTINCTIVE SHAPES, MAKING RECOGNITION SLOWER AND MORE DIFFICULT. Text in capitals also suggests emphasis (in the world of linked computers, typing in capital letters is called "shouting"). I am indebted to Laurence Hull Stookey of Wesley Seminary, Washington, for help in clarifying the above.

[18] Extract from the Prayer of St. Francis of Assisi, as formatted in the Fellowship Meal liturgy of the Christian Workers Fellowship of Sri Lanka, circa 1978.

[19] Ibid., from Philippians 4:8.

meaning complete enough to be spoken and understood as a unit, without losing the flow. In the examples above, "Where there is hatred" and "fill your thoughts" meet those criteria; lines like "where there is hatred, let us" and "fill your thoughts with" would not.

3. *Congregational speech needs clear, contemporary vocabulary, mostly in words of one, two, or three syllables.* Words like "intentionality" and "empowerment" are colorless, polysyllabic, difficult to say, and a test of comprehension skills. Phrases like "manufactured needs, material comforts, and meaningless activities" may sound impressive but fall under the same critique. They are plausible, if at all, only when the congregation has recently elaborated which needs are thus "manufactured" and which activities are "meaningless." Phrases like "after the manner of" are vague and archaic.

4. *Because it is community speech, congregational prayer should avoid idiosyncratic mannerisms like "And yes," which serve no purpose save drawing attention to themselves.*

5. *Prayer language should be sensible, not silly.* A Pentecost call to worship that has the congregation declare confidently that "the flames of the Spirit dance above our heads" is silly because it invites us to look up, see nothing, and say "What?"[20] In my composite prayer, to confess that "we cannot see beyond our own horizons" is silly, because a horizon is by definition that which one cannot see beyond. Asking that our horizons be expanded or enlarged would be more sensible.

6. *Congregational prayers should have clear structure and be metaphorically coherent.* Though metaphor is more memorable than abstraction, to have us pray that God's Spirit "may water the wasteland of our hope, set us on fire with faith, and breathe into us the breath of love" is incoherent, because it first makes us wet, then sets us on fire, then breathes on what is burning. By contrast, "water our wasteland and plant seeds of hope" coherently develops the metaphor.

7. *Objections to clunkiness in prayer language are not "merely" aesthetic.* In his exploration of liturgical prayer, Lawrence Hoffman argues that faith is generated by the discovery of patterns that give meaning to life, so that worship with satisfying patterns of word and ritual both supports faith and helps to engender it.[21] If he is right, a

[20] From a worship bulletin, circa 1989, source not found.
[21] *The Art of Public Prayer: Not for Clergy Only* (Washington: The Pastoral Press, 1988) 153–160.

preference for artistry over shapelessness in prayer language is more than a matter of taste. Even if its theology is sound, a rambling, tedious prayer shortchanges us because it mimics life's chaos instead of providing a satisfying verbal pattern.

8. *Shapeless prayers convey hidden messages.* When the pastor says, "Children are welcome," while glaring at parents whose children wriggle and talk, there is a contradiction between communication and metacommunication, communication being what is said, and metacommunication what is really meant. Metacommunication does not have to be nonverbal. Even without nonverbal cues, children generally know from the linguistic context when a parent's "maybe" means "no" and when it means "probably yes."[22] Metacommunication is rarely accidental. If paid singers try to teach a congregation to sing but without skill or commitment, so that the congregation is put off singing, the communication is "All may sing" and the metacommunication is "Don't sing, just listen." If the unstated goal of the musical leadership is to keep "quality" from being undermined by popular taste, the metacommunication is succeeding. Only if the goal of the worship system is "worship" and worship is defined as demanding participation is the singer's metacommunication a failure.[23]

This raises the scary possibility that the metacommunication of clunky prayers is functional, not merely inept. The communication that "Prayer is vitally important" or "How wonderful it is to be with God in prayer!" may cover a metacommunication that prayer is not supposed to be uplifting. Perhaps we bemoan the tedium while needing it to insulate us from holiness, so that we can pray to God while remaining untouched and unchanged. Or perhaps verbal clunkiness metacommunicates uncertainty about the value and meaning of prayer.

9. *Stock phrases and dormant metaphors have formative assumptions.* Like many other prayers, my composite presents an image of God at variance with the intent of its writer. Though it wishes to diversify from the image of God as Almighty King, the phrase "*merciful* God, we confess *before you*" implies entrance to a royal palace whose sovereign we have offended or a temporary appearance before an Other not otherwise present. The language then becomes more explicit, as

22 Ibid., 81–88, esp. 83.
23 Ibid., 85–86.

"we *come into your presence* . . . *emboldened* by the realization that *we stand before the Ruler of the nations.*" If we worship God in Christ as Immanuel, our Teacher, Friend, and Partner, transcendent yet encountered in the gathered community, we need language to match our conviction. Because "Let us pray" invites us to go with the flow of what follows, it is hard to "translate" a prayer whose language undermines our theology.

10. *Prayer language carries social presuppositions.* Though my composite prayer is communal ("*we* confess, *we* come," etc.), those who pray it are seen as autonomous selves with considerable freedom of choice. Their sin consists of actions or inaction for which they are personally responsible. They have failed to live rightly and blame themselves for everything: pride, selfishness, apathy, and being influenced by socially manufactured need. They even blame themselves for losing their sense of God's presence, as if such awareness depends not on God but on their faith and persistence. By feeding myths of autonomy, especially in middle-class settings, such prayers flagellate and depress us, yet fail to meet our needs. Confession of sin is more truthful and more liberating when it also laments our varied bondage to people, powers, stereotypes, and cultural and economic systems, and cries out for hope and deliverance.[24]

11. *Prayer language is limited by the writer's experience unless the writer has listened carefully to others.* Like the majority of prayers printed in standard liturgies and service books, my composite confession gestures a self formed by male conditioning and a stereotypical (though not necessarily actual) male experience. Thus, the selves in this prayer have a problem with pride (rebellion) but not with submissiveness, subordination, or passivity. They claim too much for themselves rather than needing help to avoid losing themselves in taking care of others. They have sinned boldly, not hidden themselves from God.[25]

---

[24] Though confession of sin serves as my case study, other categories need analysis, for example, thanksgiving, lament, petition, affirmation, and intercession.

[25] These and other insights of feminist theology need to be integrated into mainstream Christian prayer. See, for example, Mary Grey, *Feminist Redemption and the Christian Tradition* (Mystic, Conn.: Twenty-Third Publications, 1990); Susan Nelson Dunfee, *Beyond Servanthood: Christianity and the Liberation of Women*

12. *Prayer language should ensure that the congregation is gestured as praying to God, not delivering a sermon to itself.* Though the tailpiece to my composite prayer communicates that we are addressing God ("Help us to remember"), it metacommunicates a group wagging its collective finger at unspecified members who have forgotten their "blueprint" or scolding itself for not realizing that justice, peace, truth, and love are "more than words"—unless, that is, we expect a voice from heaven to answer by thundering "YES, THIS IS HOW YOU SHOULD REMEMBER!"

The above suggestions will serve their purpose if they evoke a "yes," "yes but," or "no" followed by other pertinent questions about the formative power of liturgical language. Having scrutinized prayer language, it is appropriate to conclude with prayer:

"Great Spirit, roam and reach
till we, who worship bring,
are touched by what we teach
and shaped by what we sing.
Disturbing Friend, yet welcome Guest,
be seen and heard
through table, word,
and people outcast and oppressed."[26]

(Brian Wren, © 1993, Hope Publishing Co. Reproduced by permission.)

(Lanham, Md.: University Press of America, 1989); and Valerie Saiving's pioneering essay "The Human Situation: A Feminine View" in *Womanspirit Rising: A Feminist Reader in Religion,* ed. Carol P. Christ and Judith Plaskow (New York: Harper & Row, 1979) 25–42.

[26] Brian Wren, *Piece Together Praise,* p. 76, no. 81.

Paul Westermeyer

Liturgical Music: *Soli Deo Gloria*

SOLI DEO GLORIA

Don Saliers, in the article that stimulates this Festschrift, said:

"When liturgy is regarded primarily as a means to moral exhortation or ethical motivation, it loses its essential character as praise, thanksgiving, and anamnetic enactment of the mystery of faith. Instrumentalist definitions of worship, whether Protestant or Roman Catholic, founder upon this rock."[1]

Don Saliers is not alone in this affirmation. At the risk, dear reader, of trying your patience, here are a series of quotations from other writers who make the same point. Let's start with William Willimon:

"Worship loses its integrity when it is regarded instrumentally as a means to something else—even as a means of achieving the most noble of human purposes. . . ."[2]

As if working off Saliers and Willimon, here's Harmon Smith:

". . . worship is not instrumental to any end other than the glory of God. It is, as the old formula puts it, *soli Deo gloria.*"[3]

That formula calls to mind J. S. Bach, whose ascription

---

[1] Don E. Saliers, "Liturgy and Ethics: Some New Beginnings," p. 33 above.

[2] William H. Willimon, *The Service of God: Christian Work and Worship* (Nashville: Abingdon Press, 1983) 42.

[3] Harmon L. Smith, *Where Two or Three Are Gathered: Liturgy and the Moral Life* (Cleveland: The Pilgrim Press, 1995) 135.

"'S.D.G.' at the end of his manuscripts was no empty formality . . . his aim in life was to compose and direct 'regulirte kirchen music zu Gottes Ehren[,]' well-regulated church music to the glory of God."[4]

Smith calls to mind Bach, but actually cited V. A. Demant, who said this:

". . . Christian worship—liturgical worship—has a meaning but no purpose. . . worship is the gathering up of all activities before God. In that sense it is purposeless. If we try to give it social purpose, we are destroying its nature."[5]

Patrick Miller was even more blunt:

". . . there is no more *useless* thing we do than praise God—*and that is the reason we do it.*"[6]

Aidan Kavanagh was equally blunt:

". . . educational and aesthetic fixes are not what liturgical worship is about. If one goes to liturgy for a discussion of current events or the latest ideology, one goes for the wrong reason. If one goes to liturgy for the organ prelude or choral anthem, one goes for the wrong reason. And once wrong reasons invade liturgy, or anything else for that matter, there is no end to it. For then all mutates into something else. . . ."[7]

And here's Marva Dawn, quoting Leander Keck:

"Since the worship of God is an end in itself, 'making worship useful destroys it, because this introduces an ulterior motive for praise. And ulterior motives mean manipulation, taking charge of the relation-

---

[4] Robin A. Leaver, ed., *J. S. Bach and Scripture: Glosses from the Calov Bible Commentary* (St. Louis: Concordia Publishing House, 1985) 107.

[5] Smith, 38.

[6] Patrick D. Miller, "The Psalms as Praise and Poetry," *The Hymn* 40:4 (October 1989) 15.

[7] Aidan Kavanagh, *Elements of Rite: A Handbook of Liturgical Style* (New York: Pueblo Publishing Company, 1982) 32.

ship, thereby turning the relation between creator and creature upside down.'"[8]

Both Smith and Miller realize how "startling" a claim like this is "to modern pragmatic and utilitarian ears,"[9] in a world that "measures activity by its usefulness and human worth by capabilities and accomplishments."[10] But if this logic is startling so far, look where it leads. "The *sound* of praise . . . is not speech but *music*," says Miller.[11] "Sing to the Lord a new song" means that

"singing psalms and hymns of praise and playing the organ, the flute, and the trumpet are among the definitive acts of obedience. So let the music of Bach and Handel, of Thomas Tallis and Heinrich Schuetz, John and Charles Wesley and Isaac Watts, Black spirituals and Plainsong, Ned Rorem and John Rutter ring in our churches. It will accomplish nothing. All it can do is express joy and give glory to God."[12]

It will accomplish nothing? Now we can see how truly startling this notion is. A series of the Church's teachers—in these instances from Methodist, Anglican, Lutheran, Presbyterian, and Roman Catholic backgrounds—say that Christian worship and the music in it are for the glory of God. The liturgy and its music are not means to ends. They accomplish nothing. We seldom hear such sentiments in our churches and schools today. We are most likely to consider worship and especially its music as a "tool," an evangelical tool, a means to evangelize, a social action tool, a means to get our language and thinking right, a tool for justice, a means to an end, almost always instrumental (in Saliers' sense, obviously, not in the sense of musical "instruments"), and certainly a way of accomplishing something. Not unlike the commercial culture all around us, worship and especially its music are for us the way you attract customers—"like flies," we

---

[8] Marva J. Dawn, *Reaching Out Without Dumbing Down: A Theology of Worship for Turn-of-the-Century Culture* (Grand Rapids: William B. Eerdmans Publishing Company, 1995) 88.

[9] Smith, 38.

[10] Miller, 15.

[11] Ibid.

[12] Ibid., 16. I take it that text writers like the Wesleys and Watts got into this list to make sure that the song of the people was included.

say. Music is the way you get your message across, get people to buy your product, convince, beat the competition, and always accomplish something.

Only the Glory of God?

One is immediately constrained to ask who is out of step. Does the position of Saliers and the other teachers cited above represent the position of the Church? Are worship and its music only for the glory of God and not a means to some other end? Or is the culturally conditioned way we talk about music in worship the more time-honored approach? Are worship and the music in worship indeed means to ends?

It could be argued that there are teachers of the Church who run counter to the noninstrumental view. Augustine, Calvin, and Wesley emphasized the capacity of music to move the human heart. Gelineau sees music as entry into the salvific mystery. Luther reveled in the capacity of music to carry words and thereby the work of God itself. He stimulated a whole string of composers—Bach among them with all his cantatas—who used music exegetically to break open and proclaim the word. Melva Costen links praise and empowerment. I have tried to assess the way the Church has used music and have concluded that it has been and still is quite properly used to bear the people's praise, prayer, proclamation, and story, and to articulate time in our worship. Are these not all examples of using music as a means to an end?

Liturgical Music

Now, for the moment at least, let us defer that question and come back to it after we isolate our topic more precisely. My assignment is to consider liturgical music. Such music is obviously closely related to the texts it carries and surrounds but since it is not the same as those texts and since the assignment here is about music, let us bracket out the texts insofar as possible and restrict our considerations to music itself.

I am assuming that the above logic is correct, that saying liturgy is not instrumental leads you to say that the music of the liturgy is not instrumental either. Let us bracket out the underlying question about liturgy, therefore, and restrict our discussion again, insofar as possible, to questions specifically about music.

Since the context for this discussion has to do with ethics, we could proceed in a number of ways. One would be to ask about the relationship of music to human harmony or shalom.[13] Another would be to ask about the reverse, the relationship of music to violence, pressing especially in this case beyond liturgical music.[14] Yet another would be to probe the relationship of music to the emotions and to time.[15] Here I propose to pursue none of those avenues but to ask the question that has just been deferred, that is, about the utility or instrumentality of liturgical music to some end.

IS THERE ANOTHER ALTERNATIVE?

Every time the question of the role of music in worship is raised, almost invariably only two possibilities are presumed to exist. One is to treat music as a tool, a means to an end. Then we get descriptions of, discussions about, or conferences that consider music as a "tool" for a wide variety of sometimes competing purposes, like the ones I mentioned earlier—evangelism, education, therapy, entertainment, raising our consciousness, inclusivity, teaching, promoting artistic standards, justice, attracting people to a cause, ecumenism, multicultural intentions, etc.

It is usually assumed that the only alternative to such a use is to treat music as an aesthetic reality. Here we are told music is for itself, art for art's sake. It has no utility, no instrumentality. Music is just there. We may be grasped by it, it may even be revelatory, but it has no purpose except to be. This sounds at first blush like what Miller was saying, but it is not. Is there another alternative?

[13] See Quentin Faulkner, *Wiser Than Despair: The Evolution of Ideas in the Relationship of Music to the Christian Church* (Westport, Conn.: Greenwood Press, 1996), esp. 38, 65–68, and 99–105.

[14] I attempted to do this in "Dissonance and Discordance, Consonance and Concordance: An Analysis of Late 20th Century Music as Endemic of a Violent Society?" *Review and Expositor* 93:4 (Fall 1996) 465–483.

[15] I have tried to do this in chapter 4, "Context," of *Let Justice Sing: Hymnody and Justice* (Collegeville, Minn.: The Liturgical Press, 1998).

I think the answer is yes. The other alternative is the startling answer the Church at its best—"at full stretch"—always gives. This alternative begins with *Deo*, "to God."

DEO

Saliers describes the "essential character" of liturgy as "praise, thanksgiving, and anamnetic enactment of the mystery of faith." The direction of all of that is *Deo*, "to God," and *Deo* for the Christian is through the Cross of Christ, which "gems the middle."[16] I take it, therefore, that Don Saliers means to say that he, all the rest of us, and indeed the whole creation praises, gives thanks, and remembers what God has done and does, in a welcoming circle open to the suffering of the world,[17] around and under the Cross of Christ. In the words of Demant, "worship is the gathering up of all activities [and we may add by implication all people, all things] before God."

That is, we come to worship, as Ken Medema forcefully reminds us, to bring offering. But, lo and behold—and now comes the really startling reality—the Father in Christ through the Spirit greets us and offers us the very self of God. In word and sacrament we receive new life, are adopted as daughters and sons, engrafted into the vine, made Christ's body. We gather, we welcome, we confess, we speak, we hear, we sing, we bathe, we pray, we greet, we bring offering, we remember, we eat, we go. None of that has any purpose except the glory of God. None of that accomplishes anything or gets us anything. God in Christ, out of sheer goodness and grace, turns everything upside down, or, more precisely, turns everything right-side up so that the relation between Creator and creature is "righted," comes to us, graces us. All is of God, all is for God, all is from God. We, having received, are called to be what we are, Christ's broken body in the world.

---

[16] Henry Harbaugh, "The Mystic Weaver," *Poems* (Philadelphia: Lindsay & Blakiston, 1860) 20. This poem seems to deny Harbaugh's best instincts and theological underpinnings by making humanity too puppetlike, but the Christocentric orientation of history around the Cross of Christ is a historic Christian insight.

[17] See Gordon Lathrop, *Holy Things: A Liturgical Theology* (Minneapolis: Fortress Press, 1993) 109.

As for music, it is no tool to get us anything or to get God or anybody else to do something, nor does it exist as an aesthetic entity for its own sake. Those alternatives turn out to be but two sides of the same human coin that has written on it "divorced from God." The first is the idolatry of our manipulation or tyranny, the second the idolatry of music itself. In the startling economy of the Church, music gathers around the Cross of Christ with the rest of creation and gives glory *Deo*, "to God." It, like all the rest, is simply offered to God and accomplishes nothing. And, lo and behold, God turns out to be not only the preacher and the host but the initiator of the dialogue and the chief singer.

GOING BACK

A few paragraphs back we left Augustine, Calvin, Wesley, Gelineau, Luther, Costen, and myself as possible witnesses against what I have just been saying. Are they? Let us see. Let us follow a stream of consciousness in which Augustine, Calvin, Wesley, and Gelineau put some issues into play. Following that, we'll get Luther, Costen, and others in on the conversation.

Augustine, John Calvin, and John Wesley all realized how powerful music is. Calvin put it quite succinctly: ". . . there is scarcely in the world anything which is more able to turn or bend this way and that the morals of men . . . it has a secret and almost incredible power to move hearts in one way or another."[18] Did that realization lead these three teachers of the Church to view music as a means to an end? If so, they certainly differed from late twentieth-century views of this matter. What we hear among us is that music needs to be made as attractive as possible to convince people. It is a tool that should not be throttled by any restrictions at all. Augustine, Calvin, and Wesley, however, moved in precisely the opposite direction.

Augustine toyed with Athanasius's apparent restriction of making song as close to speech as possible. He was worried about staring at music and missing the Word. He seemed to say that you have to wean yourself from music so that its power does not get in the way. For him the words breathed life and truth, not the music. He was

---

[18] Charles Garside, "Calvin's Preface to the Psalter: A Reappraisal," *The Musical Quarterly* 37 (October 1951) 570.

willing to use music in church because it was associated with the words, not because words were associated with the music.[19] *Deo* was first for Augustine, or, as Gordon Lathrop might say, music, like all things, has to be broken to the Word.[20]

The same brokenness to the Word was there for Calvin. He achieved it by restricting liturgical music to syllabic monophony and distinguishing it from the music that might be used outside worship. Calvin considered that the music one uses at home to entertain friends could be "light" and "frivolous," but music for the psalms that are sung "in the Church in the presence of God" had to have "weight" and "majesty."[21] This position led to Genevan psalm tunes, the characteristic liturgical music of the Calvinist tradition. Metrical psalms were set syllabically and sung to a monophonic line, without polyphony, without instruments, and without choirs except as a practiced group (of children) supported the congregation's unison singing.

Wesley, though he was not consistent about this, reacted against the contrapuntal music of his age with ancient monophony as his ideal.[22] He was not happy with "appointing different words to be sung by different persons at the same time!"[23] He was shocked that "this astonishing jargon has found a place even in the worship of God!"[24] Whether one can say that Wesley, like Augustine and Calvin, had a notion of music's brokenness to the Word is not yet clear to me, but he certainly introduced a restrictive note. If Saliers is where Wesley comes out, however, we may have a clue about this.

---

[19] See the famous convoluted yet perceptive passage from Augustine, *Confessions*, X.33 A translation by F. J. Sheed (1943) can be found in Erik Routley, *The Church and Music: An Inquiry into the History, the Nature, and the Scope of Christian Judgment on Music* (London: Gerald Duckworth & Co., 1950) 233–234. Another translation, by R. S. Pine-Coffin, is given in Faulkner, 59.

[20] See Lathrop, 27–31.

[21] Garside, 568.

[22] Carlton R. Young, *Music of the Heart: John and Charles Wesley on Music and Musicians* (Carol Stream, Ill.: Hope Publishing Company, 1995) 91, says, "For all his complaining about counterpoint, it is used in the anthems that Wesley included in the 1788 edition of *Sacred Harmony*." (*Sacred Harmony* was a tune book, first published in 1780.)

[23] John Wesley, "Thoughts on the Power of Music," in Young, 87.

[24] Ibid.

But Saliers is not only Wesley's heir. We have to move to another slice of the Church's heritage to get the broader context to which Saliers is responsive. Let's take Joseph Gelineau, speaking for the "catholic" tradition after the Reformation, not before it like Augustine. Augustine, Calvin, and Wesley may well be grouped together in H. Richard Niebuhr's category "Christ the Transformer of Culture."[25] Joseph Gelineau doesn't fit that category. He is best described by Niebuhr's category "Christ Above Culture." He is similar to the other three, however, in that he introduces restrictions.

"In the celebration of the Church's worship," says Gelineau, "the point at issue is not 'music-making,' but entry, by means of music, into the salvific mystery."[26] This may appear to mean that music is a tool or a means to an end, but if the term "tool" can even be applied to Gelineau, he thoroughly redefines it in the context of nature leading to grace. After asserting that music is divine—"God's daughter"— and song signifies "a reality which is not heard," Gelineau asks, "How, in a word, can singing be a mystery?" Here is his answer:

"To understand this we must first recall the natural significance of song in human life. We know from the Christian revelation that grace does not take the place of nature, but completes and fulfills it. Nothing can be a sign from God unless it has some meaning for [humanity]. However, though nature can give some presentiment of the divine, she cannot impart it; only God can communicate what is divine. And so, in the history of salvation, song takes on a significance deeper than the merely natural. . . ."[27]

Brokenness does not quite describe Gelineau's image, which is more like organic connectedness from the human to the divine. Those of us who stand in a Pauline-Lutheran heritage or resonate to the Kierkegaardian-Barthian qualitative gap between God and humanity[28] can easily perceive human merit in these words and be

[25] See H. Richard Niebuhr, *Christ and Culture* (New York: Harper & Row, 1951).

[26] Joseph Gelineau, trans. Clifford Howell, *Voices and Instruments in Christian Worship: Principles, Laws, Applications* (Collegeville, Minn.: The Liturgical Press, 1964) 10.

[27] Ibid., 14–15.

[28] For Saliers' dialogue with Karl Barth, see Don E. Saliers, *Worship as Theology: Foretaste of Glory Divine* (Nashville: Abingdon Press, 1994), chap. 4. See also Don

put off, but we need to hear that Gelineau says what we want to say: God is the communicator and only communicator of the divine, not music or anything we do. And note the parallel to Augustine, Calvin, and Wesley: Gelineau also introduces restrictions into liturgical music. In Gelineau's case, they are detailed ones comprising two categories: (1) the Church's practice and law or customs that have the force of law, and (2) artistic worth.[29]

Regarding the second of these, artistic worth, Gelineau says, "For it is only by its beauty that music can signify the sacred."[30] That leads to some aesthetic considerations and, curiously enough, back to Wesley via Erik Routley's assessment: "Wesleyan hymnody . . . shared with the universal church the conviction that music acts upon the singer with an effect corresponding in benefit to the integrity of the music."[31]

LUTHER

Luther, who fits yet a third of Niebuhr's categories—Christ and Culture in Paradox[32]—was also concerned about "artistic worth" or "the integrity of the music." He was overwhelmed by God's incredible gift of music, then emphasized humanity's responsibility to craft the gift.

". . . when [musical] learning is added . . . and artistic music which corrects, develops, and refines the natural music, then at last it is possible to taste with wonder (yet not to comprehend) God's absolute and perfect wisdom in his wondrous work of music."[33]

E. Saliers, "Prayer and Theology in Karl Barth," in Karl Barth, *Prayer*, 2nd ed., ed. Don E. Saliers (Philadelphia: Westminster Press, 1986) 9–20.

[29] Gelineau, 10.

[30] Ibid.

[31] Routley, 161.

[32] Niebuhr has two more categories: Christ of Culture and Christ Against Culture. These two are not relevant to liturgical music. The first turns music of worship into the culture and thereby destroys it, and the second writes it off altogether like Ulrich Zwingli or makes it esoteric like the Shakers.

[33] Martin Luther, "Preface to Georg Rhau's Symphoniae iucundae, 1538," trans. Ulrich S. Leupold, in *Luther's Works: Liturgy and Hymns* (LW), vol. 53, ed. Ulrich S. Leupold (Philadelphia: Fortress Press, 1965) 324.

Martin Luther, like Calvin, knew how this gift "of nature and art" could be "prostituted" by "perverted minds . . . with their erotic rantings."[34] This might imply restrictions, but these are of the "love-God-neighbor-do-as-you-please" kind. Luther never stayed with the perversion of music very long but fastened on its gift and goodness. He was not nervous about music like Augustine and Calvin and, apart from his concern for the finest crafting, never restricted it. He welcomed monophony, polyphony, instruments, folk art, high art, chant, derivatives of the Minnesingers and Meistersingers, old pieces, newly composed pieces, etc.

If anything, however, he emphasized the capacity of music to carry words and thereby the Word of God even more strongly than Augustine, Calvin, Wesley, and Gelineau did. "God," said Luther, has "preached the Gospel through music too. . . ."[35] Luther, it might seem, most clearly treated music as a tool, a means to an end.

In fact, if anybody did *not* treat music as a means to an end, it was Luther. As Philip Watson said of Luther, human beings are "in no sense in control of God, nor, it can be added, does God force Himself upon" us. "Neither the Word nor the signs furnish a coercive demonstration of the Divine presence and will. Yet in and through them God quite really confronts [us] with the inescapable alternative of faith or unbelief."[36]

Neither music nor anything else is a tool in human hands to confront us with God. God addresses us, God's word has free course among us, God's Word will do it, and "the supreme test of [Luther's] and all other doctrines [was] whether they set forth the glory of God alone.[37] Like Augustine, music was associated with the Word for Luther, or, as he said, it is next to the Word of God,[38] not the reverse.

---

[34] Ibid.

[35] *Luther's Works: Table Talk*, vol. 54 (Philadelphia: Fortress Press, 1967) 129. Luther continued with Josquin as example, like this: "as may be seen in Josquin, all of whose compositions flow freely, gently, and cheerfully, are not forced or cramped by rules, and are like the song of the finch."

[36] Philip S. Watson, *Let God Be God! An Interpretation of the Theology of Martin Luther* (Philadelphia: Fortress Books, 1947) 166.

[37] Ibid., 14.

[38] LW 53, p. 323. Of course, the Word of God is Christocentric. See Watson, 149ff.

If music is not a tool to convert us and only the Word of God can do that, is music, then, a tool to empower us? Melva Costen would seem to suggest such a thing when she speaks of worship as "both praise and empowerment."[39] Jon Michael Spencer's title *Protest and Praise* seems to express the same idea.[40] James Cone even says: "Black music is functional. Its purposes and aims are directly related to the consciousness of the black community. To be functional is to be useful in community definition, style, and movement."[41]

It's not only the African American community that knows of the power of worship and its music. Kavanagh realizes that at its heart worship is a critic of culture[42] and slays "the Trendy."[43] Marva Dawn speaks of worship as a "subversive act,"[44] and Lathrop knows that "lament . . . will ultimately undermine the most determined tyranny."[45]

Is the music of worship a tool them? Listen to James Cone again:

"At Macedonia A. M. E. Church, the Spirit of God was no abstract concept, no vague perception of philosophical speculation. The Spirit was the 'power of God unto salvation,' that 'wheel in the middle of the wheel.' The Spirit was God himself breaking into the lives of the people, 'buildin' them up where they were torn down and proppin' them up on every leanin' side.' The Spirit was God's presence with the people and his will to provide them with the courage and strength to make it through. And the people thanked him for his presence and renewed weekly their covenant to 'hold out to the end.'"[46]

---

[39] Melva Wilson Costen, *African American Christian Worship* (Nashville: Abingdon Press, 1993) 120.

[40] Jon Michael Spencer, *Protest and Praise: Sacred Music of Black Religion* (Minneapolis: Fortress Press, 1990).

[41] James H. Cone, *The Spiritual and the Blues: An Interpretation* (New York: Seabury Press, 1972) 5.

[42] Kavanagh, 32.

[43] Ibid., 104.

[44] Dawn, 57f.

[45] Lathrop, 213.

[46] Cone, 2.

There is no sense of music as tool here. The folks in this description didn't have God in their pocket any more than Luther did.[47] To read through the texts of Afro-American spirituals is to get exactly the same impression as Cone gives, page after page.[48] God in Christ is the liberator.[49] This is "soli Deo gloria," and, as usual, music expresses it. Music accomplishes nothing. God does.

Roll Down, Justice

"Elite groups" that claim "the power to interpret the whole religious tradition, the consciences and behavior of believers, through their regulation of morality, spirituality, and theology"[50] present a very different picture from the essence of Macedonia A. M. E. Church, Augustine's fifth-century North Africa, sixteenth-century Wittenberg and Geneva (the essence, remember!), or the breadth of practice to which Wesley leads and Gelineau points. When "elite groups" also control "access to the experience of community rituals of major spiritual significance," Rosemary Haughton, in a book dedicated to Don Saliers, is constrained to speak of "the social injustice of liturgy."[51] She notes that it was precisely this kind of experience that provoked the prophetic criticism of Jesus and the prophets. "I hate, I despise your festivals. . . . Take away from me the noise of your songs . . . let justice roll down like waters," thundered Amos.[52] Music is clearly included in the prophetic rebuke.

The form of the prophetic rebuke is itself musical, however. The things themselves—worship and its music—are not bad, but, as usual, our misuse and perversion of them are the problem. That is not permission to take the rebuke lightly. The message the music carries is indeed its own subversive burn on our perverse and unjust ways. To sing a song of justice in the midst of the practice of injustice

[47] See Watson, 90.
[48] Erskine Peters, ed., *Lyrics of the Afro-American Spiritual: A Documentary Collection* (Westport, Conn.: Greenwood Press, 1993).
[49] Cone, 34–57.
[50] Rosemary Haughton, "The Spirituality of Injustice," *To Do Justice and Right Upon the Earth: Papers from the Virgil Michel Symposium on Liturgy and Social Justice* (Collegeville, Minn.: The Liturgical Press, 1993) 8.
[51] Ibid., 8.
[52] Amos 5:21a, 23a, 24a.

is to turn liturgical music into noise. The prophetic rebuke turns it back to silence. It must. To be what we are as the Body of Christ is to do justice. To do injustice is to deny what we are and to turn the song into a cacophonous nightmare whose end is destruction and the silence that follows the crash.

But, lest we forget, the song is *Deo* not only of justice but even more of mercy. We are always unjust and God loves us anyway. There are times when the song needs to be silenced, as in the face of slavery, the Holocaust, apartheid, unrepentant abuse. But not all details of wrong are occasions for silence. If that were the case, we would never sing. Repentance is part of the song, as are the healing mercy, love, and grace of God.

IN CHRIST

Repentance is part of remembering. Remembering is not only related to our misdeeds, however, but to the broader "anamnetic enactment of the mystery of faith" in God and God's forgiveness. Confession and the anamnesis itself can be located at quite specific points in the service, but they take place broadly within the whole "anamnetic enactment," which, like faith itself, is God's gift. This whole is articulated by our praise, prayer, proclamation, and story— and carried by music.[53] Music is mnemonic, which in part explains its relation to worship.

Is music a tool then, especially considering its mnemonic capacity, to sell others on our worship, on Christ, or on some good Christ would have us do? No. The anamnetic enactment is in Christ, not in us or in our music. Liturgical music accompanies, even participates in, the anamnetic enactment and is its handmaiden, but it is always broken to God in Christ. The music serves and loves the neighbor[54] by growing out of the people's song and leading to choral and instrumental forces around that "popular" center. It does this freely, not as a tool of control—at its most energetic pulsing; most relaxed flow;

---

[53] Paul Westermeyer, *The Church Musician* , revised edition (Minneapolis: Augsburg Fortress, 1997) 31–35.
[54] J. S. Bach got it right. He dedicated his *Orgelbuechlein* like this: "Dem Hoechsten Gott allein zu Ehren, Dem Nechsten, draus sich zu belehren" ("To the highest God alone be glory, To my neighbor, thence to be instructed.") Service to the neighbor grows out of *Soli Deo Gloria* through one's vocation.

loudest wail or praise; quietest cry or shalom; densest counterpoint or homophony; leanest monophony; in tonal, polytonal, or atonal ways; in art or folk character; originating in many cultures and peoples; with a vocal center and instrumental (here, only here, meaning "musical instruments") adornment; in chant to jazz idioms.

Music is also gift,[55] and its crafting is important. Does that suggest that liturgical music is fundamentally aesthetic? No. Gelineau, Routley, and Luther are certainly right about beauty, integrity, and craft in relation to the music of worship. One could not imagine otherwise, given the importance of worship to human life, where humanity's true being is revealed. But the aesthetic gift itself is in Christ the Word, without whom, as John (1:3) says, "was not anything made that was made."

ALLELUIA

Saliers likes to quote William Inge's observation that "the church that marries the spirit of an age becomes a widow in the next generation."[56] That allusion follows the portion of his paragraph that begins this chapter [57] and suggests that definitions of worship which regard its music as tool or independent aesthetic reality leave succeeding generations a hopeless emptiness. Aesthetic realities once were in vogue but now have left their heirs floundering. Tools have been the trend before and are now attractive, but they have lost their appeal before and will soon lose it again.

That is, all our schemes and words finally fail. An Alleluia endures. As Miller reminds us, "the sound of praise," by which I understand all the sounds of worship—of praise, prayer, proclamation, story, accompaniment of the pilgrim people in procession—"is not *speech*, but *music*."[58] As Miller also says, the call of Psalm 150 at the end of the Psalter for everything to praise the Lord is not just a literary device but the goal toward which the whole cosmos is moving.[59]

---

[55] Westermeyer, 36f.

[56] Don E. Saliers, "Contemporary/Traditional: The Dilemma of the Church Today," *The Covenant Companion*, vol. 85, no. 1 (January 1996) 19.

[57] Saliers, "Liturgy and Ethics," p. 33 above.

[58] See footnotes 11 and 6 above.

[59] Miller, 15.

Or, as Saliers puts it in a thesis sentence, "Christian liturgy as rite and as prayer is thoroughly eschatological."[60] And music is both its handmaiden and its *telos*.

Across time and beyond time we gather around and under the Cross in a circle open to the world's suffering, singing Alleluia *soli Deo gloria*, acknowledging with gratitude those who have led us there, among them a teacher named *Saliers*.

---

[60] Saliers, *Worship as Theology*, 14.

Don E. Saliers

Afterword: Liturgy and Ethics Revisited

In an autobiographical essay, "A Confession," Leo Tolstoy tells how a friend told him how he stopped believing the Christian faith:

"On a hunting expedition, when he was already twenty-six, he once, at the place where they put up for the night, knelt down in the evening to pray—a habit retained from childhood. His elder brother, who was at the hunt with him, was lying on some hay and watching him. When the younger man had finished and was settling down for the night, his brother said to him: 'So you still do that?'

"They said nothing more to one another. But from that day he ceased to say his prayers or go to church. And now he has not prayed, received communion, or gone to church for thirty years. And this is not because he knows his brother's convictions and has joined him in them, nor because he has decided anything on his own but simply because the word spoken by his brother was like the push of a finger on a wall that was ready to fall by its own weight."[1]

This story has haunted me since first reading it nearly forty years ago. It strikes close to home for many who find their inherited liturgical and devotional religious practices suddenly empty. Religious ritual that lacks connection with real life—and the questions of how we should live—is like a carefully preserved house of cards in the wind. Soon or late, when worship becomes disconnected from how and why we live, difficult questions will be put to religious believers. The moral perplexities and sheer anguish over human suffering and

---

[1] Leo Tolstoy, *A Confession: The Gospel in Brief, and What I Believe,* trans. Aylmer Maude (London: Oxford University Press, 1974, © 1940).

oppression broadcast to us daily are a storm wind lashing against the liturgical complacencies in so many of the churches.

At the same time, for increasing numbers of people in North American society, ethical questions and moral discourse take place without reference to religious practices such as devotional prayer or public worship. Many competing ethical viewpoints and theoretical frameworks vie for attention. My concern as a Christian believer and theologian is with the struggle to live faithfully in light of what the worship of God implies and to interpret human life liturgically. I am convinced that religious practices have a profound bearing upon ethics and the moral life. Such a conviction is both more ambitious and more ambiguous than I first thought.

Questions about the *conditions* that generate and nurture human moral awareness keep drawing me back to questions about relationships between worship of God and life together as a community. Part of the task of liturgical theology, I contend, is to give an account of these relationships. What is it about a human gathering to read and proclaim stories of God in Hebrew and Christian Scripture, to sing and pray, and to feast together at a common table that motivates and empowers goodness, mercy, and justice? According to those very Scriptures, there *ought* to be a profound inner connection between worship and service, between love of God and love of neighbor, between our prayer and the lived pattern of moral life. But is this so? How is this so? Can it still be so in a contemporary situation that confronts us with seemingly endless moral ambiguity, indeed, with the suspicion of liturgy itself?

Attempts to interpret relationships between the "cultic" and "ethical" dimensions of Judaism and Christianity have a long history. My original essay was written in a time when it seemed crucial to restate, in a fresh programmatic way, the role liturgy plays in shaping a community of moral discourse. My hunch was that such a restatement would best focus on character ethics and the formation of the moral self-in-community rather than on the ethics of obligation. But today I am aware of a host of questions and issues just vaguely on the horizon of my thinking nearly twenty years ago. Insistent voices have questioned some key assumptions made in that essay.[2] These ques-

---

[2] Several lines of critique have already reshaped my thinking, as may be seen especially in chapter 11, "For the Sake of the World: Liturgy and Ethics," in my

tions must be met honestly by liturgical theology now and in the future, as several of the essays in this volume have already shown. The vulnerability of my original proposals also may allow me to see something of the promissory notes made there for work at the intersection of moral theology, liturgical studies, and Christian ethics.

I

Four major clusters of questions face any attempt to clarify the interrelatedness of liturgy and ethics. First, the "postmodernists" have resisted and often denied the possibility of any claims about a singular set of Christian liturgical practices that form moral character. Some of them see any attempt, such as I proposed—following points made by Stanley Hauerwas and others—as automatically doomed to "totalizing" only one *particular "reading"* of Scripture and tradition. If Christian moral intention and action are embedded in a form of life "portrayed and shaped by the whole biblical story," one should be able to give some satisfactory account of this. At least one should say *whose* version of the "whole" is appealed to. This is the first point of vulnerability in such a programmatic effort. What is to prevent an appeal to "the whole story" from masking cultural/liturgical imperialism—the imposition of a partial and culturally embedded view of liturgical formation on Christian communities that have very different views of the "whole story"? In one sense, nothing. There will always be such a risk in linking liturgy to ethics this way precisely because "liturgy" is always itself a culturally embodied and embedded communal action. Appeals to liturgy in the abstract are of little use when we want to know how a particular community is empowered by worship to a be a community of Christian character.

Yet, analogous to the question of what constitutes the core literature taken as revelatory, that is, the "canon of Scripture," we can ask, What constitutes a continuity of identity in Christian worship? One way or another, worshiping communities settle on basic actions and certain core narratives in their practice of Christian worship. No matter how "open textured" the canonical set may be, the question of what makes our worship "Christian" is asked, implicitly or explicitly.

Worship As Theology: Foretaste of Glory Divine (Nashville: Abingdon Press, 1994) 171–190, and *Worship Come to Its Senses* (Nashville: Abingdon Press, 1996).

A phenomenological description of how various communities worship first impresses me with *differences,* not only in order, style, and performance but also in the particular scriptural center of gravity found in hymns, prayers, and sermons. These do in fact account for differences in types of spiritualities or in particular moral/ethical styles of being Christian in the world. One thinks of the remarkable social justice witness of the Quakers and, say, the French Huguenots. Their worship styles differ greatly from that of Anglicans or Romanian Orthodox Christians. None of these differences, nor the conflict of interpretations among traditions, ought to be denied. Yet each is formed by its own history of practices—including a select range of "canonical Scriptures" that shape the moral disposition of that community in a particular way. Some traditions have been driven to radical breaks with the antecedent "received" set of dominant narratives and practices in order to be faithful to what is perceived as normative.

Any liturgical theology worth its salt in our present understanding of religious praxis begins with such rich differences. None of our traditions are static. New historical periods bring shifts in focus in the appropriation of moral norms from Scripture, and hence shifts in understandings of what the central Christian message and way of life is. Still, some sort of selective range out of a canon marks the change, especially when challenges about the way we worship arise from shifting perceptions of moral ends and means in society.

At the same time, I am deeply impressed with the extraordinary persistence of what may be called canonical elements and structures across cultures and historical periods.[3] Looking at the first five or six centuries across Christianity in Jerusalem, Asia Minor, East and West Syria, Alexandria, North Africa, Rome, northern Europe and Southwest Asia, one is struck by the appearance in all those culturally diverse forms of worship of the following elements: (1) patterns of initiation that focus on the life, teachings, suffering death and resurrection of Jesus, culminating in the water-bath and anointing in his name; (2) a holy meal in which the central prayer-action remembers a selective narrative of what Jesus said and did; (3) some form of daily prayer characteristically using the Hebrew psalms now "heard" in

---

[3] Here it is clear that I differ from my good friend and colleague James White, at least from the minimalist tone and trajectory of his essay in this volume.

light of claims about Jesus as the Messiah; (4) certain rhythms of the week (oriented on the "Lord's Day" with its eschatological promise), the day, and the year (with its principal feasts and associated Scriptures); and (5) rites of healing, forgiveness, burial, and setting aside leaders.

These great liturgical families each were formed by the act of selective remembering of the promises of God. The anamnetic force of liturgical participation focused some central stories of what Jesus said and did. This was especially true of the great feasts of Easter, Pentecost, and Epiphany that set specific scriptures, such as the passion narratives and the nativity stories, with the Eucharist and with baptismal rites.[4] Each cultural setting brought its own distinctive modes of communication and appropriation into play in these structures. Yet not all such Christian liturgical families understood fully the stories nor fully lived out the dispositions, affections, and patterns of community signified and elicited by the rites. Each variety of Christian worshiping community struggled with being faithful. Each worshiping community discovered that liturgy itself as cultic performance was not enough. Could the canonical elements themselves carry a prophetic critique of the particular cultural formation of behavior generated by the book, the table, and the place of the water-bath around which the community gathered?

This means that, in addition to criticizing the search for something common, we must also see that Christian liturgy in every culture and historical period does not simply absorb local culture. It also may criticize specific behaviors and even sub-liturgical practices discerned as incompatible with faithful worship of the God of Israel and of Jesus Christ. That liturgical imperialism has been and is still a problem is clear. That Christian communities have differed widely in what is taken to be normative in Scripture and in liturgical practice is now obvious. But neither should we deny that certain persistent practices, with their overlapping narratives (one might speak of these as "family resemblance stories"), make it possible for communities of

---

[4] The writings of Gordon Lathrop and Gail Ramshaw have been especially important on this topic in the past ten years. See their essays in this volume and *Holy Things: A Liturgical Theology* by Gordon W. Lathrop (Minneapolis: Fortress Press, 1993); and Gail Ramshaw's series *Words Around the Fire*, *Words Around the Font* and *Words Around the Table* (Chicago: Liturgy Training Publications, 1990, 1991, 1994).

worshiping Christians to rediscover, over time, a prophetic and potentially self-corrective vision of the world. This is exactly what is occurring in our period of liturgical reform and renewal, with all its attendant confusions and cultural captivities.

A second cluster of issues has come from liberationist critiques of Christian worship. Much has been written on how worship is continually being used to reinforce the political and ethical status quo. Here one thinks of the strong voices of feminist and womanist lines of critique concerning the injustice of patriarchal and hierarchical practices in many Christian liturgical traditions. Any "conceptual" account of relationships between liturgy and ethics appears to overlook the "ethics of the liturgy" itself. Here we must study how, in fact, particular Christian communities have domesticated Christian worship. As Johannes Metz has observed, Christian worship is often a kind of "eulogistic evasion of what really matters." Feminist theologians such as Marjorie Procter-Smith, Rosemary Ruether, and Elizabeth Schüssler-Fiorenza have raised questions about how liturgy actually *malforms* a community of moral discourse. Such lines of suspicion are grounded in an acute awareness of gender, racial, and social/economic class differences.

So much of the actual practice in Church life warrants suspicion of any easy normative theological reading of Christian liturgy as morally formative. The only way forward is to proceed with a detailed study and analysis of actual communities in their specific social/political context. Again, several essays in this volume suggest that only by a detailed examination of the actual practices can we understand how and why Christian communities are formed—for good or for ill. Because liturgical study of local worshiping assemblies is now aware of the dimensions of power, explicit and implicit, in any such gathering, the picture of the formative and expressive power of liturgy to form character is made more truthful and complex. The "formative" and "expressive" power of liturgy is always in context of both use and abuse.

These lines of critique have opened our eyes and ears to the ambiguity of liturgical formation. Yet, I find in liberationist moral and political critiques of Christian liturgy that the question of what "ought" to be formed does not disappear. Liturgical theology suffers when it fails to acknowledge "hidden" power issues and the malformative histories of practice. The *point* of normative questions, that is, what moral dispositions and ethical intention-action behaviors *ought* to be formed in us by liturgical celebrations of the teaching, life, death, and resurrection of Christ, can only be discerned when we gain an adequate descriptive account of what *actually* takes place.

Yet the normative questions persist. To worship God in the name of Jesus and to invoke the Spirit of God upon the assembly itself is a risk-taking act, whatever the oppressive history of its practice. The worship of God raises the question, suddenly or slowly, "How ought we to live?" just as the people of Jerusalem, hearing the first sermon of Peter, asked, "What shall we do?" The "ought" question itself signals the interrelatedness of the cultic and social/ethical features implied in the root meaning of "liturgy"—the whole "work of the people." Thus Paul, writing to the Roman church, could admonish them to present themselves as living worship to God.

It is difficult for those who have not participated in a service of worship that generates awe, wonder, lamentation, release, and thankful joy to be convinced that Christian liturgy could make a difference in the way worshipers live. To this point we must return in considering levels of symbolic participation.

A third set of issues concerns the one-sided emphasis on texts and textuality. In the past twenty years liturgical studies themselves have moved from a primarily textual orientation to more contextual, nonverbal, ritual, and performative orientation. Even though I hinted at these matters in the earlier version of the essay, I now would urge a stronger emphasis on how nonverbal aspects of liturgy are formative. It now makes far less sense to speak of our affections, attitudes, and intentions being formed only by texts (the narratives). The fundamental weakness in overly textual accounts of formation lies in their exaggerated cognitivity. Put more sharply, primary affections such as awe in the presence of God, delight in the created order, gratitude for life, and compassion for neighbor require a human ethos of respect, care, hospitality, inclusion, and the like. Beautiful and theologically "correct" texts may too easily be surrounded by means of communication in the liturgy that contradict the very teachings and stories about God's mercy, justice, and love that are ingredient in the Scriptures read and prayers prayed.

If we are to speak of allowing liturgy to shape our common life and intentions for good, we must face these problems squarely. If someone has suffered abuse from an alcoholic father and, in a period of sobriety, the father says, "Come here, I love you," ambivalence and suspicion are understandable. In fact, they are required. In our time we would say it would be foolish to trust him. What would it take for the father to gain once again the child's trust? What does it take for an individual or a group who have been alienated by "oppressive" features of Christian public worship to once again allow the liturgy to shape their lives? No general answer is available. But if the "abuses" can be held together in tension with the actual character of what it is to receive life as gift and to hold all life up to God who calls for justice and mercy, then conditions of perception are altered. The "abuses" are named for what they are because we see what ought to be in light of being created for one another in honor, respect, and love. Here the "ought" is itself a function of specific teachings of and about Jesus of Nazareth that form a normative core for assessing other teachings and stories. But these teachings are themselves embedded in ritual actions around prayer, a common meal, praise, confession, and other specific elements of worship.

Comparing liturgy to an abusive father is no casual analogy. Abuses do not teach uses. Naming liturgical "oppressions," however, highlights the vulnerability of Christian worship to immoral and unethical captivities. In part this means that formation of character requires some attention to "obligation" and command. The canon of Scripture at the heart of liturgical practice must come under reflective scrutiny here. We must specify the conditions of continual reform of the liturgy. How does Christian worship *in this particular social/cultural context* bear the seeds of its own self-critique? This question, requiring more extensive exposition and argumentation than can be provided here, is crucial to the task of liturgical theology today and tomorrow.

If the actual living performative event of a specific local community is to be taken seriously, then a phenomenological or empirical description of how the community actually thinks, feels, behaves, and makes moral judgments would seem to be essential.

Finally, a range of questions have been raised about how mass media, social rituals, and "lifestyle" options imaged in a consumerist society are far more powerfully formative of habit, perception, and moral character than are religious practices found in Christian liturgy. Does not meaning-making surrounding the rituals of sports events, the arts, entertainment, and the workplace make these non-church gatherings the "primary" liturgies? These questions were not part of my earlier concern. But in my own engagement with a wide range of worshiping communities, I find it necessary to pay attention to non-church "liturgies" that shape the very means of participation churchgoers bring to weekly liturgies.

These questions indicate "fields of force" in which sanctioned religious rituals and patterns of worship do in fact operate. What if the very notion of a gathered community with stable sets of rituals and ways of reading Scripture dedicated to the praise of God is questionable? In fact, many so-called mega-churches focusing upon "seekers" deliberately do away with specific Christian symbols and sacramental actions, using contemporary cultural media to attract persons who find "traditional" Christian liturgy inaccessible. Differences over how to be relevant to various sectors of contemporary North American society generate the tensions, debates, and the "culture wars" currently dominating both popular and more scholarly public discourse about Christian worship.

Much more obvious to me now than two decades ago is the power of mass media to influence social perception and behavior in ways liturgists have not adequately taken into account. A detailed analysis and critique cannot be given here, but two relevant aspects of the power of visual media to shape human moral sensibility deserve mention. The first has to do with images of human social interaction that pervade the world of advertising and recent popular films. The second concerns shifts in our perceptual field that render assumptions about authentic liturgical language and action problematic.

The ubiquity of television images depicting human happiness and social interaction based on possession is now a commonplace. We cannot offer a simple cause-and-effect account of the impact that sit-coms and consumer ads have on how we regard basic human relations and the role of possessions. But we know that marketing strategies based on surveys and studies of public "wants" and "responses" tend to simplify the human complexities in acquiring goods and services. In fact, human relations to possessions and to other human beings are given focused reduction in such strategies. The moral/ethical questions of "why" are left at the level of projected "wants." An illusion of social reality is projected that suppresses such matters as the growing gap between wealthy and poor. Large segments of American society are under the illusion that all have access to such goods, services, and forms of social interaction as they see. Others are angrily under no such illusion. The consumerist ways of being human form powerful symbols that are ingested. The entertainment industry mass produces and reinforces a culture of immediacy that makes the idea of character formation over time seem arcane or irrelevant. Both visually and acoustically we are part of a culture of "hype." This brings with it strongly diminished attention spans and the tendency to confuse immediacy of feeling with depth of emotion. These factors render liturgical participation more problematic.

In light of these factors, I find it necessary to claim that Christian liturgy that is faithful to its origins in those narratives of God calling for justice, righteousness, mercy, and compassion among human beings *does* offer alternative visions of what it is to be human, and invites ways of living that counter the illusions and debilitations of mass culture. This claim implicitly judges the inadequacy of our inherited liturgies to address prophetically the alternative visions; but it also judges the social images that hold us captive and cause us to resist transformation by the deeper symbolic action of Christian worship.

II

At the heart of my concern with liturgy and ethics is a theological claim. There is no knowledge of God without a form of life that corresponds to *how* God is known. The things that constitute and regulate a way of being with other human beings come before God in the assembly, whether of "high," "low," or "free" liturgical dynamics. In Christianity, those aspects of God that invite and sustain human beings together are identified in the prayers, hymns, readings, sermons, and symbolic ritual actions. So to hear of and to acknowledge in gratitude and awe the glory, holiness, compassion, and mercy of God are part of coming to know God. But this very hearing and acknowledging challenges our affections, habits, and characteristic attitudes— including those habitually ingested from both liturgy and culture. For Christians, the "hearing" and the "acknowledgment" of God are characteristically practiced in the central ritual activities of baptism, Eucharist, and prayer growing out of engagement with our lives.

It is certainly not enough that liturgical activities are done, especially if they are done without making our human life vulnerable to the mystery of God. Liturgical activity, in order to have both integrity and relevance in light of the questions now posed, must convey the deeply revelatory aspects of what "assembling before God" entails, including the destiny of the world and the fundamental images of the goodness of creation and the splendor of the incarnate life of God. There is a reciprocity between the features of divine-human interaction symbolized in the liturgy and the moral self-understanding of those who participate. The primordial cry of faithful Christian worship is "Come, Lord Jesus." The primary vision is of a world restored to its moral and social image of God. The act of assembly is thus an act of eschatological hope: "Be for us, God, who you have promised to be!"

The turn from text to symbolic ritual action now opens the way for a more adequate approach and a new agenda in the discussion between liturgy and ethics. A strong clue is found in Joseph Gelineau's observation:

"Only if we come to the liturgy without hopes or fears, without longings or hunger, will the rites symbolize nothing and remain indifferent or curious 'objects.' Moreover, people who are not accustomed to poetic, artistic, or musical language or symbolic acts among their means of expression and communication find the liturgy like a foreign country whose customs and language are strange to them."[5]

There is something intrinsically musical about the rhythm, pitch, and pace of worship—an "aesthetic" belonging to the particular culture in which Christians are evangelized and nurtured into worship forms. This is as true of reading, preaching, and praying with understanding as it is of hymns and songs and instrumental music that make participation possible.

The Christian liturgy I presuppose here is itself a complex symbolic and symbolizing event worshipers learn to dwell in. The public worship of God, whether in plain style or in highly prescribed forms, brings together many "modes of human communication" that form a multi-layered "culture." To clarify and understand how liturgy forms character requires attending equally to the canonical aspects and to the performative/participatory aspects in particular contexts. When

[5] Joseph Gelineau, *The Liturgy Today and Tomorrow*, trans. Dinah Livingstone (New York/Paramus: Paulist Press, 1978) 98–99.

liturgy is "domesticated" or made only to serve the surrounding culture's images and narrative self-understandings, it is often because of a failure of symbol. In particular, it is often the failure to distinguish the primordial symbols (the ritual act-narrative complex) from ideological and secondary ritual forms. The loss of participation in the primordial symbols often creates the "malformation" or even the subversion of the meaning and power of the narratives embedded in the symbolic actions originating in the "Christ event," with all the core variants in its earliest instantiation in actual practice.

Speaking of the post-conciliar Roman Catholic liturgy, Mary Collins addresses the effort to attend to actual local practices and to the role of symbol in liturgical participation. She observes that the attempts to reform and renew the liturgy in that tradition, especially in the American churches, have shed light on the problem. Worshipers have struggled with greater or lesser knowledge of the wider liturgical traditions. The liturgical reformers

"have drawn on the depth or superficiality of their experience and understanding of the paschal mystery, the mystery of dying and rising which is celebrated in every liturgy. They have been more or less successful in distinguishing the truly archaic ritual symbols of the Christian liturgical tradition still capable of embodying faith, from the merely antiquated ritual forms of other eras."[6]

For a tradition that struggles to come out from under certain cultural and even theological captivity, the process of retrieving the "truly archaic" symbols is crucial. But this, I would argue, is also true of traditions without a long history of highly defined liturgical books and rites. The recovery of the meal symbol behind all inherited Eucharistic theologies (and anti-theologies) is central to the recovery of the interplay of the narrative of Jesus Christ's life, teaching, suffering, death, and resurrection with how certain moral dispositions are formed by ritual participation.

At stake is the centrality of specific canonical ritual symbols and the process of participation in them. Symbols bring together many levels of meaning and experience, unify disparate and even partial

---

[6] Mary Collins, *Worship: Renewal to Practice* (Washington: The Pastoral Press, 1987) 61–62.

narratives, and accumulate affective and morally normative values around them over time. But the symbols are not "objectively" there as magical powers. They require participation for their shaping and expressive power to be activated.

Christian worship contains central signs such as bread, wine, water, oil, and light along with communal actions such as eating and drinking together, washing, laying on of hands, gestures of blessing and peace. But in specific occasions of worship only a *selected range* of the many levels of meaning potentially available in the symbol-narrative complex are activated at the conscious level of experience or reflection. It is over time that the fullness of the primary symbols may be received by the worshiping assembly. That is, it takes human experiences of suffering, joy, struggle, and yearning to make these primary symbols formative of character. The biblical narratives (however partial) and the range of sign-actions provide a shared matrix of social meaning. But this shared matrix is subject to critique by the very multivalent power of the symbol to break back into one-sided interpretations or domesticated experiences. Moral formation requires the imaginative re-visioning of social relationships.

At the heart of the Christian celebration of the Eucharist in its many and diverse interpretations is the meal shared in the name of Jesus. Despite the variety of ways of doing this meal in the earliest Christian communities, and despite the variety of ideological layers discursively attached to it, it is at heart a bedrock solidarity with Jesus' own self-giving. This asks certain behaviors of those who participate. We know that at its origin in the first communities, it was shared in the context of a meal during which the ritual breaking of bread and the drinking from the cup occurred. This was a practice, not a doctrine. Its "ethical" force was shown in the quality of regard and care for those who gathered and for those not present. The meal and the offering associated with it were also, as Justin Martyr attests, for "the orphans and widows, and those who are needy because of sickness or other cause, and the captives, and the strangers who sojourn amongst us. . . ."[7]

It was precisely this symbol of the shared meal and the density of meaning it evoked concerning the teaching, life, and dying/rising of

---

[7] Justin Martyr, *Apology*, chap. 65. Translation from *Liturgies of the Western Church*, ed. Bard Thompson (Waco, Tex.: Word Publishing, 1961).

Jesus in whose memory the meal was celebrated that caused Paul's severe criticism of the church at Corinth. There he saw that the rich arrived at the meal first, eating up the food and leaving nothing for the poor. This, he argued, was a violation of the symbol itself. This was not a theory Paul invented but an understanding of the existential entailment of participation. So he could declare, "This is not the eucharist you celebrate" (cf. 1 Cor 11:17-22).

The violations of the liturgical action were thus "ethical." Such a violation shows the unity of liturgy and its ethic; both are grounded in the same Jesus. In this way the archaic symbol at the heart of Eucharist carries a way of recognizing the abuse of its own enactment! We do not need theological uniformity in theories *about* the Eucharist to see this. Yet, as theological interpretations of its meaning and varieties of practices were made dependent upon such interpretations, it often became difficult to perceive the archaic symbol of the meal which contains specific features of God's selfgiving in Christ. I contend that whole traditions could lose sight of the original unity of the liturgical act's tacit "ethic." The same could be said of the baptism process culminating in washing, though the story there would be more complicated.

This leads me again to some notion of a "grammar" for the Christian life contained in the primary archaic symbolic actions. Many "theologies of worship" have justified a disjunction between cultic participation and the ethic it actually manifests. But the actual devolving practices of worship—excessive clericalism, exclusion of women from primary roles, lack of hospitality, lack of vital preaching juxtaposed to the ritual actions, and the loss of participation in the bread and cup—contributed to the obscuring and even the "suspicion" of the liturgy itself. This is part of the long and often unhappy divorce of liturgy and social justice, and the separation of a way of recognizing the formation of character implicit in Christian liturgical assembly.

III

We tend to begin every discussion of the moral life and Christian ethics with a suspicion born of the ambiguities in actual practice. Any discussion of the role of liturgy in moral formation starts with the seeming disunity and bad history of the Church. But is it not possible that the hermeneutics of suspicion requires some suspicion too? Particularly in light of what I have attended to in this essay, we need to discern how particular Christian communities and traditions do discover their own limitations in ecumenical encounter. Moreover, the question of faithful participation (no matter how much indifference in a local community) uncovers over time the linkages between gathering about the book, font, and table in the name of Jesus, and the larger purposes of God in the creation.

There can be no question of the reality and pervasiveness of religious self-deception with its consequent oppressions. But the search for an adequate narrative account of human life before God in relation to neighbor and the created order is the impulse behind every parochial act of invoking God. We all share in the complicities of a culture permeated with untruth and with moral fragmentation. The distrust of the language of public rituals—in church or outside the church—is fully understandable. This, in turn, contributes to our natural suspicion of any theory that identifies the achievement of a good life with mere attendance at rituals that hold before us a vision of truthfulness and goodness. But the idea that we should not participate because of this fact is strange indeed. As Rowan Williams has observed: "Because our speech and, therefore, our common life are so fragmented, we must be suspicious equally of the untruthfulness of what is offered us and of the untruthfulness of our own refusal of it."[8]

I remember how, in a very small rural church, the Lord's Prayer, repeated by rote, in season and out of season, could suddenly explode with meaning for particular folks. After routine dullness, something in their lives would allow the prayer, in its simplicity and depth, to interpret them and to make sense of events as nothing else seemed to. So in many contexts of Christian worship, both devotional and liturgical, we recognize the formation of certain dispositions in praying the petitions. "Thy will be done" is no longer a kind of resignation to what may happen. Properly understood, it becomes a cry for what God intends for us, for human beings to be realized in this community, and in the life of the ones who make themselves vulnerable

---

[8] Rowan Williams, "The Suspicion of Suspicion: Wittgenstein and Bonhoeffer," in *The Grammar of the Heart,* ed. Richard H. Bell (New York: Harper & Row, 1988) 46.

enough to pray it. Such a simple act of words and gestures in the face of such complexities and ambiguities; such a symbol that lies in wait for us: like the Eucharist, like baptism, like singing, like praying for the world.

Liturgy that resists literalizing and domesticating the symbols and the selective narratives it displays—that is the only antidote for liturgical participation lacking moral passion for justice and mercy. Mystery is central, not as mystification but as opening up dimensions of divine reality and the human being to one another. In the actual practices of such a variegated and often ideologically divided Christian faith, we need a fresh approach to the complex, mutual reciprocity between liturgy and the formation of human character if affections and virtues befitting the overlapping narratives are to be formed.

One clue is to be found in the criterion of "faithfulness" to the core narratives of the life, work, death and resurrection of Jesus Christ. Participation in the symbolic action requires more than participation in the phenomena of worship; it requires participation as a living community engaged in the struggle to show in life what is implied in the gathering. Opening up the ethical levels of meaning in the shared meal in the name of one who creates and redeems a world from itself transforms not simply the interior life of feeling and desire but the social relationships that make us human in the sight of God.

The Tolstoy experience will continue as long as Christians continue to "play church" in worship. But if the eschatological force of radical openness to God is discovered (and taught well) again, then the very act of assembling and invoking and remembering and enacting can give the clue: God continues to act in and through the gathered assembly, no matter how partial the grasp of this mystery is. This is the "fear and trembling" that continually opens, in every culture and time, the possibility of true reform and renewal—the *semper reformanda* that seems to me to be intrinsic to the Christian gospel itself.

Bibliography of Don E. Saliers

BOOKS

The Soul in Paraphrase: Prayer and the Religious Affections. New York: Seabury Press, 1980.

From Hope to Joy. Nashville: Abingdon Press, 1984.

Worship and Spirituality. Philadelphia: Westminster, 1984. Second edition, Cleveland: OSL Publications, 1996.

Worship as Theology: Foretaste of Glory Divine. Nashville: Abingdon Press, 1995.

Worship Come to Its Senses. Nashville: Abingdon Press, 1996.

With Hoyt L. Hickman, Laurence Hull Stookey, and James F. White. *Handbook of the Christian Year.* Nashville: The United Methodist Publishing House, 1987. Second edition, 1994.

With Charles Hackett. *The Lord Be with You: A Visual Handbook for Presiding in Christian Worship.* Cleveland: OSL Publications, 1990.

With Arthur W. Wainwright. *The Wesley/Langshaw Correspondence: Charles Wesley, His Sons and the Lancaster Organists.* Atlanta: Emory University, 1993.

Editor: Barth, Karl. *Prayer.* Translated by Sara F. Terrien. Philadelphia: Westminster Press, 1986.

Editor with Louis Dupré and John Meyendorff. *Christian Spirituality: Post-Reformation and Modern.* New York: Crossroad, 1989.

ESSAYS AND ARTICLES

"A Critical Appraisal of the Colloquium Man and Symbol." *Worship* 44 (October 1970): 450–445.

"On the Crisis of Liturgical Language." *Worship* 44 (August–September 1970): 399–411.

"On the 'Crisis' in the Language of Worship." *Music Ministry* (January 1970).

"A Servant Church Today." *Worship* 46 (October 1972): 473–481. Reprinted in *Journal of the American Association of Church Architects* (Summer 1972).

"Two Advent Homilies," with Julian Hartt. In *Experimental Preaching.* Ed. John Killinger. Nashville: Abingdon Press, 1973.

"The Realization of Modern Liturgical Texts: Prayers We Have in Common." *Worship* 47 (March 1973): 130–136.

"Lex orandi est lex credendi." *Thesis Theological Cassettes* 4.9 (October 1973).

"Faith and the Comic Eye: Religious Gleanings from Comic Vision." *Andover Newton Quarterly* 13 (March 1973): 259–276.

"Christian Worship and Contemporary Life." *Reflection* 71 (May 1973): 3–5.

"Theology and Prayer: Some Conceptual Reminders." *Worship* 48 (April 1974): 230–235.

"Beauty and Holiness Revisited: Some Relations Between Aesthetics and Worship." *Worship* 28 (May 1974): 278–293.

"Prayer and Emotion: Shaping and Expressing Christian Life." *Worship* 49 (October 1975): 461–475.

"The Renewal of Worship: Pastoral Intention." *The Candler Review* 3 (January 1976): 3–11.

"New Patterns of Worship: A Conversation." *The Candler Review* 3 (January 1976): 19–27.

"Recovering Our Spirituality." *The Circuit Rider* 1 (October 1976): 1–5.

"The Ecumenical Lectionary, Rich in Musical Possibilities." *Pastoral Music* 1 (February–March 1977): 27–29.

"Prayer and Emotion: Shaping and Expressing Christian Life." In *Christians at Prayer*. Ed. John Gallen. Notre Dame: University of Notre Dame Press, 1977.

"Enmity: A Deep Emotion." In *Essays on Kierkegaard and Wittgenstein: On Understanding the Self*. Ed. Richard H. Bell and R. E. Hustwit. Wooster, Ohio: The College of Wooster, 1978.

"The Connection Between Worship and Healing." *Ministry and Mission* 3 (September 1978).

"Language in the Liturgy: Where Angels Fear to Tread." *Worship* 52 (November 1978): 482–488.

"Worship as Central in Spiritual Formation." *Ministry and Mission* 3 (December 1978).

"Explanation and Understanding in the Social Sciences: A Critique." *International Journal for the Philosophy of the Social Sciences* 8 (December 1978): 367–371.

"Liturgy and Ethics: Some New Beginnings." *Journal of Religious Ethics* 7 (Fall 1979): 173–189. Reprinted in *Introduction to Christian Ethics: A Reader*. Ed. Ronald P. Hamel and K. R. Himes. New York: Paulist Press, 1989.

"Prayer and the Doctrine of God in Contemporary Theology." *Interpretation* 34 (July 1980): 265–278.

"The Integrity of Sung Prayer." *Worship* 55 (July 1981): 290–303.

"Hymns Old and New." *Pastoral Music* 5 (Spring 1981).

"Hymns and the Church Year: A Key to Faithful Worship." *Journal for Preachers* 5 (Advent 1981): 10–15.

"Worship's Hidden Tongues." *Ministry and Mission* 8 (Fall 1982).

"Anatomy: The Desert Experience." In *Spiritual Formation Resources*. Nashville: Board of Higher Education, 1982.

"Rethinking Heaven and Hell." *Ministry and Mission* 8 (March 1983).

"A Crucial Catechesis: Hymns and the Church Year." *The Hymn* 34 (July 1983).

"Essays in response to the data [from Faith and Ferment Study]." In *Faith and Ferment*. Ed. R. Bilheimer. Minneapolis: Fortress Press and Collegeville, Minn.: Liturgical Press, 1983.

"David's Song in Our Land." *Liturgy* 3 (Summer 1983): 23–29. Reprinted in *The Landscape of Praise: Readings in Liturgical Renewal*. Ed. Blair Gilmer Meeks. Valley Forge, Pa.: Trinity Press International, 1996.

"Hymns in Religious Education: Three Perspectives." With Ronald A. Nelson and William B. Rogers. *The Hymn* 34 (April 1983): 80–84.

"Liturgical Theology." In *The Westminster Dictionary of Christian Theology*. Ed. Alan Richardson and John Bowden. Philadelphia: Westminster Press, 1983.

"Music as Prayer." *Hosanna* 1 (1983): 2–5.

"Future Directions in Protestant Worship." *The Circuit Rider* 7 (July–August 1983): 6–7.

"Symbol in Liturgy: Tracing the Hidden Languages." *Worship* 58 (January 1984): 37–48.

"The Nature of Worship: Community Lived in Praise of God." In *Duty and Delight*. Ed. Carlton R. Young, Robin Leaver, and James Litton. Carol Stream, Ill.: Hope Publishing Co., 1985.

"The Church Year and Congregational Life." *Reformed Liturgy and Music* 2 (Spring 1986): 92–94.

"Liturgy, Art and Architecture: What Eye Has Not Seen, nor Ear Heard. . . ." *Faith and Form* 29 (Spring 1986): 42–45.

"Sanctifying Time and Space: Worship and the Pastor's Spirituality." *Worship Alive*. Nashville: Discipleship Resources, 1986.

"Lima at Anaheim: A Gospel Feast." *Response* 18 (March 1986): 26–29.

"An Invitation to Travel Lent." In *Expressions of Faith*. Oregon Catholic Press: Lent, 1986: Week 5, 3.

"The Church Year and Congregational Life." *Reformed Liturgy and Music* 20 (Spring 1986): 92–95.

"Living Baptism." *Weavings* 2 (March–April 1987): 6–13.

"The Gathering of the Gifted: Worship at Oakhurst Baptist Church." *Southern Baptist Church Music Journal* 4 (Spring 1987): 20–25.

"Sing to the Lord: A Rebirth of Psalmody." (In two parts.) *The American Organist* 21 (July and August 1987).

"The Daily Offices as Sung Prayer." *Reformed Liturgy and Music* 21 (Fall 1987): 208–211.

"Sanctifying Time, Place and People: Rhythms of Worship and Spirituality." *Weavings* 2 (September–October 1987): 18–29. Reprinted in *The Weavings*

Reader: Living with God in the World. Ed. John S. Mogabgab. Nashville: Abingdon Press, 1993.

"Prayers of the Faithful: Four Sundays of Easter, Cycle A." In *Prayers of the Faithful.* Ed. Gail Ramshaw. New York: Pueblo Press, 1988.

"Religious Affections and the Grammar of Prayer." In *The Grammar of the Heart.* Ed. Richard Bell. San Francisco: Harper & Row, 1988.

"Worship." In *Harper's Encyclopedia of Religious Education.* Ed. Iris V. Cully and Kendig Cully. San Francisco: Harper & Row, 1990.

"When in Our Worship God Is Glorified: Music of Liturgy and Life." *Weavings* 4 (July–August 1989): 6–14.

"Introduction." In *John Wesley on Religious Affections.* Gregory S. Clapper. Metuchen, N.J., and London: Scarecrow Press, 1989.

"Walk Through the Waters." *The Upper Room Disciplines.* Nashville: Upper Room Books, 1990.

"Christian Spirituality in an Ecumenical Age." In *Christian Spirituality: Post-Reformation and Modern.* Ed. Louis Dupré, Don Saliers, and John Meyendorff. New York: Crossroad, 1989.

"The Music of Liturgy and Life." *Weavings* 4 (July–August 1989): 6–14.

"Chronicle: Third Symposium for Church Composers." *Worship* 63 (March 1989): 154–157.

"'Behold I Make All Things New': A Vision of Life in Praise of God." *Sacramental Life* 3 (February–March 1990): 6–12.

"Liturgy as Art." *Liturgy* 8 (Spring 1990): 39–44. Reprinted in *The Landscape of Praise: Readings in Liturgical Renewal.* Ed. Blair Gilmer Meeks. Valley Forge, Pa.: Trinity Press International, 1996.

"Communion (Eucharist)." In *Dictionary of Pastoral Care and Counseling.* Ed. Rodney J. Hunter. Nashville: Abingdon Press, 1990.

"Liturgical Calendar." In *Dictionary of Pastoral Care and Counseling.* Ed. Rodney J. Hunter. Nashville: Abingdon Press, 1990.

"Worship and Celebration." In *Dictionary of Pastoral Care and Counseling.* Ed. Rodney J. Hunter. Nashville: Abingdon Press, 1990.

Introduction to the American Edition, in J. Ernest Rattenbury, *The Eucharistic Hymns of John and Charles Wesley.* Ed. Timothy J. Crouch. Cleveland: OSL Publications, 1990.

"Liturgy Teaching Us to Pray: Christian Liturgy and Grateful Liturgy." In *Liturgy and Spirituality in Context.* Ed. Eleanor Bernstein. Collegeville, Minn.: The Liturgical Press, 1990.

"Liturgical Aesthetics." In *The New Dictionary of Sacramental Worship.* Ed. Peter Fink, S.J. Collegeville, Minn.: The Liturgical Press, 1990.

"Hymns and the Song of God's People, I. *GIA Quarterly* 2 (Spring 1990): 6–9.

"Hymns and the Song of God's People, II." *GIA Quarterly* 2 (Fall 1990): 5–7.

"Ash Wednesday Through Lent: Practical Considerations." *Reformed Liturgy and Music* 24 (Winter 1990): 16–18.

"Composing for Worship." In *Church Music: The Future.* Westminster Choir College Symposium Papers. Ed. Robin Leaver. Princeton: Westminster Choir College, 1990.

Foreword to N. Lee Orr, *The Church Music Handbook for Pastors and Musicians.* Nashville: Abingdon Press, 1991.

"Seasons of the Gospel: An Overview of the Liturgical Year." *Reformed Liturgy and Music* 25 (Winter 1991): 11–14.

"Theological Reflections: Second Through the Fifth Sundays of Easter." *Lectionary Homiletics* 2 (April 1991): 4–20.

"Prayer and the Knowledge of God." *McKendree Pastoral Review* 8 (Spring 1991).

"On the Distinctiveness of Christian Emotions." *Weavings* 6 (May–June 1991): 6–16.

"Spirituality." In *A New Handbook of Christian Theology.* Ed. Donald W. Messer and Joseph L. Price. Nashville: Abingdon Press, 1992.

"Symbol in Liturgy, Liturgy as Symbol." In *The Awakening Church.* Ed. Lawrence Madden. Collegeville, Minn.: The Liturgical Press, 1992.

"The Methodist Tradition: A Musical Setting of Psalm 136 with Commentary." In *Sacred Sound and Social Change: Liturgical Music in Jewish and Christian Experience.* Ed. Lawrence A. Hoffman and Janet R. Walton. Notre Dame: Notre Dame University Press, 1992.

Introduction to Henry H. Knight, III, *The Presence of God in the Christian Life: John Wesley and the Means of Grace.* Metuchen, N.J., and London: Scarecrow Press, 1992.

"Praying Together and Alone: Humanity at Full Stretch." *Liturgical Ministry* 1 (Spring 1992): 42–47.

"This Duty Is Our Delight and the 'Place Just Right.'" *Pastoral Music* 16 (August–September 1992): 20–23.

"The Ecstatic and the Quotidian: Response to the Berakah Award." *Proceedings of the North American Academy of Liturgy* (1992): 27–38.

"Proclamation: Hymns and the Songs of God's People." *Proceedings of the North American Academy of Liturgy* (1992): 85–94.

"Knowledge and Vital Piety: Thoughts on Reading and the Love of God." *The Font* 9 (December 1993): 5–6.

"Our Hymnal Takes Hold: Initial Soundings." *Worship Arts* 9 (November–December 1993): 8–10.

"Joy." In *The New Dictionary of Catholic Spirituality.* Ed. Michael Downey. Collegeville, Minn.: The Liturgical Press, 1993.

"Goodness." In *The New Dictionary of Catholic Spirituality.* Ed. Michael Downey. Collegeville, Minn.: The Liturgical Press, 1993.

"'When in Our Music God Is Glorified': A New Hymnal Takes Hold." *Connection* (Summer 1994): 6–9.

"Feasts and Holy Days (Christian)." In *Harper's Dictionary of Religion.* Ed. Jonathan Z. Smith, William S. Green, and Lawrence S. Cunningham. New York and San Francisco: Harper & Row, 1994.

"Sacraments and Ordinances (Christian)." In *Harper's Dictionary of Religion.* Ed. Jonathan Z. Smith, William S. Green, and Lawrence S. Cunningham. New York and San Francisco: Harper & Row, 1994.

"Prayer and Preaching." In *The Concise Encyclopedia of Preaching.* Ed. Richard Lischer and William Willimon. Nashville: Abingdon Press, 1994.

"To Be Contemporary or Not to Be: Thoughts on a Liturgical Dilemma." *The Circuit Rider* 18 (November–December 1994): 7–9.

"Music and Spirituality: Listening for God's Voice." *Christian Spirituality Bulletin* 2 (Fall 1994): 9–11.

"Liturgy as Holy Play." *Weavings* 9 (November–December 1994): 40–44. Reprinted in *Communion, Community, Commonweal.* Ed. John S. Mogabgab. Nashville: Upper Room Books, 1995.

"Body Language: Eight Basic Postures Every Worship Leader Should Know." *Reformed Worship* 32 (June 1994): 18–21.

"United Methodists Celebrate All Saints." *Liturgy* 12 (Fall 1994): 32–38.

"Singing Our Faith: A Note on Hymns, Psalms and Songs." *Connection* (Summer 1995).

"Worship, Music and Technology: Identity, Integrity, and Pastoral Relevance." *The American Organist* 28 (August 1995): 30–33.

"Liturgy in a Culture of Hype: Notes on Restraint and Exuberance." *GIA Quarterly* (Fall 1995): 8–10.

"Divine Grace, Diverse Means: Sunday Worship in United Methodist Congregations." In *The Sunday Services of the Methodists: Twentieth-Century Worship in Worldwide Methodism: Essays in Honor of James F. White.* Ed. Karen B. Westerfield Tucker. Nashville: Abingdon Press, 1996.

"Celebrating Ascension and Pentecost: Some Theological and Pastoral Reflections." *Church Music Workshop* 6 (May–August 1996): 4–6.

"Singing Our Lives." In *Practicing Our Faith: A Way of Life for a Searching People.* Ed. Dorothy Bass. San Francisco: Jossey-Bass Publishing, 1997.

"Aesthetics and Theology in Congregational Song: A Hymnal Intervenes." In *Music in American Religious Experience.* Ed. Philip V. Bohlman and Edith Blumhofer. Forthcoming.

REVIEWS AND REVIEW ARTICLES

"The Failure of Language: A Review of R. Funk's *Language, Hermeneutic and Word of God.*" *Reflection* 65 (March 1968).

TeSelle (McFague), Sallie. *Literature and the Christian Life. Reflection* 66 (Fall 1969).

Davies, Horton. *Worship and Theology in England,* Vol. 1: *From Cranmer to Hooker. Worship* 45 (December 1971): 626–629.

Anderson, David. *The Tragic Protest. Journal of the American Academy of Religion* 39 (December 1971): 558–561.

White, James F. *New Forms of Worship. Worship* 46 (November 1972): 544–547.

Hoon, Paul. *The Integrity of Worship. The New Review of Books and Religion* (Summer 1972).

"The Renewal of Living Worship." *The New Review of Books and Religion* (Summer 1972).

Cell, Edward. *Language, Existence and God. Journal of the American Academy of Religion* 40 (December 1972): 582–586.

Evans, Barry, ed. *Prayer Book Renewal: Worship and the New Book of Common Prayer. New Review of Books and Religion* 2 (June 1978): 7.

Rahner, Karl and Johannes B. Metz. *The Courage to Pray. Quarterly Review* 1 (Summer 1981): 99–107.

Susman, Cornelia and Irvin Susman. *Thomas Merton. Quarterly Review* 1 (Summer 1981): 99–107.

Holmes, Urban T. *A History of Christian Spirituality: An Analytical Introduction. Quarterly Review* 1 (Summer 1981): 99–107.

"Spirituality as Embodied Prayer." Review of Kenneth Leech, *Soul Friend. Quarterly Review* 1 (Summer 1981): 99–107.

Hays, Henry B. *Swayed Pines Songbook. Worship* 56 (September 1982): 457–458.

Hays, Henry B. *Swayed Pines Songbook. The Hymn* 35 (April 1984): 125–126.

"Two Contrasting Hymn Collections: A Review of *Rejoice in the Lord* and *Glory and Praise.*" *Accent on Worship* 3 (1985): 6–7.

Ramshaw-Schmidt, Gail. *Letters for God's Name. Worship* 59 (November 1985): 549–551.

Maas, Robin, and Gabriel O'Donnell. *Spiritual Traditions for the Contemporary Church. Spiritual Life* 36 (Fall 1990).

Barth, Karl. *Wolfgang Amadeus Mozart. Weavings* 8 (November–December 1993): 47–48.

Pelikan, Jaroslav. *Bach among the Theologians. Worship* 62 (January 1988): 81–83.

Minear, Paul. *Death Set to Music: Masterworks by Bach, Brahms, Penderecki. Journal of Religion* 69 (April 1989): 294–295.

Carden, John., ed. *A World at Prayer: The New Ecumenical Prayer Cycle. Weavings* 8 (May–June 1993): 44–45.

Jackson, Pamela. *Journeybread for the Shadowlands. Worship* 68 (March 1994): 177–178.

Browning, Robert L., and Roy A. Reed. *Models of Confirmation and Baptismal Affirmation. Theological Studies* 57 (March 1996): 193–194.

Printed in the United States
41814LVS00005B/313-318